THE LIFE AND DEATH
OF A SPANISH TOWN

The
Life and Death
of a
Spanish Town

BY ELLIOT PAUL

GREENWOOD PRESS, PUBLISHERS
WESTPORT, CONNECTICUT

In order to keep this title in print and available to the academic community, this edition was produced using digital reprint technology in a relatively short print run. This would not have been attainable using traditional methods. Although the cover has been changed from its original appearance, the text remains the same and all materials and methods used still conform to the highest book-making standards.

"Christ said, 'Father, forgive them, for they know not what they do.' In this case they shall not be forgiven, for they know very well what they are doing."

The late Louis Delapré, Paris journalist, whose dispatches were distorted and rejected by the reactionary *Paris Soir*, and were given to *Humanité* by his widow, after Delapré was shot down, flying over Madrid.

The Men and Women of Santa Eulalia

THE FISHERMEN AND THEIR FAMILIES

Captain Juan
Mateo Rosa; his wife Paja; their daughter Maria
Edmundo, Mateo's brother
Toniet Pardal; his wife and children

HOTEL AND CAFÉ KEEPERS

Cosmi; his wife Anna
Antonio the cook, Cosmi's brother
Catalina, servant in Cosmi's hotel
Juanito, young proprietor of the Royalty
Pedro, the waiter at the Royalty
Xumeu Ribas, proprietor of Can Xumeu and custodian of the public telephone; his wife and daughter
Francisco Ribas, Xumeu's son
Antonia, proprietress of the fisherman's bar
Julia, her daughter
Andres, of Can Andres

STOREKEEPERS

Old Juan, of the Casa Rosita; his son Mariano; his daughter-in-law Vicenta
Toni Ferrer, of Las Delicias
Miguel Tur, of the Casa Miguel

Guarapiñada, of Tot Barat
Mousson, the butcher; his daughter Catalina; his
blind aunt

Guillermo, the blacksmith
Sindik, the carpenter
Juan Sindik, his son
Jaume, the carpenter
Primitivo, the electrician
Bonéd, fascist mason
Vicente Cruz, young republican mason
Ramon, the bus driver

Old Father Coll
Father Torres
Father Margall
And, assisting on holidays, Father Clapés and the
priest who looked like a butcher boy
The San Carlos priest and his father

Mayor Serra, republican
The fascist mayor
The Secretario
Anfita, the postmaster; his two idiot sons, Pepe and
Chicu
Sergeant Gomez, of the Guardia Civil
Guardias Ferrer, Jiminez and Bravo
The Portero

Ex-Captain Nicolau, retired army officer
Fernando, a schoolmaster
Carlos, his cousin, also a schoolmaster

Pep Salvador, Cosmi's brother
Pere des Puig
José and Catalina, of Can Josepi
Francisco Guasch
José Ribas, the diving champion
Don Ignacio Riquer
Don Carlos Roman
Don Rafael Sainz, vacationing millionaire
Pep des Horts (Algot Lange), the Dane

THE BANKER

Don Abel Matutes

ARTISTS

Andres, the young socialist
Rigoberto Soler
Derek Rogers, English painter

WOMEN AND YOUNG GIRLS

Eulalia Noguera
Marie Anfita, the postmaster's daughter
Teresa Bonéd; her daughter Juana
Maruja, the Secretario's daughter
Odila, ex-Captain Nicolau's daughter
Angeles, granddaughter of old Vicent the mason

Maria, Pep Salvador's favorite daughter
Marguerita, fiancée of Fernando the schoolmaster

MILITARY OFFICERS AND MILITIAMEN

Captain Don Alfredo Bayo, leader of government
  expedition
Captain Pastor, second in command
El Cubano, a corporal
Maño, a militiaman
Pedro, Maño's comrade
Ex-Commandant Mestres, rebel Governor of the
  island

Contents

PART TWO

JULY 14 TO SEPTEMBER 15, 1936

PART ONE

4000 B.C. *to* 1936 A.D.

1. Dawn and Moonlight

THERE is so much revolution and class war going on in all parts of the world that I believe it will be of interest to American readers to know how fascist conquest, communist and anarchist invasion, and the bloodiest war yet on record affect a peaceful town. By a town, I mean its people. I knew all of them, their means and aspirations, their politics and philosophy, their ways of life, their ties of blood, their friendships, their deep-seated hatreds and inconsequential animosities. Because Santa Eulalia is on an island, the inhabitants were unable to scatter and flee, and therefore I was able better to observe them and to know what happened to them as I shared their experience.

The town was very much like any American seaboard town except that the various races there had had six thousand years in which to be blended, and consequently the population was more homogeneous. Also the young men did not, as a rule, leave the island to seek their fortune elsewhere. Enough generalities! I feel self-conscious in writing about my dear friends with such objectivity. I loved them and their animals and the shadows of the trees that fell upon their houses. They divided their last *pesetas* and red wine and beans and gay spirit with me. I got away, and

they did not. Their land is dying. Mine is not. This
book is a debt I owe them.

Just before sunrise, the main street of Santa Eulalia
and the countryside, spread fanlike behind it, began
to awake. There was nothing reluctant or violent in
the awakening, merely a few familiar sounds which
seemed to accompany the heightening of the colors
of the dawn. In front was the sea on which a few fishing boats were moving, too, in a leisurely fashion,
leaving geometric wakes. The shutters scraped as
Antonio raised them in the act of opening the café at
Cosmi's hotel, Ferrer's donkey brayed, and because
of the rumble of an iron-wheeled cart or the footsteps
of an approaching fisherman the village dogs who had
been sleeping in the dust of the roadway cocked their
ears, stood up, stretched and walked in a dignified
way to the sidewalk. Capitan, the oldest, bravest and
most battered, was a sort of mastiff who belonged to
Sindik, a village carpenter, one of the hardest-work-
ing men in Santa Eulalia and comparatively poor.
Sindik had a gift for bonesetting and healing which
kept him constantly in demand in all parts of the island, but because he understood only dimly the mir-
acles he seemed to perform he considered that he had
no right to accept money on account of an ability he
possessed through no effort or merit of his own. Car-
pentry he had learned by painful apprenticeship, so he
was willing to be paid for that, but he liked best to
make large cartwheels and the huge devices by which
mules, walking blindfolded in circles, pulled up water
from wells to irrigate the fields. The men who needed
cartwheels and waterwheels were not over-prosperous

but they were not in a perpetual hurry, like the builders, so Sindik preferred to work for them and never
got rich or even well-to-do. Later I shall have to tell
you how his older son, as hard-working as his father
but not very bright, was shot by a firing squad and
fell back dead against a haystack, the base of which
was soaked with blood. Not now. Let's not think of it
now, for if my friends in Santa Eulalia have had misfortunes and have been ruined and destroyed, before
that for many years they had a wonderful life. I have
never seen a better life anywhere, a life more suited
to human limitations and capacities, a rhythm more
in accord with beneficent natural surroundings, a
verdant sub-tropical landscape and the sea.

The carpenter's old dog Capitan had his morning
meal in the rear of Cosmi's, just after Antonio had
opened the front shutters, built a wood fire in the
range in the kitchen, put on the coffee urn, and set
out the scraps from the previous night's meal at the
hotel. Antonio was hard of hearing and undemonstra-
tive. He never petted the dogs and seldom spoke to
them, neither did he ever forget that they liked to
eat. Franco and Fanny, both males, strange to say,
were the hotel dogs and the only ones Capitan, the
fighter, would allow to be near him while he was
eating.

This is not a dog story, and still the fate of the
men and women is inextricably interwoven with that
of their dogs and there are strays skulking fearfully
in deserted alleys all over Spain who once got regular
meals and had a name and a master.

In the happy days of Santa Eulalia, the moon shone
over the land without the chill in the air that else-

where makes the night inhospitable, and from May until November the men sat long hours after dinner in front of the cafés, drinking anis, cognac, cazalla or beer or the strong red wine of the country. They talked, argued, sang songs from Valencia or Aragon or native to Ibiza, ranging in mood from nostalgia to ribaldry. I can hear now, as I write (and I wish I could not), their voices in a favorite refrain.

Petiquita meua	*My little cigarette box,*
Que buida qu'estas	*How empty you are!*
Que buida qu'estas	
Pero demá es Diumenge	*But tomorrow is Sunday*
Yo tu rempliras	*And I'll fill you.*
Yo tu rempliras	

(Chorus)

Dos cigarros ting	*I have two cigarettes.*
Tres qui vol fumar	*Three (friends) want to smoke.*
Dos y tres fon cinq	*2 and 3 make 5,*
Y cinq fon dao	*and 5 make 10,*
Y dao fon vint	*and 10 make 20.*
Vint menus cinq fon quinze	*20 minus 5 make 15.*
Quinze menus cinq fon dao	*15 minus 5 make 10.*
Dao menus cinq fon cinq	*10 minus 5 make 5,*
Y cinq fon dao	*And 5 make 10,*
Y dao fon vint	*And 10 make 20.*

There is much in that song evocative of the character of Santa Eulalia and of Spain, the wistful attitude toward that which has contributed to pleasure, the acknowledgment of temporary material insufficiency with hope expressed immediately afterward, a joy in speculative patterns which expand and contract so effortlessly. The same feelings, translated into terms of national finance, defense or self-government, have chaotic results. They make for agreeable citizens but not zealous ones, brave soldiers who are born to lose a fight bravely.

Sindik, bonesetter and carpenter, was not to be found in front of cafés on moonlit nights. He worked with an application that vibrated in his little shop, from six in the morning until noon and from two-thirty until seven, and he slept hard at night. It was his nature to work, actually to toil without remission, and there were several others in the village whose inner forces impelled them to constant exertion, as if they were afraid to stop. Pedro, a jovial mason's helper, had an uncontrollable energy. It was gospel in Santa Eulalia that if one drop of rain fell, work was off until the next day. Pedro was the first on every job and the last to quit. Other terrific workers were Ferrer, Pep Salvador (brother of Cosmi and Antonio), José of Can Josepi, Guarapiñada the P. T. Barnum plus Patrick Henry of the town. You shall hear much more of all of these, but just now I am trying to convey that a lot of hard work, just like American hard work, went on in Santa Eulalia coincidentally with the most artistic and successful near-idleness ever achieved by pleasure-loving and lucky folk. It was the blend of everything that was charming and inspiring.

Cosmi's hotel was closed by Cosmi himself between two and three in the morning and was opened by Antonio, his older brother, an hour later. The hard-working men were friendly with the easy-going ones,

and neither envied the other. The most indolent, my
dear friend Guillermo, the blacksmith, or Toniet
Pardal, the fisherman, was expressing himself in in-
dolence as Ferrer or Pedro in work. Nature furnished
labor for those who needed it and food for those who
did not. The poorest man in town was Jaume, another
carpenter, who was poor because his wife had been ill
all their married life and had a child every year and he
could never get money enough ahead to buy a lathe.
Jaume did not starve, but he did not eat well and his
children were dirty and ragged but otherwise pretty
good kids. I am unlucky at dice, and the only times
I wanted to lose in Santa Eulalia was when Jaume was
in the game. (The stakes were drinks for the crowd,
total cost about four cents, U. S.) Instead, Jaume
almost always got stuck. I don't mean that Jaume
gambled extensively, or drank as much as his more
prosperous neighbors. He came into Xumeu's place,
the nearest café, about twice a day in good weather.
Still, Jaume asked me one of the hardest questions I
have ever been confronted with. Five minutes before
a gunboat was about to shell the town he said to me,
in a bewildered but not hysterical tone:

"What shall I do? My wife can hardly walk. And
anyway, where should we go?"

I was very tired and his question set in motion an
almost forgotten verse of T. S. Eliot. "What shall we
do? What shall we ever do?" I knew that it ended up
with something about a quiet game of chess, and as
I walked away and Jaume stayed, my absurd brain
was trying to fill in the intervening lines, over and
over, as I stumbled along a rocky road and heard the
whine of shells behind me.

Jaume was not hit, neither was his wife, nor any of his ragged children. Be reassured. No sad parts are coming for a long time in this story. The severest damage done by that particular bombardment was to the roof of the house of a wealthy retired Swiss whose last house had been destroyed in Russia and who had come to Santa Eulalia, as I had, to find tranquillity.

Most of the Ibicenca women were healthy and strong, with eyes alive and a ready smile, and because long centuries of custom had defined their lines of conduct they were able to be quickly friendly without being sexually sly. Their native costume, which occasional stray painters have made hideous, was becoming to them as good healthy women and was worn by nearly all of them who worked out-of-doors because it covered them from head to foot, several thicknesses, and kept their skin pure white in spite of Ibiza's strong sun. Catalina, who worked at Cosmi's, was one of the whitest and prettiest, a blue-eyed daughter of the Phoenicians who had once inhabited the island. The loveliest brunette, I think, was the daughter of Pere des Puig (pronounced Pooch) a dry farmer on a rocky terraced hill who played the accordion for dances in order to earn an extra *duro* each week. As he played he wore an unchanging expression of deep melancholy on his face but I think it was not because he had to work so hard to support his large family. He was lonely. He lived too far back on the hillside to see or talk with men on week days and on Sunday he had to sit apart from them, up on the stage of the local theatre, and play tunes which everybody had heard until they were tired of them. His slow smile indicated a broad sense of humor which he seldom had a chance to exercise. Pere des Puig was not driven to work by any inner necessity. He would have liked better being idle but he was fond of his seven daughters and he managed to dress them well and a little quaintly when they went to school. It was a beautiful family because, although Pere did not know it, his strong nimble hands were as beautiful as his oldest daughter's remarkable face.

In the very early morning Pere des Puig would feed his animals, hobble his sheep, stake out his goat, smear a large slab of home-made dark bread with olive oil, hitch up his mule and drive to the seashore, a mile distant all down hill, for a load of seaweed to use as fertilizer. As he bumped over the stony road, perched on his iron-rimmed two-wheel cart, he would eat the bread and oil and look out over the dawn-colored sea with about the same expression of melancholy that he wore Sunday evenings in the dance hall. At the same time, in the backyard of Cosmi's hotel the three dogs, Capitan, Franco and Fanny, would be eating the scraps Antonio had set out for them.

This was a time of day when the town belonged to those who later might have seemed the most unfortunate, the old women who had to work outside their homes and the young girls whose prospects were so poor that they had to make them poorer by working as servants. In Santa Eulalia the women were glad to work in the fields. They loved the fragrance of alfalfa, their backs were supple enough to bend for hours over sweet-potato vines. Wheat, corn and melons they understood, and nearly every family had some land of its own. Working in other folks' kitchens was the last resort.

Catalina, who worked at Cosmi's, was, as I have mentioned, one of the loveliest girls in town. She had slate blue eyes and honey-colored hair, perfect wrists and ankles, rarer still in Spain a pleasing voice, and a complete ignorance of everything that a woman does not need to know. About five o'clock she would come in through the back gate which was never locked or even closed and say good morning to old Antonia Masear, her companion in drudgery.

The Royalty Hotel, on the northwest corner of the public square, was intended for the aristocracy and transient foreigners, and had an atmosphere entirely different from Cosmi's. In its backyard stood the most beautiful palm tree on the island, and in order that the ugly structure which served for a hotel might be built, the best small specimen of Moorish architecture on the island had been torn down.

Far along the shore, among the worn and pocketed ledges, could be seen, before sunrise, a strange figure of a man, Platé, nicknamed the Admiral. He would have a short fishing rod or a staff in his hand and he knew where the fish and the small octopi would be lurking and feeding. No one knew the shores or the hills as Platé did. Each mushroom, plant or herb was his familiar friend. He had long shaggy hair and a long unkempt beard, both of which he had shaved clean once a year, in midsummer. His legs and arms were thin, his voice a resonant bass, his face was tanned and wrinkled, except for his large dark blue eyes almost hidden by his shock of hair. He laughed, grinned and talked to himself when he was alone. In company he was silent until the wine began to work on him. Then he sang, wild Moorish songs (he knew Spanish,

French, Catalan, Italian and Arabic well) and accompanied himself on the table or bar with the heel of his hand in imitation of African drums. I have heard him walking home drunk in the brightest moonlight, carrying on a reproachful and defensive conversation aloud, one voice in Spanish, the other in French, sometimes softly and persuasively, often reaching an angry crescendo so that two of his selves would be bellowing at each other.

At dawn with his trousers legs rolled up above his diminutive knees, he would be walking along the rocks at the water's edge, around the point which sheltered the harbor to the north, or the other way from town, by the mouth of the small river, looking for his breakfast. He did not catch all the fish or *poulpes* that he saw, but chose them as if the Mediterranean were his market, and its produce were laid out for him. Fish, mushrooms, wild strawberries, wild leeks, wild asparagus formed his steady diet. He did odd jobs just often enough to keep himself in wine, and tended a few flower and vegetable gardens because he was the best gardener in the Balearic Islands and was proud of his skill. Because of him, the backyards of Cosmi's and the Royalty were not like other backyards but were luxuriant with flowers—dahlias, golden glow, phlox, petunias, asters, small orange and lemon trees, all planted by Platé. They would grow for him almost like performing animals. There were many gardens in town, nearly every house had flowers growing near it, but Platé had absorbed all the arts of the Moors in his long stay in Africa and had learned from the French how to trim and take care of trees.

When I first went to Santa Eulalia, I hired a house

for a friend who was coming and asked Platé if he would make a garden in front of it. He refused, politely but firmly, and later that day Cosmi told me why. The land had formerly been Platé's own. In fact, Platé had been one of the largest landowners in the town, years back. It seemed that he had had a wife of whom he was very fond, and the wife had developed some ailment that baffled not only the island doctors (of whom the least said the better) but doctors on the mainland as well. Platé had worried until he was ill, too, and had spent a fortune trying to cure her. After she died, Platé started drinking and gambling until he had lost everything he had left. He was unhappy and morose to the point of madness until the remains of his property and money were gone. Then suddenly he became aloof and merry. He moved into a little shack not larger than eight feet by four, on the top of the hill beside the church, slept on straw, fished for his meals and worked only when he needed wine, maybe six hours a week. One of the jobs he would consent to do now and then was to fetch bundles of rosemary for kindling fires, and each morning the fragrant smoke of rosemary would pervade the town.

Old friends! Beloved island of Ibiza! My chosen town! How can I believe that you are of the past, cut off from me as irrevocably as the legendary days of the Moors, the camps of the Romans, the settlements of Carthaginians, Phoenicians, Iberians, all lost in the mirrors of history? You are not all dead, my former comrades. There are dawns in unending series to come, and the rising moon will lift the identical shape of Ibiza from the darkened sea. Shall I ever find your equal or your equivalent? Can I survive another transplantation? Shall I be always saying, "Those were the good days. They have been destroyed." Or can I keep those scenes a while by re-enacting them, with a pin on the discs of my brain, until they are worn and emit false tones and eventually are discarded?

2. *Of Fish and Fishermen*

FROM the depths of the sea and the hidden ledges and alternating patches of seaweed and sand came daily the evidence of seasons more mysterious than those familiar ones of the verdant slopes of hills. In approaching Ibiza from the sea, at night, after pitching and swaying in the rough cross currents which had menaced the Phoenicians and the Greeks, one would see in the distance a constellation of low lights, rising and falling with the swell, sometimes obscured, then reappearing. It was the fishing fleet. And later, when the passenger ship passed between them, just as the starlight was thinning, one would stand at the rail and try to guess which boat was Captain Juan's, which was manned by Mateo Rosa and his cousins, which by the curly-headed man whose child was sick in the alley leading to Jaume's carpenter shop, and in which of the dories was Edmundo, peering through steel-rimmed glasses, or Toniet Pardal, who had borrowed fifty *pesetas* from me to buy his skiff and was repaying me, through all eternity, with presents of lobsters, ink-fish, daggers forbidden by the Guardia Civil, rare shells, old coins and his unending conversation.

I think there are no better fishing grounds than those lying north and east of Ibiza, and let no one imagine that the tales of hardship and death and per-

petual danger (such as those of Hugo or Melville or
the chroniclers of the Newfoundland Banks) apply to
the happy-go-lucky crews who set out from Santa
Eulalia. There was no ice in the rigging, no bullying
skipper, no waiting women wringing their hands on
the shore. On the contrary, if the weather was the
least bit rough they stayed in town, strolling from
café to café, and by nightfall would be roaring but
never belligerent. There was no reason for them to
risk their necks. For thousands of years, the sea which
lay within convenient rowing distance had yielded
richly whenever the waters were calm and if the people
who remained on land, either in Ibiza or Valencia or
Barcelona, could not have fish a certain day, they
could eat lamb or goat, and, in the winter, pork or
sobresada. As to Fridays, the fishermen liked nothing
better than to annoy the priests by failing to have
fish that day. The fishermen never knew when they
were going to work, and did not care. When their luck
was good they spent more, that was all. I never knew
of a fisherman getting rich, or even starting a bank
account. Captain Juan had got hold of enough *pesetas*
to buy a thirty-foot boat and a reliable motor, but
most of them got along with crude equipment and
still were able to eat and drink.

After passing through the fishing fleet, the passenger ship headed straight for the Tagomago light, which
stood on a rocky island almost touching the northern
coast of Ibiza. Around Tagomago, on which the fishermen often camped at night, were other dories and
quite different varieties of fish. It is a dangerous
coast, much like Norman's Woe, except for the ab-
scence of tides. Reefs show a ragged crest just above

the water surface or lurk just below. One large rock with scrubby vegetation on it, about one hundred yards square, bears the name of Santa Eulalia and can be seen from the hill roads behind the town. In the lee of the rocks the nets are spread, buoyed up with corks and green glass buoys and each morning when they are hauled up they yield an unimaginable assortment, in shapes, colors and sizes, of sea-creatures, gasping, flopping in futile convulsions.

To see them overflowing the baskets or lying side by side—huge meros with red open mouths a foot in circumference and six jagged sets of teeth, smooth cirviolas like torpedoes with green and indigo markings on their steel-colored sides, daurade with golden flecks of imitation sunshine to hide their lurking eyes, tuna, great and small, bonitos, snake-like picados with long sharp bills—to see them is not like seeing sheaves of wheat or tubs of grapes. If a fisherman had to plant a mero, bend over in the hot sun for months at a stretch in order to pluck it, then thresh it and gather it into barns no fish would be available for mankind. On the days when the big fish were plentiful, that is, when the season was right and the weather calm enough to permit the fishermen to go out three or four miles from shore without discomfort, there was a quickening of the pulse of the town. The fishermen's families knew there would be money in larger than everyday quantities, the wives began to look for chickens for the rice, children thought of candy, clothes and possible bus-rides to the port city, storekeepers looked forward to an active day and Antonia, whose café was opposite the Royalty, on the eastern corner of the public square, prepared herself and her grown daughters for hard and profitable work. Antonia's was the fishermen's hangout. First, because it was situated nearest the great spreading tree in the shade of which the fish were sold from baskets and also because fishermen liked to have women near by when they drank.

So each calm morning, hours before the dawn, while the card playing, and discussions and songs were still in progress up and down the main street, far off shore the fishing boats were rising and falling with the swell. Nearer the shore, among the ledges, nets were spread and the buoys made strange hieroglyphics in the calmer water. Around Tagomago and the island of Santa Eulalia a few men were fishing with a handline for sarks, or catching langostas (similar to the Pacific lobster) or large crabs called *krankas*. After daylight, the fishermen farthest out would come inshore, haul in the nets, and with their craft and tenders gleaming with their catch would come into Santa Eulalia's small harbor, just inside the point which sheltered it on the north. All the fish would be dumped into flat-bottomed skiffs and ranged in large wicker baskets on the shore. The cirviola, tuna, bonito or dentuls were like battleships with eyes, designed for speed and high pressure, having nothing to fear or pity. Burnished steel, reflecting all the colors of the dawn, smooth sides, torpedo tails, the force of battle in their strain. And around them their lesser brethren, whose environment had made them flabby or grotesque or crafty. Large skates with their deathlike bellies on which was a false ghost's face, flounders with eyes staring out at forty-five degrees, the flat limande (or Mediterranean sole), all the fish that lived on the bottom, their backs marked and tinted like veined clay, their undersides light so that when they rose from the sand and mud in their defenseless condition the fish of prey could pass beneath them without seeing them. The large-mouthed fish caught near the shore had heads like traditional monsters. Because they were likely to be left stranded by the waves, they were built to live longer in the air and breathed heavily with their gills long after the big fighting fish had lost their power. They were not colored like the currents in deep water, nor stained to look like mud, but had all the weird colors of the sea plants and wet rocks, brick-red, dark-violet, brown-green, green-grey. The largest of their kind was the mero, a giant Mediterranean bass that lurked among the largest ledges. The smallest was no larger than a man's little finger and looked like a dragon carved in green gumdrop. Then there would be eels, dark mo-renos six feet long, grey eels with triangular heads, small sharks with their wicked underslung jaws, sea butterflies with antennae and ribbed wings marked like peacock feathers, vacas with streaks of gold and a thumb-print of violet on each side, mahogany-colored fish with scarlet slashes to make them invisible in red reeds, light pink prophet fish with pale staring eyes, spider crabs with legs a foot long, pajels with blue and turquoise like changeable silk, sea snails, lobsters, and shellfish called *cigales* built like steam shovels with saw teeth on their powerful tails.

These creatures, in damp baskets on the shore and the fishermen standing around them, were not like anything on the earth. Still, in looking at them one could see the beginning of machines, the grimaces of actors on the screen, the glitter of the ballroom, the fighting fleets, the gardens of Babylon, the sidewalks of New York, projectiles, kitchenware, whatever there is or has been. And Captain Juan, the cleverest of all the fishermen, would often look at his catch and shake his head in a pleased and bewildered way, and chuckle about the vagaries of chance and the prodigality of nature, as evidenced by what came daily from the sea. He thought of the big fish in terms of *pesetas* and spending money, but he knew the fish seasons and migrations, where they lived, how they behaved toward one another, what they fed on. He was happy whenever he could add to his store of fish facts.

As the different boats came in, their owners and the helpers would load the baskets and start the half-mile walk to town in pairs, each man holding one handle of the heaviest basket and carrying another on his outside hip. Frequently they would stop to rest, or to roll cigarettes. They were strong men, with great endurance, but none of them wished to make an ordeal of a job which could be done in easy stages.

Usually they got in with their catch about a half hour before bus time, if there were big fish to be shipped to Ibiza and from there to Palma, Barcelona, Valencia or Alicante. The first stop for Captain Juan would be Cosmi's hotel, where Antonio, Catalina, Anna Cosmi and old Antonia Masear would come out to see what he had. Antonio or Anna would select what was needed for the hotel, the fishermen would stop at the bar for coffee and *cazalla*, then the Captain would go on to the Royalty, where Juanito, the young proprietor, or his mother, Isabel, would buy the day's supply. The big fish remaining would then be iced and placed on top of the bus which left for Ibiza at seven in summer and seven-thirty in winter. In the Ibicenco dialect, there are only two words for seasons, *estiu* meaning summer (April to November) and *ivern* for the rest of the year.

The men carrying baskets of smaller fish made many more stops. As they approached the town from their mooring place, they blew a horn made of a large sea-snail shell. The first stop was at Gork's, the theatre café. There a group would gather from the nearby houses. After that, they would go as far as Can Xumeu, in which was the public telephone office and exchange. Xumeu, the proprietor, his sedate wife and melancholy daughter, Sindik and his helpers from the carpenter shop next door, Guarapiñada and his wife from across the street, the *barberet* (so-called because he was the smallest of the barbers), the new baker's wife and sister-in-law from the back street, and others would take their pick. Each fish was weighed on hand balances which probably had not been checked for twenty years and paid for in copper coins, including French, Italian, Algerian *sous* and English pennies.

And so it was, as the fishermen proceeded from north to south along the main street of Santa Eulalia, the great fish and the small gasping ones would be spread back through the countryside according to a plan or a system whose ramifications had to do with the structure of human society and fish destiny. The small rock fish, pale garnet or brick red, the ones which lived longest out of water, had known nothing but terror, and were cheap, found their way into houses like that of Jaume the carpenter, and the poorest little shacks. Large lobsters, cirviolas, the choicest and most belligerent in their own environment, went

straight to the houses of the rich. The hotels got the
middle-class fish, salmonetas like over-sized Wag-
nerian goldfish and merluzas so insipid in taste and
texture that even English tourists could eat them.
Flabby and defenseless fish got into soup, relentless
ones were baked or fried. The big ones were packed in
ice, some stopped off at Ibiza, others went on to Barcelona, Valencia and Alicante and were relayed to
Madrid.

Captain Juan was not an avaricious man. Because
of his superior knowledge and equipment, he could
have made it more difficult for his competitors but it
is doubtful if ever he thought of Mateo Rosa, or old
Pere the deaf man, or Edmundo in that light. He accepted a bit more responsibility, could be depended
upon to fill large orders, took care of the customers he
liked in case they did not show up while the best of
the fish were going. He was one of those who listened
most carefully, with a pleased benevolent smile, when
Cosmi, late at night, or old Mousson, who ran a com-
munistic pottery in a nearby cove, would say that all
men were brothers. He did not hate the rich, who
made it difficult for friends of his on land, but he
feared them less than most men did. When he saw a
Guardia Civil he looked at him frankly, knowing the
officer would like to shoot him but aware that no pretext was likely to arise. A priest he thought was
grotesque, without being funny like a clown.

The fishermen and the police were natural enemies,
partly because long centuries of coercion had failed
utterly to make fishermen attend or respect the
church. Also, the fishermen augmented their income
by smuggling in tobacco from Africa and thus weak-

ened a government monopoly. Captain Juan was
not outspoken in his defiance of constituted authority and dogma, as was Edmundo, nor a member of a secret political committee like Matco Rosa.
He was small in stature, mild in manner, but he was
fearless. He was dangerous because the other fishermen, whom he had never tried to put out of business,
considered him as their leader. All he seemed to do was
to lead them from bar to bar, but in those bars he
frequented, Cosmi's, Andres', and Antonia's, talk went
on, irreverent, suggestive of change. It was hushed
when a Guardia entered—passing priests or deacons
caught only the rumble of it. Unmistakably, however,
the police and the clergy were happier in the inland
towns.

My modest friend Juan was a Spanish Red. He had
scarcely heard of Moscow, had never slit a throat. He
had not aspired to political office, never made a
speech, but he could not be imposed upon and he complained when any of his acquaintances got an unfair
deal. He had no selfish interest in a change of the
social plan. He wanted most of all for the children to
be saved from religious instruction and for countless
officials who were being paid for doing nothing to be
dropped from the rolls.

Juan, the best fisherman in a fisherman's town,
knew nothing of Karl Marx. The ideas which pleased
him, when he heard them expounded, and harmonized
with his temperament and the lessons of the sea,
would correspond with those of American patriots.
Freedom of thought and expression, freedom of action
within reasonable social limits, separation of church
and state, re-division of idle land, abolition of special

privilege and the poor old brotherhood of man—nothing more.

The only man Juan ever fired was Toniet Pardal. And this was done gently. The Captain waited for their twelve-months agreement to expire and then did not renew it. It was a painful moment for him. He dreaded it several days in advance, blushed, made false explanations more kindly than the real ones, stood on one foot, then the other. In the end he probably would have embarrassed himself to the point of relenting had not Toniet, who was capable of tactful or even noble gestures, made it impossible. Both men were drunk for days afterward, in their different fashions. Toniet was sorry for himself and went about seeking sympathy, which no one gave him. Juan was very quiet, and sought out a few of his intimate friends, like Cosmi, to explain that he really had to do it.

What the town hadn't understood was why Juan had kept Toniet so long in his boat, for Toniet was lazy and undependable to a degree that made him lag behind even the gentle rhythm of Santa Eulalia's activities. Worse than that, he talked too much. He was always apologizing. Sometimes he was quarrelsome.

"*My pobre madre*," Toniet had said to me one day when his sixty-year-old mother passed us in the heat of the day with a basket of fish on her head. Toniet was doing nothing at the time, but his pity for his mother and her lifetime of toil was as genuine as that of Villon, who began a stanza of his testament with the same words. The poet would have liked the rich intonation of Toniet's deep voice when he said "My poor mother" and turned away from the sight of her misery.

There is a sort of poetic justice, however, in the fact that Toniet, who had been a burden to his fellow-fishermen many years, did them a service in the class struggle they so dimly understood. The point of land and rocks behind which for centuries Santa Eulalia fishermen had moored their boats, and on which they had loaded their baskets and often slept under trees on warm nights, was owned by Don Carlos Roman, a red-faced genial man whose father had been an antiquarian and an expert on Phoenician relics. Don Carlos knew nothing of relics, but he had been appointed curator of the excellent Ibiza museum when his father had died. That was the way in Spain. The King's agents kept a few families loyal everywhere by giving them whatever they could not themselves take away. The Romans were such a family, and owned large tracts of land, had several houses, and enjoyed complete immunity from the law. By that I do not mean that Don Carlos was a bad fellow. Decidedly he was not. Nearly everyone liked him, and that is the test. That is what saved his life later on, when nothing else would have done it. His town house in Ibiza was near that of his aristocratic neighbors and inconvenient for the purposes of orgies, so he decided to build a house in Santa Eulalia on the point the fishermen had always used. It was far enough from other houses in Santa Eulalia and could be enclosed by a wall. The fishermen knew nothing of this until one day some workmen began building the wall. The boss mason informed the fishermen that they must trespass there no longer.

That night the shack in which the workmen kept their materials, a motorboat and tender belonging to

Don Carlos were burned. The Guardias slung their rifles and searched the countryside and, unable to find a bit of evidence, arrested Cosmi's brother-in-law, Marc Colomar, in order to show their superiors that they had not been idle.

Marc's arrest was not known in town until the next morning, and immediately Toniet came to my room. What should he do? I told him to be quiet until nightfall, that Marc would be released that day, and exonerated. I told him also to be careful what he did with matches in the future. He started to go away, but I could see he was hurt and disappointed, and suddenly it occurred to me that he wanted me to judge him. Moral questions were too difficult for him.

"You did a good job, Toniet," I said, and I wish you could have seen him smile.

Nearly always, however, there was an acceptance of things as they were, few outbreaks, few protests, extreme smoothness of the flow of life. Sea moods. States of sea. The rise and fall of the dories and motorboats in the stillness of the night, the oncoming lights and then the bulk of the steamer from the mainland, firelight and pans of rice among the rocks and the pale buff beaches. The fishermen saw each other and their friends and customers daily, rode over expanses of the sea, sorted our miraculous draughts of fishes, eels; crustaceans and bivalves, lugged baskets, blew soft horns made from conks, made change, while the Guardias dozed and loafed in the *Cuartel* or patrolled wooded roads in a desultory way and the black gowns of the priests made spirals in the middle distance as they wound upward and trickled downward over Santa Eulalia's hill. The fishermen seldom read letters or wrote them. They saw their wives infrequently, except for the noon meal and in bed on rainy nights. Santa Eulalia and its coast to them was a countless number of superimposed vistas from the sea, with the green slopes spreading upward toward the skyline, the best of the trees and the white plaster houses gliding slowly in concentric movements, crossing one another, falling into new alignments, resolving themselves in a stationary pattern when the harbor was reached. The main street was fed by streams of morning customers. Don Abel Matutes made all the money because he controlled all the means of transportation, gave out the licenses, filled or emptied cash boxes, mended or neglected roads. Who cared? It is possible that the fishermen considered men lucky who were born with unlimited acres, funds and exemption from all laws except that against murder. They were certainly friendly with Don Carlos and Don Ignacio and Don Mariano Riquer. The visiting millionaire banker who had built a summer house in Santa Eulalia, Don Rafael Sainz, they pitied because his wife was so holy and he was afraid to behave as he liked. But Don Abel Matutes, who spent all his hours making his money in divers ways and forgot to shave as he sat among his ledgers and clerks, was as foreign to them as a spider might be.

Toniet Pardal's wife had five children to care for. She made all their clothes and mended them. That took all her time that was not needed for preparing meals. She had no women friends and her relatives avoided her because she was so often in need. Her manner to her husband was respectful but not submissive or fearful. She showed her age much less than most of the other women who had much less to do. Probably her work was less arduous than that of a poor farmer's wife, but her life lacked the farm festivals and the church holidays and the other pleasures in which women were permitted to share. Patience makes women beautiful in middle age, and Toniet's wife radiated a part of the calm which was Santa Eulalia's best attribute. At any moment she could have begun to enjoy herself if she had had time. And in front of her door was one of the town's most magnificent grapevines. The gnarled stock was thicker than a man's arm, the leaves spread luxuriously on a wooden trellis, offering always a sharp patch of shade on the dust of the back street. As the clusters swelled and grew, Toniet's children would stand in a row, looking up at them, and others would stop and express their admiration. Señora Pardal loved the vine because it was her only possession that others might envy, and the bunches of sweet white grapes, as they grew and took on that faint tinge of brown that sweet grapes should have, were singled out by Toniet and his wife and the children to give as presents to those they liked best, and Toniet's manner, bringing grapes, was something one can never forget and for which he may be forgiven anything.

I cannot leave the fishermen without a word about Edmundo. In a town where the lives of the inhabitants were so closely inter-related there are few men who always stand alone in one's memory. Edmundo was such a one. He was the only man on the island with that name. He was the only one who habitually wore a black shirt, and that had nothing to do with the meaning of black shirts elsewhere. Edmundo was the most thorough and outspoken republican I ever saw, under no matter what regime. The protests others might think about or whisper, he would shout at the top of his lungs when a Guardia or a priest was passing by. Drunk or sober, he would defy arrest or constraint of any kind. He was the only fisherman who wore spectacles. These spectacles had nickel-plated rims, with small lenses which must have been out of alignment, and they gave Edmundo's face a particularly villainous appearance, although his features were much like those of his brother, Mateo Rosa, the best-looking man in town.

Edmundo had a small motorboat and fished alone. When he walked or staggered up the street, he would be alone. He would join his friends for a drink or a song, but even then something about him made him seem to stand apart from them. He had been married once, to celebrate the 1931 revolution, had been left with a couple of children and for their sake had married again, but his wife stayed at home on the back street, did her housework well and was sound asleep long before Edmundo left the cafés each night. There was a purely unsentimental arrangement between them.

Mateo Rosa and Edmundo might have started out as young brothers with similar instincts and inclinations, but since Mateo had tried to appear as respectable as he could, considering the demands of his temperament, Edmundo had emphasized his iconoclastic views in every possible way. Against the formidable inertia of custom and the force of coercion, he had set himself resolutely. He was tough, and the authorities were afraid of him. He said and did what he pleased, knowing he was right and the others were wrong, and nobody dared lay a finger on him. He was one of the best sailors, one of the best dancers, a good companion and a loyal friend. Later I shall tell you what happened when someone tried to force him to take up arms against himself and the other republicans.

And I must not forget the fisherman named Carlos who had a very small house in a narrow alley between the main street and the back street. He was tall, with curly hair and dark-brown eyes and his wife was slender and wore a pigtail, in the ancient style. They did their cooking in a black pot over a small wood fire outside their doorstep, and had only one child. They were together, the slender woman and big curly-haired man and the small child, grouped near their outdoor fire, much more than other fishermen's families. Once the child lost his appetite, and ate almost nothing for about a year, and the mother and father moved through the alley and the town with listless steps and downcast faces. Their fire burned with a duller gleam, and whoever passed through the narrow alley heard the child weakly crying. Then suddenly the child began to eat again, and the woman smiled and danced by the doorstep with the baby in her arms, one step forward, one step back, singing a Moorish lullaby. Carlos walked briskly to and from the harbor, and caught huge baskets of fish and almost laughed aloud as he shouted "*Bon dia*" all the way from Gork's to the tree in the square, where he put down his basket and blew merrily on his horn.

3. The Morning Bus

JUST before six o'clock every morning tremendous and explosive noises would issue from a shed adjacent to Can Xumeu, just about half way between the square and the theatre on the main road. Ramon, the bus driver, would be tuning up his motorcycle. The more noise Ramon could make, the better he liked it. His round tanned face, with deep wrinkles at the outside corners of his eyes, would beam with pleasure when the machine mounted a strong crescendo like many riveting hammers. When it choked and wheezed and died, as it frequently did, his forehead would wrinkle, he would unscrew this or that, take off a part or two and look at them, put them back and start the engine again. The more it balked, the more he raced it afterward. No one complained. Nearly everyone was willing to think about getting up at six, and those already up would saunter down to the shed in time to hear the last few moments of the racket and to see Ramon start shooting toward San Carlos at a murderous pace, leaving a trail of dust in dry weather or splashing house fronts on either side of the road if it were raining. The inhabitants of Santa Eulalia, and particularly Ramon, had an Oriental love of noise. They let doors bang, raced their engines, pounded on tables, shouted all conversation that did not have to

31

be whispered, encouraged dogs to bark and donkeys to bray. When pigs were killed, by having their throats slit and slowly bleeding to death while a man held each leg, the terrific shrieks, diminishing ever so slowly to a final gasp through ten terrible minutes, was music to the ears of gentle girl children with curls and white-haired benevolent grandmothers. If a child fell down and bumped his head, the whole village street would throb with sympathy. Not so when animals howled or cried with pain.

I told at least a thousand persons that pigs should be knocked on the head before their throats were cut, and each one shrugged his shoulders and smiled indulgently, as if nothing mattered less in the world. So cool mornings were punctuated with fiendish sounds, the firing and back-firing of Ramon's motorcycle, death shrieks of pigs and the braying of Guarapiñada's donkey Napoleon.

As a matter of fact, Ramon was the best mechanic on the island, which is not saying much. Mechanical work is not a Latin gift, neither is it Arabic or Catalan. The reason the motorcycle acted so badly was because it was old and worn and would have been discarded by a man of lesser talents than Ramon. He always ran it full speed and only his skill as a driver kept his neck intact, for the road between Santa Eulalia and San Carlos was in all states of disrepair. The dust was almost as treacherous as the mud, and the part that had been macadamized under Primo de Rivera was as full of holes and man traps as nature's own bed rock in other stretches that had echoed the boots of the troops of Julius Caesar.

A few peasants with market baskets filled with pro-

duce, live chickens, etc., got on the bus at San Carlos
and at quarter to seven Ramon would drive the bus
into Santa Eulalia and stop just beyond the post
office. If he overshot his mark, his front fenders would
come up even with the first tubbed palm in front of
the Royalty. He would honk his horn until his arm
muscles ached, and as he honked there would be a
mild outpouring from doorways all along the street.
The fishermen, squatting around their baskets just
ahead, would cross the street languidly to load on
the bus roof boxes of fish packed in ice. The bow-
legged proprietor of Casa Rosita, the grocery store
and bus terminal, would saunter over with a battered
ledger in which were written the names of those who
had reserved places. He looked like an American cowboy. Certain days of the week, on Tuesday when the
Barcelona boat arrived, or on Saturday, the biggest
market day, the bus would be overcrowded and those
who had had the foresight to inscribe their names on
the list had first right to the seats. If there were more
customers than could be jammed without headroom
into the aisles, another and even more rickety camion
would be urged out of its garage and a second-string
driver pressed into service to take care of the over-
flow. Often the second-string bus broke down and
Ramon would have to make two trips.

The inside of the bus, on days when the windows
had to be closed, smelled like a deserted cheese factory that had just been used for shoeing camels. That
was because the Ibicenco men smoked home-grown
tobacco they called *pota*, which means horse's hoof.
Their town clothes were invariably black, made of a
thick absorbent material like velvet only much

cheaper, and once they became permeated with *pota* smoke they never lost their flavor. The men who smoked *pota* were proud of the stuff, as a local product, and insisted that it was good. I have seen them try the best English sliced plug and dump it from their pipes in disgust.

As a whole, though, Santa Eulalia was especially fragrant in the morning at bus time, for the household fires and the larger ones in the hotels and bakers' ovens, were kindled with rosemary twigs which Platé had gathered on the hills and sold for wine money. And the climate was such that on very few days was it necessary to close the windows of the bus or the doors of the cafés. Men lived out of doors nearly all their waking time.

To many of the women from the outlying farms, a trip to Ibiza (nine miles) was an important voyage, to be undertaken twice a year only after much discussion and preparation. A few of them, dressed in holiday attire (head kerchief, of dull greenish gold, plum-colored shawl, full accordion-pleated skirt of Veronese green, and a gay turquoise ribbon at the nape of the neck), would be standing in a group and the moment the bus rolled in would take their places, chattering in high-pitched voices, changing from one side to the other, finally settling down and sitting close together as if for mutual protection. No young women ever travelled alone, or even crossed the street alone after dark. A mother or an aunt accompanied them, and she would be as picturesquely and tastefully dressed, but in darker hues. Eighty percent of the women wore black because they were in mourning. That custom, one of the blights on the lives of the women that depressed and inconvenienced them most, seemed to be unbreakable. One of the smartest young girls, Eulalia Noguera, told me when she was nineteen that she had been out of mourning only six months of her life and her family was one of the most radical, politically. Even Cosmi, for a few months after Anna's grandfather died, selected a black necktie on the two or three occasions in that period when he wore a necktie. He muttered and grinned sheepishly when I commented on his choice of cravat, but still he made that slight concession to the conventions. Had he worn a colored tie, he knew that the women of the family would have given him no peace, and Cosmi loved peace dearly.

Each morning, Ramon, after honking the horn until his hand was tired, would step down to the sidewalk and those who had errands for him to do would gather round. It is hard to say how large a percentage of the objects which found their way from Ibiza to Santa Eulalia and the messages between relatives or business men which were exchanged passed through Ramon's head or his hands. If a housewife needed a teapot, or a foreign visitor had to have a check cashed, when a baby needed medicine—no matter what there was to be done, Ramon accepted the commission. He was not paid for these services, except in rare cases, but he performed them in an effortless and efficient way. Whenever I saw him, in his dark flannel shirt, with a leather cap into which he stuffed written memoranda, slapping his trousers legs with his driving gauntlets, I thought of some stage driver out West in the early years of the century. It is astonishing how much I found in Santa Eulalia that reminded me of American life of thirty years ago. To enter the village never seemed to me like entering a foreign town. Instead I had the sensation of getting back home, back to old days I had been led to believe were beyond recall. That is why now I feel shaken and desolate.

Through doorways, the broad tree-lined *paseo* leading up from the sea and the cool public well, the narrow passages or the fields between the houses, men strolled toward the bus as Ramon honked. Guillermo, the blacksmith, in a blue striped shirt rolled up on his lean hairy arms, his shock of curly hair awry, moved slowly toward the center of activities. No one hurried, except a few half-hysterical peasant women who were in fear that the bus would go away without them. Guillermo stood near Ramon when the latter was receiving requests for this and that, apparently inattentive, and still nothing escaped his notice. He knew everything that happened in town, and said little about it unless it was especially comical. Life, for Guillermo, was a leisurely pageant, enlivened by comical trivialities. His sense of humor was extremely broad, not to say Rabelaisian, but it was capable also of refinement. In certain ways he was the most proper man I ever knew.

Early in the morning there was never music, but only the babble of voices, and the men with the strongest voices made themselves heard most frequently. Nicolau had the strongest voice in town. He was a short stocky man with a large nose and a very red face, an army officer who had been retired with full pay just after Alfonso had been chased from the throne. Each morning he emerged from his house, a rather spacious one very neatly kept which stood on the southeast corner of the public square. Nicolau did practically nothing, day in day out. While Guillermo and his other friends worked according to their temperaments in their shops or cafés or stores, Nicolau would sit in a chair on the shady side of the street and talk with them at various distances up to a hundred yards. His voice was ideal for giving commands and his brain well equipped for receiving them. He put no other strain upon it. Like most army men, he liked hunting and he had a fine pair of Ibicenco hounds, lean white dogs with pointed noses like greyhounds and capable of more speed. In the autumn afternoons, Nicolau would tramp through the woods between Santa Eulalia and San Carlos and once in a while would kill a small wild rabbit or a grouse. Sometimes in rainy weather he would play dominoes noisily in Cosmi's café. He was not a heavy drinker but he tried to be a good fellow and at the time of which I am writing, the early days of the Republic, he had a number of friends, none of them intimate, but all of them ready enough to drink or play dominoes with him.

When the government that succeeded Alfonso's was organized, Azaña, who was President in the tragic days of 1936, was made Minister of War. He knew that the Spanish army had been built up by the monarchists to take care of sons and relatives and that of the inordinate number of officers there were few who were not hostile to republican ideas. Instead of disbanding the army, which was of no use except as a threat to free government, Azaña proceeded more cautiously. He retired the officers who were most flagrantly hostile to his regime but in order not to stir them up too much he consented to pay them their full wages as long as they lived. They had done practically nothing when they were on active service, but that did not satisfy their ideal. The prospect of full pay, and no work whatsoever, was alluring. It bolstered up their disrespect of a government of the people and made them feel that their enemies, the people, were afraid of them. Nicolau got one thousand *pesetas* a month for staying out of the army, and among the monarchists joked about it freely. Branches of the family were rich, otherwise he would never have been a captain in the first place. His immediate family lived comfortably on his pay, had a rather large house, better clothes than the average in Santa Eulalia, and his wife held herself slightly aloof from the other women and was assiduous about going to mass. Nicolau, as far as I know, never went to church himself. If his wife kept up her religious practices, it was enough to cover him. That was as near piety as the average Spanish man ever got.

Between the post office and the Royalty, Andres the painter would be standing in front of his father's café, and from time to time his mother, Magdalena, would look out, her broad shapely arms wet with suds or dusted with flour. Young Andres would be talking in a way that pleased his father and caused his mother much anxiety. The lad did not look like a café keeper or a farmer. He was a painter, and a talented one. His parents, bewildered by his aptitude for drawing, had sent him to Valencia to study and he had fulfilled their hopes as far as his progress was concerned. In the academy, though, he had heard of socialism and some of the simpler and most humane of its doctrines had touched his heart. He spoke of social justice wistfully, without bitterness, for although his mother and father were not rich, he had suffered none of the hardships usually associated with poverty. He had worked hard, but not excessively. His influence among the young men of the town was considerable. Soon after young Andres had returned from school, he had been talking in his father's café about the right of workers to control the machinery of production, and Captain Nicolau, shocked and angry, had told him he had better be careful what he said. Andres' father, who had been a revolutionist long before 1931, spoke up and told Nicolau to mind his own business, and from that time on, Nicolau ceased to patronize the café.

Once in a while Don Ignacio Riquer's auto would break down and he would ride to Ibiza on the bus. Don Ignacio was a pleasant cherub-faced little man. He wore a neat black suit, with the coat unbuttoned, a white cotton shirt and a black bow tie. His shoes were shined and his trousers, while they were seldom newly pressed, were not so baggy as those of the peasants. His Santa Eulalia house, built in U shape around a broad patio, was just south of the plaza. The front was covered with climbing vines and the windows were broad, in French style, in contrast to the small Arab windows of the neighboring smaller houses. He had had an English ancestor way back in the time of the Catholic sovereigns (his name was Wallis y Riquer) and took pride in his vocabulary of thirty English words. All the land along the south bank of Santa Eulalia's river belonged to Don Ignacio. He owned miles of the shore, with its rocky caverns and sandy coves. He owned groves of mariner's pines and thickets of cane twelve feet tall, fields of wheat, corn, sweet potatoes, olive trees, *garobas* trees, rows of hunchbacked fig trees with props holding up the branches. He was proud of having twenty pure-bred Holstein cows, but his most cherished possession was his well. It was situated along the Ibiza bus road, about a mile from Santa Eulalia, and if Don Ignacio gave you a lift to town, as he frequently did when his auto was running, he would stop and gaze admiringly at the small white plaster structure, dome-covered like a shrine, beneath which cool waters eternally bubbled. Don Ignacio had worked out the number of gallons which could be pumped from this well without lowering the water level more than a centimeter, and I think it came to 90,000. He loved his farm, his cattle, his hills and coves and trees, but the well, fed by inexhaustible hidden springs, seemed to him the mark of God's special favor.

During the summer, the sun was well up in the sky at seven o'clock in the morning. Sometimes I thought it was the hottest hour of the day. I suppose the heat reached its peak of intensity between one and two in the afternoon, but few of us in Santa Eulalia were on the street in the *siesta* hours. At seven, the low buildings adjacent to the fishermen's café and on the other side of the street from where the bus stood threw a deep comforting shadow. In front of Casa Rosita and the sheds and small storerooms used by Ferrer, proprietor of Las Delicias, scattered groups would stand and talk a while as the seats of the bus were filling and its roof was being laden with fish, empty siphons, battered suitcases, straw hampers, bundles tied up in black cloth and straw-vested demijohns to be filled with wine.

The Secretario, always smiling, wore a light grey cotton jacket, and had his hair cut pompadour style. He was usually to be seen with the municipal doctor, whose aristocratic origin prompted him to wear a black coat in hot weather and to walk mincingly among the townspeople as if he could not tell them apart. Nearly everyone disliked Doctor Torres. Some of the peasants had a superstitious fear of passing near him on the street, but at that time he was the only doctor available in Santa Eulalia and in extreme cases it was necessary to call him. Under the monarchy he had done as he pleased, refusing to go out at night, making excuses if the roads were rough or muddy, neglecting families who owed him money or whom he disliked because one of their members had died on his hands. The Republic had required him to hold a free clinic twice each week, which he did with the utmost disgust.

The Secretario had been given his job in the days of the old regime and had contrived to keep it when the republicans took over the administration. His work did not touch on matters of life and death but had to do with ink and papers and he mixed with his neighbors cheerfully enough.

"Which party does the Secretario favor?" I asked one day much later, after I had seen him perform his functions with at least five of them.

"The one that wins," Cosmi answered.

Still, the Secretario did small favors for nearly

everyone now and then and was never known to do any harm. Evenings he did not appear in the cafés but sat in a wooden chair in front of his doorstep, his family and a few friends gathered around, and would play the guitar as best he could in view of the handicap of a missing finger.

The owner of the bus and the holder of the concession was named Julian, pronounced Houlianne. He looked and acted more like a chimpanzee than any man I ever saw. He hopped about, cackling and smiling, jerking his arms and his moustaches, volunteering eloquent opinions that invariably were wrong. Always he was one of the most active elements of the morning crowd, but his activities had nothing to do with the bus line he owned. That he left entirely to Ramon. Julian played dominoes and the simpler card games in the Spanish style, that is, with vociferous disputes over every point and a fiendish pleasure in seeing the loser pay. His bus line, except for the extra and gratuitous services performed for the public by Ramon, was conducted with a fantastic disregard for public convenience. That was accepted as the normal state of affairs.

As the moment drew nearer when Ramon must pull out for Ibiza, he would stand near the horn and sound it again until his hand got tired. The peasants in the bus would count their bundles, hitch themselves more firmly in their seats, and often there would be the sound of women sobbing and crescendos of mournful exchanges of farewell. Every family in Santa Eulalia had relatives in Mallorca or Catalonia or the Levantine shore, and when visits were at an end scenes of grief would occur around the bus that were unrestrained and almost contagious. Women would sob and scream, hide their faces in one another's shoulders, others would stand silently and miserably on the outskirts of the crowd, weeping softly into handkerchiefs, stealing a last fond look at the cousin or niece who was going away, and shivering as if the warm sun were attached like a kite to Ramon's spare tire and would follow the bus and the loved ones past the fountain, the broad residence of Ignacio Riquer, the villas with their bright gardens, the rocky hill on which stood the ancient church, the flour mill, the Roman bridge and along the white road south to the utmost ends of the earth.

4. Stores and Storekeepers

THE Casa Rosita, the general store nearest the plaza, was named for a little girl aged five with large brown eyes, dark curls neatly parted, who wore pink and white dresses and smiled at all the men. Her grandfather Juan, the proprietor who looked like an American cowboy, had short bow legs, a black moustache with twirled ends, wore a black slouch hat and rolled his own cigarettes.

I never saw Juan work hard, and he never was completely idle, except on Sundays. He was amiable with his customers and neighbors but in all his life he had never formed but one close friendship. That was with José Ribas, the diving champion.

Early Sunday morning José would walk in from his dry farm in the hills northwest of town. Juan would be strolling up and down the main street waiting for him.

They would greet one another gleefully, with smiles, handshakes and slaps on the back and would head directly for Cosmi's to get a drink. In passing Can Xumeu's, his brother's place, the diving champion would glance guiltily inside, knowing that he should greet Xumeu forthwith but fearing that in case he did Xumeu would caution him mildly about drinking. At Cosmi's, the old friends would select a

small round table for two and would order *cazalla*. I
would have given a lot to know what old Juan and
his friend talked about on Sunday mornings. They
leaned close together and José would stoop so that
Juan's moustache was within an inch of his ear. They
would whisper in turn, glancing furtively around
them from time to time, sometimes bursting suddenly
into hilarious laughter, again sighing and shaking
their heads in a deprecatory way. It was in 1932
that the incident occurred which gave José the title
of Diving Champion.

Just after the 1931 revolution there had been a stir
of civic pride in Santa Eulalia and a number of the
leading citizens and a few of the foreign residents
had banded together in an effort to beautify the
town. Two long parallel rows of pink azaleas were
transplanted from distant dry-creek bottoms to the
borders of the town *paseo*. Holes about the size and
depth of graves were dug on either side of the main
street at fifty-meter intervals for the planting of plane
trees. Before the trees were bought, however, the
funds and enthusiasm ran low and the committee
broke up in discord over the question of the use of a
street sprinkler.

One Sunday morning when the tree holes were
filled with rain water, just as the women who had attended mass were filing down the street, Juan and
José stepped out of Gork's. They started up the street
together, arm in arm, trying to be as unconcerned
and dignified as possible, as they threaded their way
through the colorful procession. But José stepped a
little too near the edge of the concrete sidewalk,
waved his arms wildly on the brink, lost his balance

and fell with a great splash into one of the deepest
tree holes near by. Everyone in town witnessed the
mishap, saw José's head come up, saw old Juan risking his own safety in an effort to get his friend's floating hat, saw Guillermo the blacksmith and others
rush out from Gork's and pull José to safety. The
crowd was awestruck as the dripping farmer, sobered
by his sudden immersion, walked penitently to his
brother Xumeu's and disappeared from view. I expected to hear roars of laughter, but there were none.
They were all so impressed with the enormity of the
misfortune that they reserved their mirth until José
was out of sight. Even then the men joked only in
whispers and the women shook their heads and
thought of the shame that would be visited upon his
family forever more. Had Edmundo or Toniet Pardal
or Platé or any of the hard-drinking infidels fallen
into a hole, no one would have been so much impressed, least of all the victim. But for José, brother
of a priest and of the respectable Xumeu, a public
exhibition of drunkenness meant deep disgrace.

Next time I saw the diving champion he had lost
twenty pounds. His eyes were haggard and deep-set
and he hurried along the street, looking neither right
nor left, and slipped into Xumeu's, going directly to
the kitchen without a glance at the bar. For at least
two months, on Sunday mornings, Juan the grocer
wandered aimlessly up and down, snatching a quick
drink now and then but obviously sad and lonely.
Then very gradually the two friends resumed their
former convivial habit, the champion regained his
weight and good spirits, and the next year the trees
arrived from Valencia, were planted, the holes filled

in, and one of the hazards of the town disappeared.

There was no sense of keen trade rivalry between the storekeepers. Customers usually went to the nearest store and if they could not get what they wanted, they went on to the next one. The Casa Rosita, being nearest the plaza, got the trade from the southern end of town. It was due to Mariano, old Juan's son, that the store was comparatively orderly and systematic. The goods were ranged conveniently and Mariano knew where everything was. He was like Guillermo the blacksmith in that respect. Without the appearance of effort or industry he seemed to be able to accomplish what was necessary. He never tried to advertise, as Guarapiñada did. He didn't attempt to carry everything in stock like the proprietor of the Casa Miguel. Business, he thought, should proceed in a natural way as trees grew, and not become an obsession.

Of the four general stores in Santa Eulalia, however, the Casa Rosita was the one for the respectable minority, the primitive peasants, the Guardias and the clergy. It would not occur to a priest to enter Las Delicias, from the doorway of which Ferrer, the proprietor, shot sky rockets and pointed upward, roaring with laughter when the church bells would ring on Ascension Day. The reverend father would not dare go into Guarapiñada's "Tot Barat" for fear of being doused with a siphon. And Miguel Tur, of the Casa Miguel, was a socialist and revolutionary from birth.

If General George Washington had marched with a flag down the main street of Santa Eulalia, beginning at the plaza and proceeding north toward Gork's, I think there is no doubt who would have been the first to drop whatever he was doing and join him. I refer to Toni Ferrer, ex-blacksmith and proprietor of Las Delicias. He was a stocky man with broad shoulders, a hearty laugh and mischievous eyes that looked fierce at a distance because of his heavy black eyebrows. As a young man he had been apprenticed to a blacksmith and had learned to shoe mules, mend cartwheels and iron tires, make door latches and the heavy iron keys in use in the town. Although no one locked the door of his home, the shopkeepers always locked their doors at closing time and the proprietor carried the key in his pocket until the next day. Even at noon, when shops were closed until two or three o'clock, this custom was followed. So often the apprentices had to go all over town to find the boss and get the key. Ferrer kept his store open until ten or eleven o'clock at night. There was not much trade in the grocery line at that hour, but men from the country around dropped in during the evening to buy odds and ends. The electric-light plant broke down about three times a week and sent everyone scurrying to the stores for candles. Ferrer kept a stock of wine on tap, a bottle of cognac and a few liqueurs. But at ten he usually closed the place, sent his wife, sons and daughters to bed, and went across the street to Cosmi's. There, after nearly everyone had gone home, he and a few other patriots could talk freely.

In saying that Ferrer would have been the first to join General Washington, I did not mean to slight Cosmi himself, by far the highest-minded and ablest man in Santa Eulalia. Cosmi would have known the General was coming and would have been with him before he got as far as Santa Eulalia. Cosmi was the natural leader of liberal thinkers and courageous men, and he and Ferrer were good friends. I do not mean that there were revolutionary plots, or involved Marxian discussions at Cosmi's in the late reaches of each night. Merely that Ferrer, if he felt like it, could say aloud that it was a damn shame Matutes' second cousin (sole contractor for building roads) had left the gravel piled on the muddy sidewalks for two years. And Cosmi could call attention to the fact that the Guardia Civil permitted young monarchists to hold meetings whenever they liked but that all republican organizations were refused permission on the ground of public safety. To those American readers who have never yet lived in a country where a man could not speak his mind on such simple subjects, this may sound trivial. To others, whose fathers or grandfathers remember long years during which everything they really meant had to be whispered, after hurried glances around them, Cosmi's oasis in a desert of hushed voices and circumspect thoughts, will be green and cool, with sheltering branches of palms and the odor of clean growing fruits in the air.

Additions, subtractions, and what simple bookkeeping was required in Ferrer's Las Delicias were performed by a slim girl of twelve with large dark eyes and a gentle voice. The mother and father watched her proudly and somewhat wistfully as if, had they known it was as easy as it looked when their child did it, they themselves would somehow have learned to add. At the time they were young, however, Alfonso's government was spending one-third of the national income in paying salaries to priests and practically nothing on secular education. Ferrer, as a boy, distrusted the priests and everything in which they had a hand and preferred to work, hard and honestly, in a blacksmith shop rather than to sit mumbling prayers and reading the lives of the saints with a minimum of A.B.C.'s and two plus two make four. What did he gain or lose? Is it worth while to blight your understanding and squander your time in order to learn to read a newspaper in which not one word of essential truth would appear in a year? Two-thirds of the inhabitants of the central part of Santa Eulalia could read, but I never found more than a half dozen who read anything interesting. The two daily newspapers, four-page sheets, were both controlled by Matutes and censored by the bishop. I doubt if six books could have been found in the combined libraries of Don Carlos Roman, Ignacio Riquer and Don Rafael Sainz, all millionaires. And sometimes I wonder if they, in that single instance, might not have acted for the best. I wonder if Don Carlos, having ploughed through the *Saturday Evening Post* and the *New York Times*, would have enjoyed his cognac or his boys with more relish or less? Or whether he would have dusted his Phœnician and Carthaginian relics in the museum oftener, or tried to find our where his father had learned so much about them?

I can only be sure of this. That if the rich men in the United States had bought out the army and the police with foreign money, turned loose the Indians with guns and driven the people's government from Washington, Ferrer in Ibiza would have understood the situation better than literate Americans seem to understand affairs in Spain right now. And his sympathies in the matter would be straight-forwardly and sincerely with the people.

Señora Ferrer was a short strong woman with bright dark eyes, a high forehead, bobbed hair straight and black as an Indian's, and small though capable hands and feet. She wore a sort of Mother Hubbard print dress and no stockings. All the Ibicenco women wore old-style white ruffled drawers and although they stooped in the fields and climbed in and out of high-wheeled carts, they never exposed themselves above their ankles or below their throats. I cannot remember having seen any other portion of any native woman in Santa Eulalia, not even a glimpse, in the years I spent there. Keeping their persons safe from the sun and men's eyes was among their strongest instincts and most thorough accomplishments. Women who had worked all their lives in the fields had complexions pure white. Nevertheless, young mothers would nurse their babies in a crowded café without the least embarrrassment and without drawing a glance or comment from the males. So one knew the faces, hands, ankles and breasts of all the delightful young women, and nothing else except clothes.

Ferrer's first child, a girl, was feeble-minded. There was a chair for her in a small alcove just off the main room of the store and all day she used to sit smiling, replying happily when anyone took the trouble to greet her.

As if to compensate the Ferrers for their first disappointment or to reward them for their patience, the other three children were exceptionally promising. Little Maria, who kept the cash box, was not only graceful and amiable, but what the French call *spirit-uelle*. It pleased her when lists of figures resolved themselves into a correct total or her father brought her a flower to put in her hair. On feast days, when the other girls were parading up and down the street, dancing and singing songs in chorus. Ferrer always sent her out to join them. The younger boy delivered siphons up and down the street and in summer carted chunks of ice to the foreigners. He was always busy, raffling off a fish, cleaning old horseshoes, running to the garden for vegetables demanded in the store. Soon he was to have his turn at the school in Barcelona, where his brother who drove the donkey and later the automobiles had learned so much. In certain American comedies I have seen instances where children returning from school attempted to lord it over their less-educated parents. Such an idea certainly never entered the head of one of the Ferrers.

The store was small, half the size of the Casa Rosita, smelling of wine, fresh onions, and Ibicenco tobacco. Dry beans, peas, macaroni, and rice were ranged in boxes and sacks on the floor. The shelves were covered with canned goods, cooking utensils, chamber pots and alpargatas, the native sandals with cactus-fibre soles, cloth tops and ankle strings. When a customer ordered a can of tuna, for instance, Ferrer would hop up on a box, take down a can from the top shelf and hand it to the customer tentatively.

"I think that's tuna," he would say. Quite often he was right. If the can was marked *calamares*, the customer would hand it back and Ferrer would look at it carefully for identifying marks before he put it away and selected another.

The family slept in a series of small rooms extending back into the garden. One alcove was used as a dining room, another for the wine and the older daughter's chair. Next door was the blacksmith shop, with the forge cold, and beside that a small room used for storage of cases and in the fall and winter for butchering pigs and making the marvellous Ibicenco sausage called *sobresada*. Pep Salvador, Cosmi's brother, killed the pigs on the sidewalk outside Las Delicias and then lugged in the carcasses and stretched them on a bench. Pep Salvador was master of ceremonies at nearly all the pig-killing festivals, working like a demon, drinking more than any other man, always the buffoon. At carnival time, the principal clowns were always Pep Salvador and Ferrer. They put on acts in the plaza, visited all the houses and nearly wrecked some of them, caroused from café to café, trailing half the population behind them. One year Pep was the dentist and Ferrer his patient. They would set up a hideous chair, ring a bell to attract the crowd, then Pep, with a set of tools the Fratellini could not excel, would yank out a huge horse's tooth from Ferrer's mouth while the latter made noises that put dying pigs to shame.

It is Monday morning and Santa Eulalia begins as usual. The Sunday night *ooks* (Balearic cries of challenge and exuberance which helped make Caesar's slingers formidable) have died, spreading fanwise, in the country roads. Lights twinkle on the fishing boats, dogs stretch and seek food, the motorcycle's bombardment, the early men and women appearing at doors, the rosemary smoke, the bus, then the women, with fibre baskets called *cenayons*, go out for the day's supplies. On the northern edge of the town, just across a lane leading westward to the hills, is the Casa Miguel the old general store of the pioneer days, dim and roomy inside, the windows obscured by flyspecks and dandling ladles, skimmers, strings of onions and red peppers, fly swatters, shovels and hoe handles. No one, not even the proprietor, Miguel Tur, could have told you what his shelves contained. When you asked for a beanpot, for instance, he would raise his spectacles slowly over his forehead, sigh, look at you with frank, almost challenging eyes and repeat the word "beanpot" as he rose to his feet. He was always sitting by a littered window, reading. He could recite Don Juan Tenario and whole acts of Lope de Vega's plays, long passages of Cervantes, Shakespeare, Voltaire and (duck your heads, legion) Thoreau and Tom Paine.

"Beanpot," he would say again, as if in looking for a beanpot he was indulging one of your mild eccentricities. His head wagged from side to side, like that of a mechanical toy, partly to help him preserve a state of open-mindedness and partly on account of a nervous affliction.

"Beanpot."

His wife, old and dropsical and completely un-literary, would rise at this point from her low chair in the kitchen and appear at the doorway, pushing back her spectacles over her smooth high forehead. They would start out in opposite directions, pottering through nuts and bolts, cans of sardines, cornstarch, flour, cans of olive oil, washboards and other assorted articles. Miguel Tur would pause, rub his back with one hand, brush dust from the other hand on his trousers leg, and remark that he was sure he had a beanpot.

"Yes," his wife would say. "There's one here somewhere."

If you, the customer, were lucky, a young fat boy with round face, plump cheeks and prominent buttocks would come in from a football game in the streets or a siege with other customers.

"What is it you want?" he would ask, and upon being told would get you a beanpot promptly. He did not look bright, but he was. The fat boy was Miguel Tur's adopted son. When he was outdoors, which was frequently, the turnover in the store was very slow, but Miguel Tur was as conscientious about the boy's freedom as he was solicitous about the affairs of Spain and the oppressed throughout the earth. To me that is by no means funny, but to most of his neighbors Miguel's earnestness, I must admit, had a comical aspect.

Miguel's neighbors' doctrine of "let well enough alone" weighed heavily on his mind and patiently, always, he tried to make them understand that things could and should be better. For this unwelcome attention to public welfare he had been obliged to leave Ibiza in the days of Primo de Rivera. Luckily Miguel Tur's father had been serious-minded, too, and had said that every boy must learn a trade. One could never tell what was going to happen. So Miguel Tur, when chased out of his home by Primo (I know he built wonderful roads and the trains ran on time), was fully equipped to make a living as a pastry cook. He got a ride to Cuba with another grand man who found it safer to absent himself in that golden period of road construction and assassination, our friend Mateo Rosa, master mariner, diver and fisherman. They made their getaway to Cuba, where Mateo Rosa fished and Miguel Tur cooked pastry. Miguel Tur's wife was very pretty and sprightly then and she took a job with a rich American family (who did not suspect they were harboring radicals) and the Americans liked her so well they cried when Ibiza was safe again and the pink laurel bloomed in all the dry creek beds and Miguel Tur and his wife came sailing back on the *Isabel Matutes*, with money enough to stock their store in such a way that it remains well stocked to this day.

O eighty-foot schooner, beloved *Isabel!* Do not let our readers forget you! Impress yourself somehow, gently, upon their minds, your sturdy lines, the lift of your masts and spars, the paths through the sea you have left to disappear in sea behind you, the hearts and the heads of the men you have borne away from death and dungeons. There is another voyage ahead, most needful of all, and the saddest, when again you shall sail from the harbor with the sunset astern and the future as uncertain as the wind.

The latest comer among the Santa Eulalia store-keepers was Guarapiñada, whose hearty and somewhat derisive laughter could be heard whenever a customer entered his shop called "Tot Barat." All by himself, without ever having seen America or read a correspondence course, he had discovered advertising. He was the local P. T. Barnum. The other store-keepers never thought of calling attention to their wares. They took it for granted that their customers

knew what they wanted and would ask for it. Not so
Guarapiñada. One day he would have candied pine-
nuts on display, in tissue-paper packages, with a huge
placard he had painted and lettered. If they did not
sell fast enough to satisfy his enthusiasm (not greed)
he would improvise a gambling machine and offer
packages of candied pine-nuts as prizes. The children
would flock to his doorway and he laughed and sang
with them until they would scatter to their homes
and the shops of their fathers to asks for *sous* to spend.
The tomatoes and deep purple eggplants, all the
fruits and vegetables at "Tot Barat" were cleaned
and polished until they shone. Guarapiñada had invented a liqueur he called *Aigu de tots boscs* (Water
of all the groves) which was a strong concoction of
alcohol and herbs like the Italian *grappa*, only much
stronger.

There was much that suggested the Italian in
Guarapiñada, his mirth and expansiveness, his love
of the center of the stage, his effervescent romanti-
cism. He was tall, with twinkling dark-blue eyes and
grey hair, a square forehead, determined jaw and a
most contagious laugh. As a young man he had been
too restless to remain in San Carlos. On the mainland,
after much adventure, he thoughtlessly joined the
Guardia Civil. He liked the uniform, the black patent-
leather three-cornered hat, the capes, the dark-blue
full-dress regalia, the green-grey uniform for every
day. He took naturally to drill, became a crack shot,
in every way a credit to his organization, until it began to dawn on him what the Guardia Civil really
was. He was not allowed to fraternize with the population, he could not question orders, he found himself

pierced by the smouldering hatred in the eyes of his countrymen he had been trained to intimidate and, at the word of his sergeant, to slaughter. For several years, his orders were such that either he could evade them or carry them out without the loss of his soul. He became a corporal, then a sergeant, because it was impossible for a man of his distinction not to get ahead. Then, before the 1931 revolution, in the last days of Alfonso, he was detailed to shoot two young aviators who were suspected of being republicans. Guarapiñada took off his natty uniform and threw it into the latrine of his *cuartel*, he broke his rifle across a stone bench, then he walked out and for one year was a fugitive from Alfonso's justice.

While hiding in Barcelona, Guarapiñada worked in a bicycle shop, but ordinary bicycles lacked something for him, so he invented a three-wheeled conveyance with tread pedals and an armchair seat, and when 1931 came and he was free to go where he pleased, he returned to his home town, and astonished the natives by riding back and forth on Primo de Rivera's paved roads in his unique vehicle. He bought a mouse-colored young donkey, Napoleon, who learned to respond to Guarapiñada's conversation. Napoleon would follow his master like a kitten, roll over, count up to five, trot, single-foot or walk, according to command. His coat was sleek and beautiful but one day he playfully nipped one of Guarapiñada's children and in a fit of rage Guarapiñada sold him to Ferrer and never spoke to him again.

At the time Guarapiñada returned to the island he was a bachelor in his late forties. A pretty San Carlos girl, fourteen years of age, fell madly in love with him. He liked her and thought it was time he was married, but the parents, among the most backward and old-fashioned people in the town, objected with all their might and locked the daughter in an upper room. The old folks thought Guarapiñada was crazy, and everyone knew he had been wanted by the authorities for more than a year. Besides, he rode tricycles, talked to donkeys, organized counter-processions of unbelievers with brooms when the faithful marched around the churchyard on Palm Sunday, and generally comported himself in an unorthodox manner. He was three times the girl's age and not rich. The girl soved the problem by jumping out of the window at night and rousing Guarapiñada out of a sound sleep. They were married next morning, the first civil marriage ever to take place in San Carlos, and moved at once to Santa Eulalia where business opportunities were better and the townspeople more liberal-minded.

Guarapiñada and I addressed one another in French, with elaborate titles such as *Monsieur le Directeur* and *Monsieur le President* and were always on the best of terms. Imagine my surprise and chagrin one day when I entered his store to make a small purchase, was greeted in an angry and surly fashion and told to get out and mind my business. I learned not many minutes later that his oldest child was ill. For more than two weeks, during the child's illness and for a day or two after its death, Guarapiñada would speak to no one. He did not try to do business, dust collected on his shelves, the tomatoes and eggplants lost their gloss. I have never seen such fierce parental love or such profound despair. His wife moved furtively through the back rooms of the house, dull-eyed, afraid, repenting unknown sins of omission. Then suddenly one day Guarapiñada laughed again and carved a marvellous doll for the other baby, not a copy of a doll he had seen but a new and strange one that no ancient Aztec or Chinese or South Sea Islander or any living man had imagined or set eyes upon.

It was an intense and happy family in Tot Barat. The young wife worshipped Guarapiñada and he was harsh with her only when the children were concerned. They both watched young Eulalia, who had a grave face and large grey eyes which looked terribly intelligent, followed every move she made and were paralyzed with terror if her appetite failed or she slept badly. The next year another baby was born, a boy, and Guarapiñada expressed his joy in billboards and posters and a huge new gambling machine that caught the Sunday crowds. He built himself a thatched terrace, whitewashed his walls out of season, and printed on them in letters four inches high

ON PARLE FRANCAIS
(and untruthfully) SPEEK ENGLISH.

5. The Church

THE church of Santa Eulalia stood aloof from the town on the crest of a high hill, set back a quarter of a mile from the sea but rocky like the sea cliffs far below, a stranded coast-line of some previous age. An old Moorish fortress commanding miles of country and shore formed the front of the structure, semi-circular to fit the shape of the crag foundation, walls immensely thick with battlement windows so small they looked like slits. A dome, the shape of which accentuated the hilly horizon, had been placed on top and behind the old fort was a long sweep of white wall against which small pines and fig trees threw sharp shadows. A small belfry topped by a cross looked like an afterthought. The cemetery wall rose up and dipped down according to the contours of the hill, and inside was rich earth which had been carried up in baskets from the lower levels by the Moors. Where the gravestones stood had flourished a high green garden.

Except for a very few women from the center of the town, the worshippers came long distances from the white plaster houses which dotted the outlying hills. About ten o'clock Sunday morning they would begin to converge toward the rocky hill from farms and groves, terraced orchards, stony pasture lands. The

roads curved and twisted through the valleys, zigzagged around the stone fences, approaching the
church and the town in devious ways. The costumes
of the women, always with a touch of gold, showed
spots and flashes of red, blue, purple and orange,
which heightened the colors of spring or of harvest
and stirred to holiday vibrations the vivid greens of
the trees and the fields, the buff of the wheat and the
beaches, and the blue of the sea and the sky. The
black coats and hats of the men intensified the white
walls of the houses. The two-wheeled carts creaked
and bumped in the ruts. On they came from all directions, obscured by thickets of cane, then reappearing,
pausing as the occupants shouted greetings to friends
in doorways, continuing without reference to the bell
which rang lazily and frantically by turns, according
to the mood of the sexton. Each woman carried a
small camp stool on the woodwork of which was
carved her name or that of her deceased mother or
grandmother.

It seemed almost as if whoever planned the island
roads, in Phoenician, Carthaginian or Roman times,
had suspected that the inhabitants of the main settle-
ment of Santa Eulalia would not be pious, for the
country roads nearly all reached the hill on which
stood the church without passing through the principal street of the town. There was no room on the
hilltop for the mules and carts, so the animals were
tied to trees at the foot of the hill and many of the
men and women who had ridden together parted
there, the men intent on visiting their favorite cafés,
while the women trudged up the spiral paths in chat-

tering groups until the whole rocky hill was kaleido-
scopic with bright silks and alive with shrill voices.
A few of the men, perhaps twenty, got as far as the
café just below the church, from which could be seen
far below five miles of the road to Ibiza, the summit
of the Cala Llonga slope, the twisting and turning
of the river bed, with cane and oleanders to mark its
course through the corn fields and alfalfa patches.
The beat of the Ibicenco drum would be heard, first
softly then imperatively, the sharp horse-castanets
would join in, clicking demoniacally, then the shrill
flutes, two or three in imperfect unison, would embark upon an Ibicenco melody. Every musician
knows what it means to hear, suddenly and unexpectedly for the first time a kind of music he has never
heard before—new timbre, a different beat, a tune
from some weird and unknown inspiration. I wept
with joy when first that music burst upon me, not
because it was sentimental or in any way sad, but as
a botanist might have wept in finding without warning a new kind of orchid or striped satanic vine. I
shall try to say more of the Ibicenco music, of which
Primo de Rivera and all his Guardias disapproved
and which has been extinguished by war. I am glad
that I have some decades and acres and even centuries of it in my head, which some time, if ever I feel
equal to hearing it again, I can commit to paper.
There are ballads and children's songs, invocations
and quicksteps, chants that must have had their
origin in Solomon's temple.

Only the women sat in the main body of the church,
packed tightly together on their stools, chattering
even more loudly in anticipation of the entrance of

the officiating priest and his assistants. They filled the
broad area and leaning toward them at odd angles
from the walls were wood and plaster saints in stiff
and characteristic gestures, flat-faced painted virgins
with haloed children, bearded patriarchs, tinselled
suffering and stereotyped ecstasy. Santa Eulalia, pa-
troness of the town, was a young Catalan virgin who
was done to death for her faith in Barcelona in the
days of one of the Caesars. Like Saint Peter, Saint
Paul, Saint Joseph and the other favorites, Santa
Eulalia was mounted on a platform with wooden
handles and on certain holy days was carried in
bumpy procession through the churchyard and
around the top of the hill. Never had the saints ventured down town, as they did in San José at the
southern end of the island or in the town of Jesus
which could be seen from the summit of the Cala
Llonga ridge. High on the wall, left of the altar, was
a wooden statue of God the Father with a purely accidental expression of ferocity on his face, due not to
Old Testament traditions so much as to the uncer-
tainty of the sculptor's hand. The stained-glass windows in the modern part of the church, that is, the
rear annex built since the days of the Moors, were
tawdry and unbeautiful and the patches of colored
light they threw on the walls and the floor were not
up to the standard of the silks and gold lavallières of
the women assembled for conversation and prayer.

I think that the twenty men who climbed the hill
did so because of their love of music. In all the years
I passed in Spain I never met a truly pious Spanish
man. Plenty of them thought the church was useful
for keeping wives in order while the husband went his

way. Others had relatives or employers who wished them to keep up appearances now and then. Others feared that if the church declined terrible things would happen. Most of them thought very little about the church at all. In Santa Eulalia I never saw Don Ignacio Riquer, Don Carlos Roman or any of the big landowners in church. The fact that Don Rafael Sainz was in such fear of his wife that he went shame-facedly with her to mass caused chuckles and laughter to follow their auto all the way from the theatre to the plaza. His wife, Secora, breathed nothing but in-cense. She kept their house half filled with visiting priests. When not actually in childbed she was busy with catechisms and first communions. Don Rafael, round-faced and grotesquely heavy in the poop, wad-dled dismally where she led, escaping whenever he could to snatch a bottle of beer in the grape arbor behind the Royalty. He had wanted to build his house by the sea. Secora said no, because of possible danger to the children, so the ungainly mansion he erected north of Santa Eulalia was situated just off the San Carlos road, where the passing vehicles constituted such a menace to child life that Secora was in hysterics between prayers. Ironically enough, it was Don Rafael's long domestic martyrdom that saved his great fat neck in 1936. The militiamen all thought he had suffered enough and forgave his riches in a comradely way.

Not even Xumeu, of the telephone office bar, ever mounted the hill except for family funerals, and his brother was a priest. Ex-Captain Nicolau's wife was always in attendance at the Sunday evening dance, but she seldom bothered to go to mass. Mass was primarily, in Santa Eulalia, an occasion for young farm women to get together weekly and to meet the young men after service was over. I think the local priests, and most of the priests in Spain, preferred it that way. Whatever criticism of them or their actions had ever been offered had been offered by men. Men had tender political sensibilities, the Spanish women none. Men had a liking for privacy, the women were not reticent by nature. As long as the men contributed, the clergy were not severe with them.

There were three priests in Santa Eulalia, and on special religious occasions two other young ones came out from the city of Ibiza. The oldest one took little part in the Sunday services and was seldom seen on the main street. On weekdays one would often meet him on unfrequented roads or see him vanish into doorways where old people lived, especially old women. He belonged to a generation whose ideals and mode of life had disappeared before its hardiest members were dead and it always seemed to me as if old Father Coll got more comfort from his surviving parishioners than he was able to give them. The younger priests took advantage of Father Coll's popularity with the oldest and poorest of the peasant women by placing the collection of funeral and other fees in his hands in cases where they would not have dared to exert pressure themselves. The old priest was lonely. There were no marks on his wrinkled face of intellectual or spiritual attainments. He haunted the country roads like a daylight ghost in black and nothing he said or did gave the slightest indication that he had grasped the passing of Alfonso's monarchy or the Middle Ages. In the center of the town he had no

friends. One of the houses in the *paseo*, the one occupied by Guillermo the blacksmith on the ground floor
and a priest upstairs, had come to Father Coll by inheritance, and whenever the old priest hobbled down
to collect the rent, the crowd around the fishermen's
bar would look after him and grin, as if they were
mildly surprised that he was still alive.

Father Torres, who had owned the building torn
down to make way for the Royalty, was tall, very
pasty, about thirty-five years of age. It was he who
was thoroughly detested in town, and I never heard
even one of the most assiduous church-going women
say a good word for him. His round flat face wore a
look of perpetual disdain. He walked through a crowd
as if he were afraid of contaminating his robes, contemptuous of the ignorant because of their ignorance,
suspicious of the clever men because they knew more
than they should know. He had been born in Santa
Eulalia, in the shade of the magnificent palm tree
which stood before the Estanco, and it was said that
he had tuberculosis. I saw no signs of it except his
unusual pallor. It was Father Torres who lived in the
magnificent old Arab house just below the church.
There was a connecting passageway into the church
vestry and a communicating tunnel which had been
walled up by Bonéd, the fascist mason, after it had
been filled with firearms. Father Torres preached the
political sermons and went from house to house incessantly, speaking venomously of the Republic and
all republicans and impressing upon the newly en-
franchised women that to vote liberal was a mortal
sin. This gem of information was also included in the
children's catechism. His sister augmented the family

income by keeping rabbits which fed on the luxuriant grass in the walled cemetery around the church. About a year after the 1931 revolution, Father Torres preached a sermon one Sunday in which he spoke of the sinful way in which the new government had cut off the priests' salaries. He asked for contributions for his own and his colleagues' support and passed around written receipts which, he said, would insure the bearer's being buried in consecrated ground. Before the day was out, his words had been repeated to Miguel Tur who immediately wrote a petition to the new municipal authorities. The result was that the keys of the cemetery were taken from Father Torres and deposited with the embarrassed Secretario. The priest's sister made a bitter complaint because of her rabbits, but the Secretario did not dare give her the keys, so the rabbits had to be sold in a hurry and for a day or two rabbit was cheap and plentiful.

Three years later, in 1934, Father Torres had a serious clash with the civil population. The government of that year, under Gil Robles and Lerroux, was more anti-republican than Father Torres himself and the priests had become bolder. A meeting was announced in the theatre on a Sunday afternoon and it was advertised on the posters, to attract a crowd, that a concert was to be given by musicians from Barcelona. The men of Santa Eulalia and San Carlos would go anywhere to hear music, and the theatre was crowded to capacity. No musicians appeared, and a priest from Ibiza began the proceedings by speaking in favor of the return to the Jesuits of the property confiscated in 1931. I was standing near the rear of the hall and heard ominous comments. A few of the young men began to ask aloud when the music would begin. Still no musicians appeared, and when Father Torres began an anti-republican tirade, the men began to *ook* and cat-call until the din was magnificent. The priests, in a panic of fear, tried to run out the stage door but found it locked and were obliged to hurry through the yelling angry crowd all the way to the main entrance. Wild yells and laughter followed them down the street, and when they passed Cosmi's their robes were flowing behind them, so great was their haste.

That was the only instance in which the priests invaded the town itself. Always they kept to their hill and the more circuitous roads. When they rode in the bus, they read breviaries assiduously. If one of them was called to a death bed, he hurried through the back street. Once in a while a man from one of the official families would say "Good day" to a priest but there were no long conversations out of doors. Surely the clergy was cut off from the general population more definitely than the Guardia Civil.

I must make an exception of Father Margall, who lived upstairs from my dear friend Guillermo. Father Margall was a Madrileño who had been banished from the city he loved probably because he loved it too well. He had bought himself an upright piano and spent his leisure hours trying to learn to play the simplest tunes. As is often the case, he had enthusiasm and persistence but no talent. He had as little as possible to do with the native priests, downed a quick drink now and then in the Royalty grape arbor and when the communists searched his house, in the lively days of August 1936, they found not machine guns

and ammunition but two years' files of a nudist
magazine.

The only one of the priests who looked to me as if
he might be helpful to one in the throes of spiritual
suffering was young Father Clapés, who was sent to
Santa Eulalia from Ibiza each Sunday and on important holidays. He was courteous and responsive, sensitive to a high degree, really good to look upon. I
could only think of Aloysha Karamazov every time
I saw him, except that young Father Clapés was not
beset with doubts. He had Aloysha's all-embracing
love for the human race, his naïveté and impractica-
bility and a thorough aesthetic appreciation of his
offices. To see his gesture as he raised the chalice, or
hear the inflection of his perfect voice as he gave God's
blessing was a touching experience from any point of
view. One would have thought that because of his
youth and beauty he would have been the favorite of
all the women, but it seemed to me as if the women
were afraid of him. The other priests who looked like
clerks or butchers or tired old men were approachable
in ordinary ways. Father Clapés had an air that was
truly unearthly, and therefore, to the simple mind,
disconcerting. Of course Don Ignacio Riquer and
others among the rich had wives, but their women's
mentality was in no way superior to that of the farm
girls. In fact, it had been dulled by torpor and neglect,
while that of their poor neighbors had been sharpened
by daily activity and closer companionship. Whether
in Santa Eulalia or Madrid or Seville, the female aristocracy was a pale and bloodless imitation of the
common women, their clothes, their amusements—
everything was copied and devitalized. The factory

girls and shop girls and farm girls had the colors, the
wives of the rich the tints. The gypsies danced wildly
with their bodies, the rich girls languidly with their
fans.

One day, a short time before one of the most important saint's days, Father Clapés sought out Pep
Torres (no relation to Father Torres) and me to ask
if we would play the violin and harmonium for the
Mass of the Angels, which was to be sung by a group
of fifteen or twenty of the girls. The harmonium had
been in the church seven years but no one had ever
played it, probably because the chief resident priest
disliked innovations and did not wish to pay the bus
fare and lunch of an organist from the town of Ibiza,
if there was one to spare. There was a strong under-
current of friendship between Pep Torres and Father
Clapés. They had been classmates in the seminary
where Pep had found doubts and torment while his
friend had found peace.

Pep Torres, without outside contacts, had discovered free thought as Guarapiñada had discovered
advertising. Raised on a farm in an inland town, with
six hard-working brothers and three sisters, he had
been singled out by his mother and father for the
priesthood. His mother was gently devout, his father
harshly pious. Pep, with boyish misgivings, had consented, thinking principally of a possible musical
training. It had been impossible for him to continue.
He was honest, outspoken, obstinate and courageous.
He suffered for himself, on account of abstract truth
and justice as he saw it, and much more on account of
of his mother who he feared would die of disappointment. Nevertheless, after the beginnings of a brilliant

career in the college he felt obliged to leave. He had
no money to go away and had to carry on his struggle
under the eyes of all his lifelong acquaintances. His
father cursed him bitterly, his mother was ill for a long
time. The pressure of ecclesiastical displeasure kept
him from any of the lucrative Matutes jobs for which
his education fitted him. So he came to Santa Eulalia
and got a job as mason's helper with Costa, one of the
republican builders and the rival of Bonéd the fascist.
I shall have much more to write of Pep Torres, who
lived in my house and played and studied with me
every evening. Enough now to say that he and I consented to play the mass, to the great amusement,
when the word got round, of all our anti-clerical
friends. Father Clapés had brought us the score, a
Georgorian chant of great beauty which for me had all
the flavor of antiquity and to the Ibicenco farm
women would sound as modern as the "Sacre du
Printemps."

Pep and I together had built up quite a competent
little orchestra to play for weekly dances and on feast
days. Also we were much in demand for weddings and
pig-killing festivals in the country. During the fall and
winter season we nearly ate and drank ourselves to
death. Pep played the violin and trumpet and had a
rich tenor voice. I played my accordion and an amazing wreck of a piano the proprietors of the town
theatre had bought for two hundred *pesetas* (about
eighteen dollars). Pep had taught a young mason's
helper to play the lute, and two young girls to play the
Spanish mandolin. Guillermo the blacksmith played
the guitar. A fine Catalan laborer played the castanets, tambourine, chimbumba, and triangle. On the

night before the Mass of the Angels was to be performed in the church there was a big dance in the
theatre, especially well attended. The importance of
the weekly dances had been growing steadily since
the orchestra was organized, until the townspeople
had learned to look forward to the dance as a happy
social occasion and could recognize not only the Spanish *paso-dobles* we played, but could follow the Amer-
can dance tunes I had arranged for our odd group of
instruments. "Tammany" was a favorite, and "Harvest Moon" a close second. "*No pod se que plogi mes*"
("It Ain't Goin' to Rain No More") always brought
out resounding *olés* and glasses of cognac and gin
which were ranged along the piano top for the adult
members of the band. On the night in question, the
crowd responded with eagerness to the music, the
young couples dancing with gusto and applauding
each tune until it was repeated. The boxes formed a
horseshoe around the dance floor and in them the
older women and children sat in an animated half-
circle around us, talking, smiling and visiting with
their friends in other boxes. The men cheered, took
off their coats, danced always more furiously. The
graceful peasants' skirts swung wider as the beat was
quickened. Outside, in the corridor, the older men's
voices rose and fell around the bar like the drone of a
huge bagpipe. When we got tired, Pere des Puig
played a dance or two on his accordion. At half past
twelve, the hour when ordinarily we would have
begun to think about closing, the crowd was having
such a good time I did not have the heart to quit. My
mandolinists, aged twelve and thirteen, respectively,
were bright and wide awake and their parents gazed

on them with pride and on Pep Torres, their teacher, with touching gratitude.

The dance that night broke up at half past three, after which most of the people had a walk of two or three miles to reach their homes. Guillermo, Pep and I were detained at the bar and served with dark home-made bread, red wine and *sobresada*. Nevertheless Pep and I wrenched ourselves out of bed at half past eight the next morning, doused our heads in cold well water and after coffee at Cosmi's started up the long stony hill. Guillermo joined us at the plaza. He had no guitar part in the mass but could not see us venture into strange territory without him.

Father Clapés the seraph and his colleague from Ibiza, who looked like a Shakespearean lout, met us at the entrance of Father Torres' house. They are both dead this day, and I pause to say I am as sorry for one as for the other, only now and then I reflect that if they were right, and are now in the kingdom of heaven side by side, with wings and snowy raiment, they will afford in the radiance of the presence of the Most High as incongruous a picture as they did in black robes on the steps of the Arab house high on Santa Eulalia's hill.

That morning, alive and gracious, the seraph-faced Father Clapés brought in a tray on which were glasses of *cazalla*. We all touched glasses and drank, and what with my long night of banging the piano and the generous dose of spiced sausage I had eaten before going to bed, I can say that that drink warmed my heart to the clergy. Very soon it was repeated. The furnishings of the house were sparse but the room did contain a clock and I saw with some uneasiness that the hands pointed to quarter past nine. The church bell, which had been ringing spasmodically for some time, slowed down, then stopped altogether. I began to feel bad. Except for Pep, Guillermo and me not a soul had climbed the hill. Father Torres started through the corridor toward the church at half past nine and timidly I followed him. We glanced around the corner, left of the altar. The spacious auditorium was empty. I expected Father Torres would be angry, even that he might be reproachful to me as an instigator of dances. Nothing of the kind. He turned back philosophically and we joined the others in his living room. More glasses of *cazalla* were passed around. At half past eleven a few women entered the church and the noise of their shrill chatter reached our ears. Some time after noon the girls who were to sing arrived. I think I was the only one present who thought it strange that the mass should begin three hours and a half after schedule time.

I had my troubles with the harmonium that morning. Seven years of disuse had left the action frightfully stiff and the bellows somewhat uncertain. The instrument was placed just to the left and in front of the altar. The girls were grouped behind Pep, Guillermo and me. A few minutes after the priests entered, the beat of an Ibicenco drum sounded in the church doorway and the men marched down the middle aisle in ragged formation, following the drum, flute, castanets and triangle. They took their seats on the platform around the altar, on a level two feet above the women massed behind us. Men and women never sit together in an Ibicenco church.

After a few instrumental solos three of the men rose

and began a native chant called *Caramelos*, more of a declamation than a song, in a plaintive supplicating tone with many measures of "ai, ai, ai, ai, ai, ai, ai." None of the priests knew its origin, but it had a definite Hebraic quality, with endless verses of lamentation and repentance. Finally the mass got under way. When the first chords from the organ sounded through the church there was a stir of surprise, almost of fright, among the women, but once they got used to the unaccustomed sound and the girls' voices, led by Father Torres' uncertain baritone, joined in, everyone settled down and enjoyed it thoroughly. Pep had the hardest task trying to keep the priest from running ahead of the violin. Guillermo, in his shirt sleeves as always, turned the pages faithfully. After the mass was over, the men on the platform, the priests and the musicians were invited to lunch at the Royalty, where at my request the *Caramelos* was repeated.

It will be remarked that an Ibicenco church service was not at all banal, from the point of view of ordinary Roman Catholic practice. The Ibicencos had, in a measure, taken it out of the hands of their priests and impressed their peculiar quality upon it. They were likely to do that with whatever came to their island. A German waltz tune that strayed out into the Ibicenco hills would soon be transformed until it would pass for a native melody to untrained ears. Modern styles of clothes were being adopted by many of the women, but never slavishly. The final garment would reveal somewhere an Ibicenco line which might have come from a frieze from the ruins of Tyre. French cooking, brought back by a wanderer such as Cosmi, was modified in some indefinable way until it had an

Ibicenco tang. There is much sound experience and vitality in an old civilization, a tremendous share of what Henry Adams would term "education." My town, my island will die hard.

And now, Santa Eulalia's hill in early evening, the ancient rocks swept clean by the winds, the earth-clinging shrubs, rosemary, thyme and bay, where the earth has held on thinly, the scrub pines, the dark shimmering splendor of an olive tree. Spread before us, far below, are the sharp streets and clustered rooftops of the town, the mosaic of ploughed fields and small gardens. A large bird is flying slow and straight for the Cala Llonga hill. Gulls are floating in the cove, near the black lace of the buoys. Miles of coastline, rich red earth. White houses scattered on the hillsides. A palm for the tropics, a pine for the north. Wild plover. Domestic fowl. Seaweed moving with the heave of the sea, seaweed dried on the strand, in carts along the roads, stacked in barnyards. The same figure that at dawn was seen against the sea is seen against the sky at evening—Platé. His hovel, his refuge from riches and grief, is close by the church. Next door is the café in which the churchmen gather and linger and tune up their flutes and drums.

I would like to have seen all that has been seen through those battlement windows, and before the ancient fortress was built. What hordes approaching, what sails, what galleys! What centuries between events! But I cannot complain, for in all Ibiza's six thousand years the watchers on her hills saw no stranger sights than I did, nothing more unreal, more unexpected. The tramp of feet from neighboring or distant shores, the trumpets and the dust.

Nineteen thirty-six, take your place in the corridor of bloody years! Be proud, if you can, of what you have evoked and produced and spilt. No redder blood has trickled down the rocks, no more innocent victims have been led to the sacrifice. The smell of tripes and incense. Your shrieks are the equal of old echoes, your bones will lie in a layer, nineteen thirty-six, which is now the top but will sift down gradually.

One might have waited seven hundred years and seen nothing violent at all.

6. Cosmi and the Punta de Arabie

THE northeastern corner of the township of Santa
Eulalia, between the shore and the San Carlos road
which strayed a mile and a half inland in that area,
was called Arabie, after the Punta de Arabie, which
sheltered Cosmi's cove and the pebble beach. It was
Arabie Cosmi had chosen for his farm and where he
and his brothers, the Antonio who opened the café
each morning and Pep Salvador, master of ceremonies
at the pig-killing feasts, had added by purchase to the
land their father had left them. From one of the
terraces of Cosmi's still only partly developed truck
garden the church and the central part of town seemed
unified, a compact clear-cut view. A narrow road
which never had had the benefit of Primo de Rivera's
macadamistic genius continued on a tangent from the
main road of Santa Eulalia near the electric light
plant where the San Carlos bus road took a turn to
the left. First was the house of Pere, a small deaf fisherman, farther along was Can Josepi where José and
Catalina (heroic pair) worked as tenants. Another
half mile, after passing two more farms, one found
oneself in the shade of the largest mariner's pine in all
Santa Eulalia. Another enormous and perfect tree, almost a twin of the first, stood fifty yards away.

"Me, I love the earth," Cosmi would say, looking

proudly over the beginnings of his project. "Antonio likes the hotel." During the years Cosmi had wandered as a boy aboard French ships in wartime, through the principal cities of France just later (where he had studied French methods of cooking and serving), in Algeria where he had worked for the large fruit companies and finally established a café and hotel in Alger, Cosmi had dreamed of the day when he could return to the town of his birth and develop the acres surrounding his father's old place. Nothing Cosmi planned was small or in any way unthorough. He wanted his land to bloom and yield as did the gardens of the Moors, with all their ancient wisdom and the benefit of modern science, too. He wanted water flowing freely through his conduits and ditches, bubbling and gushing over the ground. One lot had been chosen for goats and pigs, up-to-date hen coops and runs, with a pure race of Brahma hens that would make the restless little Minorcas look like insects by comparison. Antonio, his older brother, had been like a father to him and so Cosmi planned for him as well. Since Antonio loved hotelkeeping they were to have jointly Ibiza's best hotel. They were to build one which, because of its architecture, would fit in ideally with the landscape and the town but which, inside, would be fitted up as the best Swiss hotels were, with fly screens and window shades, running water, baths, all the comforts to match nature's gifts of sea and sunshine and fertility.

To accomplish anything on a large scale in Ibiza is difficult. No one knew that better than Cosmi, and no one was more confident that big things could be

done. He did not want riches for himself, or to pass on
to his son. His needs were modest in the extreme. But
in the wistful way in which he had hoped for the bet-
terment of Spanish society and of the conditions of
workers everywhere, he longed for his island to shake
off its historic inertia in a healthy moderate way and
keep step with the modern world.

As I say, Cosmi's plans were in their initial stage.
The hotel he had rented, while waiting to get capital
enough to build, was by no means the last word in
appointments. The rooms were badly placed, the windows constructed in such a way as to make screening
almost impossible. There were toilets in American
style, as contrasted with the Turkish pattern in
vogue, but the women in the hotel understood their
significance and care imperfectly, to say the least, so
to foreign visitors they were practically useless most
of the time. However, the food was good, one got used
to the flies, and Cosmi's own service and courtesy
were so magnificent that it made up for many small
difficulties.

Cosmi was dark and tall, with sloping shoulders and
immensely strong hands. He moved about with a sure,
pantherlike tread. His eyes were black and bright, his
forehead high and wrinkled by the facial gestures with
which he emphasized his earnest conversation. Always
he had dignity and distinction. They rested upon him
and went wherever he went, like an invisible garment.
He was the first man to whom anyone in straits would
go to borrow money. He knew everybody's business
and never talked about it.

"What we need is a little more humanity," I have
heard him say, again and again. That was his solution

for the ills of society. That was his reason for detesting
the church with all its intrigue and rigmarole. His
employees knew themselves to be lucky. His enemies
could find no footholds by which to impede him. No
official, no native millionaire, no active politician had
such an influence as Cosmi. Good men just naturally
stood behind him. To the earth and the sea for sus-
tenance, to the heart of man for better living and
fairer relationships. Where have we heard that simple
creed before?

How pleased Cosmi was when his well was finished
and proved to have an almost limitless supply of cool
spring water! He had struck an underground spring
and the thought of giving such superior water to his
livestock, plants and trees made him very happy.
About that time his first and only son was born.
Cosmi worked in the hotel until two or later in the
morning, slept until ten, then took a lunch and a
bottle of wine under his arm and walked briskly out
the Arabie road. He would stay on his land until sundown, never seeming to exert himself too much,
always having time to talk with his passing neighbors,
his brother Pep Salvador, a large good-natured Dane
nicknamed Pep des Horts (Garden Joe), the loquacious Barberet whose land lay west of his near the
San Carlos bus road. Cosmi had a few acres of corn,
two large fields of sweet potatoes. He had selected his
house lot and liked to stand upon it, sampling the
view, the great expanse of sea, the coastline, each
rock and cove of which was familiar, the distant
town. Best of all he liked to watch his pump.

Cosmi's pump had earned him much friendly ridicule, for it threw a lusty four-inch stream and seemed

to the tight-fisted farmers from the dry hills behind the fertile Arabie much bigger and more powerful than was necessary. As a matter of fact, it was. Cosmi could have done with a pump one-sixth the size of the one he had installed, but he wanted water in abundance. He wanted to sell it or give it away, to pipe it all through Arabie and make his neighbors' farms as luxuriant as his would be. Cosmi enjoyed tinkering with the motor, and thinking how powerful it was. He understood the sly amusement of the peasants' faces and took pleasure in it, knowing they were partly right and fundamentally quite wrong.

Pep Salvador, Cosmi's brother, had been a farmer all his life, except two fantastic years he had spent in what he called *La Fabrika de Curas* (priest factory) in Ibiza. Probably Pep Salvador was the hardest worker on the island, and besides that he was the hardest drinker and the most consummate clown. When his mother and father, dismayed by Cosmi's congenital aversion to the church, had suggested to Pep Salvador that he become a priest Pep kept his face straight and said "Sure." He knew his friends would laugh themselves sick, that his teachers at the seminary would always half-suspect he was having fun at their expense. Cosmi was away or he would have put a stop to it. As it was, Pep Salvador stayed two years in the *Fabrika* and came away able to give the best parody of the mass I have ever witnessed. Sometimes Pep Torres helped him with it, and what with the candlelight and dimness of Cosmi's bar, the potent liquor and the healthy air of abandon, to say nothing of the organ responses I furnished with my accordion, the performance was effective and enjoyed by all. Pep

Salvador's clowning, however, was mostly done in the evening. All day he worked in the fields, his wife, their seven children and a boy cousin with a face like Baudelaire working with him or in distant plots, their backs bent, their movements quick and steady as they advanced along the rows. Pep got his water through an old Moorish irrigation system that still was functioning admirably. His animals had spirit like his. I am convinced that men choose animals like themselves, and influence their character. Guarapiñada had this gift in the highest degree, Pep Salvador was not far behind him. Pep's black horse had hardly had a line on him for years. He simply did what Pep told him to do, in a slightly clownish manner, now and then taking a playful nip at Pep's old felt hat or his shoulder. The corn on Pep's fields had a wonderful sheen, and in a grove of his trees the nightingales spent a week or ten days each year, resting in their flight from Africa to Europe. The creek that ran through his property and turned toward the sea to form Cosmi's boundary was hidden by tall clumps of cane and thousands of flowering bushes with pink petals and glossy green leaves. The old farm house was white, with grape arbors and a white-domed well near the doorway which faced a peanut field and a plot of scarlet peppers.

No other family cultivated so much land as Pep Salvador's and made it thrive year after year, and still each Saturday afternoon Pep was one of the first to drop his tools and light out for the cafés. His oldest daughter, Maria, went with him. While he was carousing she would sit in the café kitchen talking with the women or would walk up and down the street, arm in

arm with Eulalia Colomar, her slender cousin. Maria
by no means represented the father-dear-father-
come-home-with-me idea. She had her father's hun-
ger for life and loved to see him enjoying himself.
Some time before dawn they would walk together
along the Arabie road, Pep singing or talking to himself, Maria smiling happily and carrying the lantern.
Pep Salvador's wife was a fine woman, and a happy
one, too, but after the week of farm work she liked
best the luxury of a long uninterrupted sleep. She
seldom came into town until Sunday afternoon, and
even then she returned in time for the evening milking. She was strong and sturdy and certainly had not
been broken by childbearing. The striking contrast
between Pep and Cosmi, or between Pep's wife and
Anna Cosmi, or Pep's daughter and Anna's sister,
Eulalia, was that of island tradition and modernity.
Pep and his family dressed always in the old Ibicenco
style, the shawl, the kerchief, the full pleated skirt to
the ground. Anna and Eulalia at their best would have
attracted admiring glances in the rue de la Paix. Pep
never changed his old felt hat or wore a necktie. On
infrequent occasions Cosmi wore the conventional
black and looked as a nobleman should but seldom
does. Pep sang Ibicenco songs, danced the wild
Ibicenco dances with breath-taking grace and agility,
was never at a loss for a word or an antic. Cosmi could
not sing or dance. He blushed when he tried to talk.
He envied his young brother his loquacity and never-
ending fun-making, and in his dreams for Arabie,
transformed and outdoing itself, he foresaw that Pep
Salvador's acres would be exactly as they had been
for a thousand or more years and knew his own al-

ready were different. Maria, Pep's daughter, wore her
old-fashioned Ibicenco clothes proudly while all her
friends changed to conform to modern style, knowing
that she was pleasing her father. I can't say which was
lovelier, Pep's Maria or Eulalia Colomar. Maria was
brown, intense, far stronger, a type that seemed pure
Arab, like her father. Eulalia was lithe and frivolous
with a slim figure that would have brought out
genius in a Paris couturier. Ibiza's nightingales were
from Africa. One could almost catch the scents of
Arabia in the breeze that carried across to Santa
Eulalia's shore.

Antonio, Cosmi's older brother, had neither Cosmi's
vision nor Pep Salvador's perverse energy. He was
somewhat cut off from the general gaiety because he
was hard of hearing. His smouldering black eyes were
alert but wistful. His slow smile bespoke detachment.
I loved to see him working in the kitchen, proceeding
so surely, with no lost motion, making meat, fowl, fish
and vegetables and condiments advance, to the rear
march, join forces, go to opposite ends of the drill
field. I imagined him sometimes raising his arms like
Toscanini and evoking the harmonized odor of stew,
a great chord in D or F-sharp minor. He had style, the
trait of Cosmi's whole family. And when later there
was a rumor that Cosmi was to be arrested, Antonio
with one of his effectual motions reached to a nearby
shelf, closed his fingers around the handle of an
Ibicenco dagger (forbidden of course) and tucked it
into his belt and he looked at me with his smouldering
Arab's eyes and smiled slowly and went on with his
work with fishes and peppers, not saying one word.

No doubt in centuries past the romantic quality of

Arabie had appealed to susceptible hearts among those now silent hordes who had passed by sea and noticed the inviting cove and the mouth of the creek quite smothered with shrubs and flowers, or who had wandered there by land in search of fruits or wild birds or fragrant pine-nuts. There was that appeal in the setting of green mountains streaked with Venetian red, the grace of distant roads, the spiked marsh grass at the water's edge and the pasture lands beyond. Just lately its idyllic touch has been supplied by a rare young Valencian painter, Rigoberto Soler. I don't mean that he painted it successfully. He had not Gauguin's gift of seeing that a tropical landscape and a picturesque race could not be represented literally upon a yard-square canvas. But Rigoberto had the gift of song, of impetuous joy and sorrow, and particularly of falling in love. He had come to Santa Eulalia from Valencia as a very young man, having quarrelled with his father who wanted him to spend his days in a bank, and he had brought with him one of his models, the enchanting, almost-frightening type of Spanish beauty to which Spanish calendars and cigarette ads do not do justice. Rigoberto had put up a small shack near the mouth of the creek, just across from the land Cosmi began to develop a few years later. There was one room and an alcove, to serve as studio, living room, dining room and all. For the *siesta* there were sheltering pines and thick cushions of pine needles. The cooking was done on an oven of stones at the water's edge. Pilar, the model, was painted in all kinds of Spanish costumes, in the nude, half-draped in the bath. She was so Spanish that she preferred to wash in a basin indoors rather than plunge into the sea, not fifty feet distant. She was represented picking orange blossoms, grapes, pink oleanders, reclining on rocks, grass, imaginary doorsteps. A phonograph played Flamencos all evening. As he worked with the palette or the frying pan, Rigoberto sang Valencian songs. He knew a thousand, I am sure. In one time of stress, when the town needed music, he agreed to furnish one good song a day and did so by singing them to me until I could note them down. After that Pep Torres, Guillermo and I played the melody until the singers around us caught on. The words were soon memorized.

The love-nest existence has no counterpart in Spanish life. Rigoberto, in Valencia, had spent his off hours in cafés, singing, drinking *manzanilla*, of which he was enthusiastically fond, telling and exchanging anecdotes or discussing the happier forms of philosophy, with occasional nostalgic relief. The town of Santa Eulalia, so enticingly within view, lured him away from *Niu Blau* (the Blue Nest, as his shack in Arabie was called) each day at mail time and frequently in the late afternoon. Pilar, much bored to be alone with nature and stacks of paintings of herself which she did not fancy, inflamed his jealousy by whatever means the countryside offered. They fought and were reconciled so passionately that Rigoberto, always a slight little man, grew thin and pale until his dark expressive eyes seemed larger. She retained or even improved her languid beauty, but even quarrelling eventually bored her and she took a boat for the mainland suddenly one day. Rigoberto devoted himself to *manzanilla* for some time afterward and so endeared himself to the semi-idle men that members of the local aristocracy began giving him commissions in order to keep him in town. Also he received notice that one of his paintings of Pilar had won second prize (one thousand dollars cash) in the national exhibition at Madrid. He forgot his sorrow and started building a house on the slope behind the center of town, far enough removed so that he could enjoy comparative quiet, near enough to reach the cafés without exertion. When Rigoberto entered any company he transformed it. He was always ready to sing, he had stories to tell. By that time he knew every native within miles and relished their strange gossip. His dark eyes showed traces of boredom, even suffering at times, but always in a crowd they sparkled. Ferrer, Guillermo, Pedro of the Royalty, all the men along the main street who had laughed a little at his expense in the days of Pilar began to find him indispensable. The few foreigners took to him immediately, because of his natural grace and geniality and also on account of his magnificent Castillano. I am sure that anyone who had not heard Spanish spoken before could understand Rigoberto.

The experience at *Niu Blau* did not break Rigoberto's volatile heart, but it convinced him that he should not marry a Spanish woman. He admired the American way of life, as exemplified by the rare specimens in Santa Eulalia, but any foreign girl was a prospect. His romances succeeded one another with varying degrees of comedy and tragedy through the early years of the Spanish Republic. He wanted twelve children, one for each month in the year. Each girl to whom he proposed was tempted by his qualities, his now quite wonderful house overlooking the rooftops of the town and great stretches of sea, his *Canto Flamencos* on the phonograph, his Valencian rice with rabbit made in his broad fireplace over the coals. Nevertheless, one after another decided she must go away to think it over and none of them came back. Finally he married a charming German woman who, however, was not of child-bearing age and he was somewhat lost to cafés, for he took his responsibilities quite gravely. It took the war to bring him back to his place in the town life again, but that must wait.

7. *Of Farms and Farmers*

IN SANTA EULALIA there were several kinds of farmer. Let us consider Don Ignacio Riquer, a merry, round-faced man slightly below medium height, plump but not fat, with a ruddy complexion that got ruddier when he smiled and shook your hand.

"*Bon dia*, Don Ignacio. *Commen' vos trubau?*"

"Very well," he replied, smiling ruddily. He was proud of his few words of English. "My great-great-grandfather on my father's side was English," he would say. His name was Wallis (probably Wallace). Don Ignacio would be found at Cosmi's bar quite often in the afternoon with Rigoberto, whom he admired. Most of the other aristocrats went to the Royalty, where not so many of the natives would see them drinking, but Don Ignacio thought it was more important that his cousins and uncles should not see him indulging and that occasional visits to Cosmi's, in his shirtsleeves, improved his standing with his neighbors. Also, that his wife was less likely to hear about it.

Señora Riquer was plumper than her husband but quite good-looking. She must have been twenty years younger than Don Ignacio. Like most Spanish women of her class, she did absolutely nothing and didn't seem to mind it. She slept late every morning, ate

heartily in the heat of the day, took a good long *siesta*
in the afternoon, had another tremendous meal consisting of soup, rice, fish, eggs, meat, fruit and cheese
with plenty of red wine, played the piano in a vigorous
perfunctory way, sat in a rocking-chair observing the
moonlight on the sea, leaf shadows on the dusty road,
listened to the night birds (the periodical soft whistle
of the butcher-shop owl, F-sharp, timed to the second,
the reply of its mate, G-flat; the *chiboli* or rock plover
whose clear night song was heard from the shore and
the intermediate slopes although the bird was seldom
seen), ate a handful of chocolates and bonbons and let
the winking of the lighthouses stir her consciousness
in a night island pattern, Tagomago which blazed forth
once a second without turning, Formentera which
turned dash dot-dot, blood-orange, sharp yellow,
blaze, dash-dot-dot. If Ignacio were in the room she
would make a remark now and then that required no
answer, "I saw Esperanza today," "I tore my black
lace dress" (she always wore black lace), some obser-
vation like that with no bearing on the human struggle, the rising of man from the muck to the trees to
the dry land, no reflections on the march of great
nations and peoples over the ground which supported
the stones which held up her rocking-chair. No Iberians in the mists of history, no Phoenicians spreading
through unexplored sea paths as the fish found the
way to strange caverns, Carthage not a word, Rome
poof, ditto Arabia. Señora tore her dress, saw her
cousin, dropped a melon on the dining-room floor,
spied a lighthouse, heard a bird. Her husband, in his
shirtsleeves, glanced at her ample bare arms and her

ankles in black silk stockings, adjusted his spectacles
and smiled. Later in his nightshirt he would smile as
she undressed. They were happy. Oh, yes. I do not
mean that they were bored. Damp night grass and
plover's song. *Jai-alai* of familiar lighthouses. The
champing of Holstein cattle in a long old-fashioned
barn. Don Ignacio's red face on the pillow, smiling.
Señora's stretch of contentment with her corsets off.
In March, wild strawberries. They were placidly
happy in March as they were in May, unless it rained
two or three days at a stretch in March or in November. Then the plump white-skinned twenty-year-
younger Señora thumped the piano harder and stood
by the rain-swept windows watching the stain of
Santa Eulalia's river encroach upon an angry sea, and
ate chocolate creams, and right after dinner they went
to bed, Ignacio smiling.

I repeat that the Señora was not bored. There was
not that frozen death in her face that marked the faces
of most of her aunts and cousins. No priests sniffed in
the offing. She never thought about God. Her gossip
was not malicious and she liked a good joke. And when
wheat grew and the corn fields shimmered, when geraniums were red and petunias pale, if the sea pounded
steadily against the shore and the moon rose new and
each night changed her shape and hour, Señora
Riquer, thirty years of age and sound, felt the sea-
sonal stirrings and the daily warmth and coolness and
breathed in a rhythm of our island and had nothing
whatever to worry about.

There must have been something about Don Ignacio
besides his physical appearance to single him out
from his brothers, the tall saturnine Don Mariano

who lived on the Casino balcony at the port, or Don Antonio who had transformed a large sea cave on his estate in San Antonio into a lobster pound. I say there must have been something because Don Ignacio as a young man was sent to Madrid to study medicine.

"Did you want to study medicine?" I asked him once.

He smiled even more broadly than usual. "Me? No," he said. "I wanted to study Madrid."

He studied Madrid so minutely that, before his course was half finished, he got syphilis. That is odd, is it not? Don Ignacio, heir of hundreds of acres and employer of a hundred tenant farmers, caught the same old bug that waylaid the fisherman Mateo Rosa. There was that bond between them. Don Ignacio, then aged twenty-four, made use of what he had gleaned in the medical school to cure himself in the old-fashioned way and then, later, when 606 came along, he took a few shots of that, for luck, administered by his old professor.

"That's nothing," Don Ignacio said to me.

In an earlier chapter I have told how Don Ignacio several mornings each week rode in to Ibiza and sat for a couple of hours in his municipal office. Also that he had an almost miraculous well. Next to his well, he prized his Holstein cows. He loved to walk along the row of cow-sheds admiring the animals and he took pride in telling all foreigners that he could send them milk each day that was rich and pure. He lost a few *sous* on each litre he sold, because the price of cattle was very high and delivery very difficult. Never having had to worry about money, Don Ignacio was able to view his fields and barns with an eye for their beauty and productiveness. When wheat yielded full and firm kernels and the corn was tall, he beamed with pleasure. If crops were scant he shrugged his shoulders and said, "Well, another year." His tenants knew they would never be cheated or starve and if they added to his riches they increased their own profits in equal proportion.

If there is injustice in the system by which Don Ignacio (doing nothing but pleasantly stroll around) reaped half the fruits of the labor of the farmers (who with their wives and children worked every daylight hour) no one blamed Don Ignacio. He had always taken things as they had come, without disturbing doubts or complicated analyses. He was generous, unexacting and, when bad moments came to him later, unmistakably game. If I have portrayed him in one or two of his less dignified moments, do not be deceived. There were instances of his charity which he never talked about at Cosmi's bar. His tenants were not hounded through life with a feeling of insecurity, for neither Don Ignacio nor his father nor his grandfather had ever let one of them down. They are lucky, no matter what happens to Ibiza or to good men there who dreamed of freedom, that Don Ignacio is still alive. He will do his best for them, good-naturedly, thinking only on the surface, enjoying what he can of life. Let it be written of him that his dependents were his friends as well, that he really loved his land and never neglected it, and that his wife, twenty years his junior, was not restless or bored.

What exactly is an estate? Is it the people who own it? The people who live on it? The acres of red earth, brown loam, waving grasses, shrubs, blossoms, the ragged shore line and the straight stone walls, pines, olives, *garobas*, almonds, orange and lemon trees, apricots, wheat, corn, alfalfa, melon and sweet potato vines, the roots in the soil and the stalks, fronds and branches in the sunlight, the water bubbling under the earth and coursing through creeks and irrigation ditches, the birds, fowls, colored fish around the ledges, the smell of earth and leaves and hay, up-rooted vegetables, plucked fruit, of livestock and manure and seaweed? Is it a succession of days, passing east to west across a slowly changing landscape? One sees, standing on the hill just south of Santa Eulalia's river, wide expanses of Don Ignacio's real estate and what is known as tangible property. The tangibility of trees obscures the tangibility of low white walls and thatched rooftops. What remains is good to look upon. There is the large house in the town, the city house inside the battlement walls of Ibiza, the new house on the shore opposite Cosmi's, the farm house on the Cala Llonga slope, the houses of the tenant families. These cannot be seen all at once but one knows where they are, in this or that knoll, behind this or that mountain, on the Calle San Jaume. In Don Abel Matutes' bank are *pesetas*, *duros*, sheaves of 25-*peseta* notes, 50-*peseta* notes, 100- and 500- and 1000-*peseta* notes, and legal papers, contracts, promises to pay and be paid, mortgages, stacks of closely written pages in elaborate legal Castillano. There is good will all over the place, and credit. Why, certainly, Don Ignacio, let me lend you 50,000 *pesetas*. Don't mention it. Of course.

The estate is beautiful, the people were beautiful, the earth, sea, sky, cereals, vegetables are beautiful.

The good will is still beautiful. Nobody knows what to think of the *pesetas* or the promises to pay. Don Ignacio, who never had had to worry before, did it in a gentlemanly way when the moment came, with bows and smiles and uplifted *chattos* of *manzanilla*. There were those who squealed like stuck pigs, but not Don Ignacio. Not at all. He had had syphilis and a lot of wholesome fun. The Lord giveth and the Lord taketh away.

Still, whenever I think of the slopes and woods and acres under cultivation, the shapes of my favorite trees and the smell of rosemary and laurel, the gait of the peasant girls and the greetings of peasant men, I cannot forget the produce. Perhaps that was most beautiful of all. I am in the stores of Santa Eulalia, or the market place in Ibiza, Valencia, Palma, Barcelona, Alicante, Madrid. I shall not say Nineveh because I was never there. As a child I regretted lost cities, but what need have we of such reminders now? Madrid. Oh, yes. There was Madrid, and I carry it like a photograph in the inside-pocket of my mind and each day it wears, is soiled, gets thinner, cracks, wrinkles—still it is Madrid. And a ghostly bombardment continues night and day and what crumbles is the petrified meat of my heart. We are all Madrid and we all must be shot to pieces, quarter by quarter, until the shells begin to fall in the quarter of our self-respect, and then God knows what we shall do.

I am thinking of what comes from the earth, what grows and is harvested and moved away toward far and distant markets from Don Ignacio's estate. How cool and beautiful, how comforting and non-inflammatory! There are eggplants in straw baskets, royal purple, black at the larger end, ivory and magenta near the stalk, so many shapes and reflections. Tomatoes in huge clusters, ranged singly side by side in boxes, deep ox-blood, pale vermilion streaked with green, defiantly green. Braids of garlic, onions in sacks, potatoes, sweet potatoes; and the melons, cumbersome purveyors of Oriental perfumes. How many melons have been carted along Don Ignacio's narrow winding roads to the Ibiza bus road, over the divide through Jesus to the harbor? Neat footsteps of mules and silence of men driving, perfunctory whacks with the stick, short naps, so many overtakings and being overtaken and proceeding in single file. To walk through the market in Ibiza, brushing the leaves of carrots or of spinach, seeing peas in the pod and string beans. How many sacks of grain and corn, in carts, trucks, in the holds of Matutes' ships (he had them all), in trains! How much bending of backs and creaking of tackle to hoist the produce into lofts! The mental calculations, the scribbled notations, the coins and bills, profit and loss, gross and tare, weights and measures. All this set in motion before the days of the Phoenicians and continuing and growing day by day except when interrupted by a state of war. I should like to dream of a warehouse and an outdoor market place and to wander there through all the produce of Don Ignacio's acres, looking up to pyramids of cauliflower, across prairies of melons, pausing to bury my arms in a wheat-bin the contents of which would be bought by Hannibal, selecting from a million eggplants the richest purple and most pleasing shape and finding it was one I had bought myself at Las Delicias.

Would the contrast be too cruel if, on awakening, I

should lead you across the Roman bridge, through the plaza, along the main street of the town as far as the theatre and there turn westward up an unpromising lane which rises slowly until we can see over the town rooftops, up the coast as far as the Tagomago cliffs and far out to sea? Just before we reach Rigoberto's land, the lane takes a right-angle turn to the north and we face the San Carlos mountains. On the mainland they would not be mountains, perhaps, but relatively, on the island, they loom high and voluminous, about five miles away. We follow the lane and the slopes around us bulge with uncovered ledges and are littered with stones. Between the stones, although we shall never see them, are plovers' eggs in pairs. That elusive night bird, so seldom seen, comes to such slopes as fell to Pere des Puig in order to lay her eggs. They build no nests but the eggs are so perfectly camouflaged to represent the Scriptural stony ground that they pass unnoticed and hatch in safety. So that melodious night bird, whose song far surpasses that of the nightingale or mocking bird or any of the others whose names lend themselves to verse so readily, sings as sweetly for Pere des Puig, outside whose walls she comes to rear her young, as for Don Ignacio, in whose lush seaside meadows she finds her food.

Pere's house fits against the hillside. The roof is flat and built to catch rainwater, for Pere has no well. Inside there are steps between the front room (combination kitchen, dining room and living room) and the bedrooms behind it. The walls are of plaster, whitewashed inside and out. All the houses in Santa Eulalia are whitewashed once a year, just before the important feast day which occurs the first Sunday in

May. The ceiling of Pere's living room has narrow
rough-hewn beams from which hang strings of red
peppers, garlic, *sobresada*, *butifara* (short thick dark
sausages that look like blackjacks) and wild leeks.
Fish stew, with potatoes and tomatoes, fish rice fla-
vored with saffron, home-made sausages, wine and
peasant bread form the principal diet of Pere and his
family of daughters. For dessert they eat dried black
figs (called *churracas*) and almonds, or pomegranates
in season. The cooking and light housework is done
by Pere's oldest daughter (a child of ten in 1930, a
girl of striking grace and beauty in 1936). Pere's wife
died when the youngest of the seven girls was born.

The sheep and the goats on Pere's few acres found
just enough to eat if they applied themselves constantly to the task. All day and on quiet nights they
stumbled around, sometimes on their knees, sometimes stretched erect on their hind legs to reach the
tops of shrubs or the low branches of trees. They were
not fat, but neither were they painfully thin. Pere,
who had the appearance of a grave man, was never
harsh with them. He spoke to them gravely, only
when it was necessary. When it was necessary he
lifted them in his strong and beautiful hands. He had
no names for them but thought of them according to
their color or their size. If Pere worked steadily from
daylight until dark he managed to earn about the
equivalent of two dollars and a half a week. Not that
he handled that much cash. He traded his labor for
pork and wine, as well as *pesetas*. It was good labor,
not the sweating resentful kind, but an hour or a day
of steady work, handling things gravely, carting seaweed, pausing to look around him or to say "Good

day," giving what he had (his time and strength) for what he needed at home. Each Sunday evening he went with his accordion to the dance hall and received a *duro* (about fifty cents) for playing. He had to buy salt, sugar, coffee, saffron and some of the small rock fishes with many fins and bones. He had a few almond trees, enough for his year's supply, and a few squat fig trees. Now and then he accepted as part payment for one of his animals a few ribs or a leg after the butcher had slaughtered it. Probably Pere and his family ate meat once a week. Vegetables were plentiful in the stores and very cheap, so he was able to buy sweet potatoes and white potatoes. Bay leaves and rosemary for seasoning were to be found on any nearby slope.

It was usual in Santa Eulalia for a man who had lost his wife and been left with a growing family to marry again as soon as the period of mourning was over. Three years was about enough mourning for a wife. Pere had not married a second time. His bleak farm on the crest of the hill was not attractive to marriageable girls or even to widows, so the women did not make advances to Pere and he was too busy, what with the Sunday dances, to think much about them. Then, about the time when he could have looked around for a second wife, his oldest daughter, Eulalia, suddenly was transformed into the most beautiful young woman for miles around. Had one of the worn rocks split open and produced a rare flower which never faded and which he could silently admire, Pere could not have been more pleased. He was pleased also that he had lived to see the Republic and that his daughter would have a chance for decent schooling without the degrading influence of priests. He was stunned, almost, by the respect and admiration Eulalia had for him.

The school children were released about half past eleven each morning, just before the bus got back from Ibiza. Those who lived at a distance, like Eulalia des Puig, waited in and around the post office until the mail was distributed. Then Eulalia, marshalling her small sisters, would proceed down the main street to the lane that turned westward just beyond the theatre. If I had nothing else to do at that moment I would contrive to meet her somewhere along the way, just to ask how her father was and send him my regards. Eulalia would stop very politely and gracefully and her hands would rise and pause gently clasped on her breast and she would smile in anticipation of my question, her eyes glad and her lips parted to reply.

"Oh, thank you. My father is well," she would say, and the stony farm would be turned to gold, and Pere, in new driving clothes with smart leather gloves, would be standing by a blooded Arab horse and all the landscape and the glittering sea would sing with noontime praise.

"Please give him my regards and say that I hope to see him Sunday."

"It is very kind of you to have inquired about him. He will come down Sunday I am sure."

I was proud of Eulalia, and of the Spanish Republic, and of so many good men and lovely girls for whom vistas were opening. I liked young girls' dresses made from faded cloth from a dead mother's hand-carved dowry chest. I respected respectable goats and sheep who foraged on stony ground so worthily. I liked grey stones, in fact. There were certain grey trees that were very bare in certain seasons and whose bare colors vibrated with those of the rocks on bare hillsides and produced a silver mystery. I liked to think of Pere being served at lunch in a cool whitewashed room that contained so much admiration.

And still, when Pere played the accordion he appeared to be melancholy. Some old and sad wisdom seemed to steal over him and deepen the lines of his face. I suppose now and then he pondered as to how it would have been had Eulalia been rich and handsome instead of poor and handsome, and undoubtedly he was tired of hearing the tunes he played, for he never had time to learn a new one. From my seat at the piano I used to watch him on the stage, just a few feet away, and when the Royalty's Pedro or Anna Cosmi's brother Marc or some other enthusiastic dancer brought drinks for the orchestra I would hand Pere's glass to him and receive his amazing smile. Eulalia never attended the dances because someone had to be at home with the younger children, but on Monday at noon she took the Sunday *duro* from her dress pocket and spent some of it with dignity for salt or potatoes, which she carried with her up the hill.

No water bubbled from the ground on Pere des Puig's hill. The Moors had terraced what land they could find there and had walled it with the plentiful stones. The sun beat down from early in the morning until late in the afternoon and the goats and sheep sought the deep shade of the *garobas* trees or the thin ghostly shade of an apricot tree. Of table scraps for the pig there were few, so he ate corn and raw sweet potatoes. I think Pere's mule enjoyed the view. I have seen him spread his nostrils, raise his long ears at the afternoon stirring of the breeze and turn gravely toward the San Carlos mountains, the Tagomago cliffs and follow with his attentive mule's eyes the shore line. And dry lizard lightning snapped and crackled in the rocks.

Can Josepi was on the Arabie road not more than three hundred yards from where it branched off from the San Carlos stage road. The house stood with its back to the road, with flat and fertile acres at its feet, facing the fishermen's cove, with Don Carlos Roman's new house and the cliff called *Vei Isglesi* in the left foreground. Over the doorway and along the front of the house beams had been extended to support magnificent grape vines with twisted stalks as thick as your wrist. The leaves and clusters shaded the house front and a long cool corridor through which José's cart could be driven past the house to the adjacent stable. Inside there was the long living room, with three bedrooms behind, and a short stairway led upward to a balcony, also shaded with vines, behind which was another room quite detached from the rest of the house. Adjacent to the kitchen alcove but with no connecting door were the pig sty and the stalls for the mule and the cows. By God knows how much labor and years of saving José and Catalina had achieved the price of a queenly black cow which they loved and fed with the best they had and cleaned carefully her glossy coat, not from tenderness regarding animals (of which they had less than might be expected), but in memory of painful gettings out of bed and staggering through dawns and of shelling corn at night. Then later the cow had had a calf, a mouse-colored daughter which soon had turned black, like her mother, and in due time gave milk as well.

The owner of Can Josepi was a sergeant in the Guardia Civil, born in Ibiza and stationed in Formentera, a narrow sandy island that lay southeast of Ibiza and could be seen from the balcony of Can Josepi. He was a mean man, detested by the inhabitants of the small island he ruled with arbitrary power, and particularly by José and Catalina from whom he squeezed the last ounce of work in order to cheat them more at the time of the yearly reckoning. Because the house was larger than most farm houses, the sergeant insisted on crowding José, Catalina and the four children into two back bedrooms (in one of which a kitchen was rigged up) and renting the main room, downstairs bedroom and upstairs balcony and bedroom to visiting foreigners. Thus José and Catalina, although inconvenienced beyond the endurance of any lower animals, began to learn something of the outside world.

The land around Can Josepi was not as extensive as Pep Salvador's, nor quite as fertile, but it was good rich earth and around it ran the raised irrigation flume left by the Moors. It never lacked water. Wheat, corn and sweet potatoes were the principal crops, but due to Catalina's initiative and José's strong back they had also planted tomatoes, peppers, white potatoes, carrots, cabbage and, at the request of a Frenchwoman, a bed of leeks. José and Catalina were quite different in character, but they shared an immense capacity for work. Not a moment were they

idle. Before dawn they got out of bed, half stunned
with fatigue. Catalina made coffee and gave the children bread and oil while José fed the animals. From
that time on they both were busy, milking, hoeing,
planting, reaping.

When I mention José's broad back I do not mean
that Catalina's was frail. I have seen her obscured by
a load any man could be proud to have shouldered.
Her childbearing had not been the complicated and
expensive affair which is associated with the process
in America and elsewhere. A neighbor midwife (five
duros) and two weeks out of the fields were enough
for her. The boys, her children were all boys, grew up
in the mud around the animal sheds, began doing odd
errands and trivial jobs as soon as they could walk,
and in the days of the Republic went sullenly to
school. In spite of a lifetime of work that would have
raised a countrywide scandal had it been imposed on
an American convict, four haphazard confinements
without benefit of *medico*, and the absence of a fairly
important tooth, Catalina was not an unsightly
woman. Her warm brown eyes had the light of understanding, her greeting was shrill and cordial, she
waved at one in a comradely way from a distant corn
field or potato patch, surprised one when on Sunday
sometimes one saw her in holiday clothes. One night
I saw her dance the Ibicenco dance in which the
woman circles demurely while her partner leaps like
an amorous bird, and the graceful simplicity of her
movements, the sureness with which she dodged her
partner's flying knees and feet, the way in which she
modified her style for each succeeding man, made me
thoughtful, and thereafter I looked at her more care-

fully. Good work, human race, I said to myself. What a lot of vigor and endurance! Why be reluctant and ashamed? It is possible to love one another.

Would you have thought that a man like José, who had never signed his name, who could count to forty only with difficulty, who toiled prodigiously sixteen hours or more each day, would have taken the trouble on Saturday night to amuse himself and even on weekday evenings sometimes, when the wind was right and the sound of my accordion and Pep Torres' trumpet reached the back bedroom windows of Can Josepi? It is true. José had still the instinct of play. In a situation where he had had to work a little less, he would have enjoyed himself more.

One paid José for the milk once a month, but he did not appear to make collection on the first, unless the first of the month fell on Saturday. José had splendid manners out of doors. He gave other mule drivers a fair share of the road, greeted passers-by spontaneously, was sorry, in fact momentarily deeply affected, if someone was bereaved and shook one's hand joyously if all was well. On the first Saturday after the first day of the month there would be a timid knock on the door, if it were closed. Otherwise suddenly one would be aware that José was standing nearby. He would be wearing a cap which should have been worn by a Paris *voyou* or a Hollywood gangster, but his sturdy carriage and open smile would more than counteract the desperate effect of the cap. His expression would be like that of a boy who had just decided to skip school and go fishing. He would ask *"Comm vos trubau?"* or *"Tot va be?"* (Is everything going well?), inquire for absent members of the family, then stand there heroically, hands at his sides and submit to a painful moment of silence.

"How about a glass of wine, José?" one would say, and his tenseness would relax. A glass of wine was another social objective to and through which he could steer.

"*Un poc de vi pajes*" (a little wine of the country), he would say happily.

Still he would remain standing, not like a statue but like a model for a statue who is momentarily awaiting the word to step down from the platform.

"Won't you sit down?" one would ask.

He would obey. There is no other word for his method of accepting a chair. Then he would sit erectly, cap in hand, glass of wine in the other hand, poised.

"Have you heard from Señor Page?"

"Oh, yes," José would reply. "He and the Señora sent us two dollars last Christmas. That was very kind. He was a good man, Señor Page. Worked very hard with his head. Sometimes I used to hear his typewriter going half the night."

Richmond and Phyllis Page had lived two years at Can Josepi and had become a part of Santa Eulalia and of the struggling family whose toil above, below and around them had filled them with awe and admiration. José and Catalina spoke of them affectionately and wistfully. And the two-dollar Christmas gift, months, even years later, would make José pause, shake his head thoughtfully and grope for a time in metaphysical areas.

I have no idea how long José would have sat and tried to make light conversation in case I had not

mentioned the matter of the milk bill. Often I was
tempted to try the experiment. Always José's uneasiness and tension, his scarcity of words, the sweat on
his bronzed forehead, made me ashamed of myself. I
was careful, in fact, never to pay the milk bill directly
to Catalina because José, once a month on a Saturday
night, liked to feel the weight of *duros* in his pocket.
Otherwise he never handled money. Whatever small
cash transactions were necessary were carried out by
his wife, who spoke a little Castillano and understood
foreigners more easily. José never spent too much of
the milk money, but he felt different, fingering it in
his pocket on a Saturday night at the café. He knew
he could toss a *duro* on the bar when it came time to
pay, instead of searching his pockets for small change
and fearing between drinks that he might not have
enough. He would sit quietly at a table watching a
card game, or on the fringe of some conversation
touching on politics or life. When the others asked
for drinks he would have another, too, and he would
recognize his friends proudly when they passed by on
the way to the bar or the door. Days and nights of
work had not extinguished him. The mild excitement
kept him awake, his eyes wide open and smiling. He
nodded when someone made a clever play at cards
or when Cosmi, defender of the faith, said something
in favor of humanity. Broad back, noble head without
words. Man who lifted and strained. Sitter among
men, in clouds of candle and tobacco smoke. You
could shoulder a two-hundred-pound sack of potatoes
without batting an eyelash, and still the weight of
fifteen *pesetas* in your pocket made you free. I suppose José would spend about sixty *centimes* (less than

a dime) and go down the Arabie road to his home with fourteen *pesetas* forty.

Such a man would have liked to have land of his own. He would have been glad not to worry, for the owner of Can Josepi had threatened now and then to expel the family and could do so at a moment's notice. Perhaps, in that case, José could have found another farm to work on shares, more likely he would have become a hired man.

Catalina, whose outlook was broader and whose mind was more flexible than her husband's, was the more cheerful of the two. They enjoyed their food and ate plenty. They shivered when the sun was not shining, but the sun shone nearly every day. They suffered from no superstitions. The trouble was that they had to work too hard all their lives, and it was getting them nowhere. Their sons will have a harder time. It is best not to think of what they are in for. It is best not to think at all.

8. A Group on the Main Street

THERE was seldom a group of five or six men on the shady side of the street in the center of town that did not include Guillermo the blacksmith. His blue shirt, imperceptibly striped, his shock of curly hair and his indolent and at the same time attentive attitude were easy to identify at almost any distance. His forge was in a little shed next to Sindik's carpenter shop and almost opposite Cuarapiñada's "Tot Barat." His vise stood on the covered sidewalk which was littered with bars, sheets and scraps of iron. Several times a day, whenever a customer appeared, Bernardo, the hardworking apprentice, would wipe the sweat from his eyes with his bare arm and go looking for Guillermo. Usually he found him at Cosmi's or Gork's, sometimes at Can Xumeu in the next building, now and then at Andres' small bar near the Royalty or Antonia's fishermen's bar on the edge of the square.

"I'll be back in five minutes," Guillermo would assure his companions. And usually he rejoined them within an hour.

It would have seemed to a casual observer that Guillermo did almost no work at all, he was so often on the street and in and out of the various bars. His sour-faced father-in-law who sat all day in front of Las Delicias snorted and ground his teeth disgustedly each time Guillermo appeared. Bernardo, the assistant, did all the steady tedious work. Nevertheless, without Guillermo very little iron work would have been done in Santa Eulalia. He had a wonderful eye and an understanding of iron. He could design a gate that would fit its concrete posts. His door and window fastenings were not unsightly and they functioned well. He could estimate quantities and stresses and strains. There was almost nothing he could not repair, if the customer was a friend of his. Guillermo did his blacksmithing in the way Rubens accomplished his murals. The spade work was Bernardo's—Guillermo was called in for the finishing touch.

The contrast between Guillermo's shop and that of Sindik, the carpenter, next door was amazing. Neither Sindik nor his sons nor his assistants paused a moment in their work. They were bent over lathes or benches, hammering, planing, sawing or sandpapering every minute of the working day. Conversation was discouraged, drinking forbidden during working hours. And still, because Sindik's honest head worked slowly and contained no ingenuity, the results of his frightening energy and application to duty were meagre. Guillermo, who loafed nine-tenths of the time, accomplished as much or more. As a matter of fact, the work Guillermo agreed to do was usually delivered within a day or two of the time he had said it would be finished, while with Sindik it was a matter of weeks.

Unshaven and collarless, his arms and his clothes soiled with soot and cinders, Guillermo was not prepossessing. On Sunday, with a clean shirt and a clean shave he was a strikingly handsome man. His blue eyes, made more expressive by long lashes and finely turned eyebrows, twinkled sardonically but never maliciously. There was nothing happened on our end of the island that he did not know about. Ideas, for Guillermo, did not exist. He had never given one moment's thought to the brotherhood of man or to economic interpretations of history. But he knew all about the men and women around Santa Eulalia and he enjoyed hugely their minor and major predicaments.

Some very bad writers have spread much misinformation about absinthe, and the government of France, which permits nearly everything within reason, forbade the sale of absinthe years ago because of its supposed effect on the birth rate. I simply wish to submit, in the interest of science, the following facts: Guillermo, on a dull day, drank twenty glasses of absinthe and on Sundays and holidays forty or more. He was forty-five years old, unusually sound and strong, had seven sons conspicuously healthy and bright (the youngest born in 1931), ran his shop, supported his large family and never was disorderly. Sometimes, I must admit, he had difficulty in following the music in the late hours of the weekly dances. If Guillermo arose early on Sunday, as he almost always did, everything went well with the orchestra that night. He would drink enough in the morning to put him soundly to sleep after lunch. Then he would wake up at five o'clock, refreshed and completely sober, and would not have time before the dance began to drink enough to impair his coordination. On rainy Sundays now and then he would sleep late in the morning. That was bad. He would not feel the need of his *siesta* and by nine o'clock at night whole notes, half notes, quarters and eighths streamed and capered like seaweed under troubled water. He was loyal and conscientious, however. I have seen him continue long after he was unable to tune his guitar. I would tune it for him, place it in his hands, put the right sheet of music on his music stand and tell him when to start.

Few men were as fond of music as Guillermo. Of course there were no music stores in Ibiza and it was difficult to order music from Barcelona. We got several Spanish *paso-dobles* that way, but most of the dance music I arranged for our strange group of instruments, and the guitar was very important to us because so many strings and keys were missing in the bass section of the piano. Whenever I had finished an arrangement, I would stroll past Guillermo's shop with the music in my hand. He would drop whatever he was doing and come with me to the theatre to try out the new piece. At first it was difficult for him. He had had almost no musical instruction and had to learn his part by painful repetitions. Within a few months he could read quite complicated scores at sight. Pep Torres, who played the violin and trumpet, had all the industry of Sindik the carpenter. He had raised himself to his fair degree of efficiency by hard work and dogged persistence. Guillermo learned as much or more without effort, and always his performance had a touch of something not to be written on paper, a lilt, a subtle *rubato*, a twang, an inner voice. His expressive blue eyes twinkled. If I threw in an extra note or two on the piano, he gleefully

shouted *Olé*! Moments of music were perfect moments
with him. His thoughts, unhampered by ideas, had
formed moving patterns, like fringes on a pantry
shelf. Guitar strings, tones of trumpets, click of castanets. The dancers caught the beat, became more
male or more female. *Olé!* Guillermo, swaying and
holding his guitar, was like Casey Jones at the throttle. We had some breath-taking engine rides, I sitting
on a stool and Guillermo on a chair. Always when we
were practising in the empty theatre Gork and his
customers would come in, one by one. They would
take seats quietly, in chairs near the piano or in the
empty boxes which formed a horseshoe around the
bare concrete floor. If the day was rainy, the masons,
Vicente Cruz and Juan Costa, and their *quadrilles* of
helpers would sit around us. And Pep Torres would
join us, Pep, splashed with mortar, freed by the rain
from his work, pulling up a chair, grabbing up his
trumpet and hopping the melody, *Olé!*, in the midst
of a chorus. Once in a while a mason's helper in his
overalls would bashfully sing a tune and ask if we
could play it, and I would note it down, scribble a
guitar part and a violin part hastily, and the man
would be overcome with appreciation and pleasure.
Gork—his sacristan's face would break into a bashful
smile. He would leave us, baggy knees of corduroy
trousers, and shuffle back with a bottle of cognac or
gin. Yes. I liked best the rainy days like that. It was
pleasant when the sun shone, too, and the theatre was
cool and the woman whose house was next door and
who used the same well would open up the well doors
on both sides, and smiling women, too timid to enter,
would listen from there.

On the broad *paseo*, Guillermo had a home, but he was almost never in it except to eat and sleep. That was true of nearly all the men who lived in the town. The Ibicenco women found that state of affairs quite natural. They did not scold or rant, least of all Guillermo's wife. Her job was to cook, keep house and take care of seven growing boys. She did it scrupulously well. Her father, the sour-faced retired sea captain who sat all day in front of Ferrer's in order to watch Guillermo, would have liked to make trouble but Paja was severe with him. Whose business was it if Guillermo took a drink now and then, as long as the *pesetas* kept coming in? The father-in-law could only scowl and mutter, but Guillermo was sensitive to approval or disapproval and often chose the back entrances and the back street in his progress from bar to bar.

One of Guillermo's important functions was to act as town scribe. For this he made no charge, no matter how many hours he put in. Many of the brightest men in town, as I have said, could not read and write, and their business correspondence and letters to the many members of their families Guillermo wrote for them in his meticulous handwriting, almost like engraving, of which he was justly proud. Thus it was that Ferrer and others were able to gather around with the rest at noon when the bus came in and accept from the postmaster's green-eyed daughter their share of letters and postal cards. It was a common sight to see Guillermo leave his shop with a letter in his hand and a neighbor walking beside him interpolating voluble explanations as Guillermo read. The blacksmith's curly head would be bent wisely. His sloping shoulders stooped a little as he walked. There was always a certain jauntiness in Guillermo's walk. He was graceful with the cape. He swung a beautiful *muleta*. Guillermo, in gold and silver spangles, a matador's queue at the back of his neck, silent bull-fight music to guide him along the main-street arena, on his way to take up his pen and write Gutierrez and Company in Barcelona about a shipment of canned sardines and inkfish. The neighbor would follow admiringly each flourish of the pen and Guillermo would read his careful Castillano phrases, sign the man's name, seal the letter, search the box-office drawer for stamps (he always did his writing in the theatre bar) and then they both would shout for Gork and drink together. Often farmers coming in from the country would tell their needs to Gork and he, with baggy pants, would amble up the street to the blacksmith's shop. Guillermo would always respond. He never seemed to be too busy with his own affairs. In the end, the man from the hills would offer to pay, and Guillermo would make a marvellous gesture, all the fingers of his right hand spread, his arm flung upward, tossing payments to the skies, destroying the thought of payments, scattering aloft torn payments and all exploitations of art for coins, and, smiling, he would glance at the bar and the farmer would shout loudly for Gork even if Gork were only two feet away.

The Ibicencos never forget small favors done them and invariably find an opportunity to reciprocate.

One Sunday morning I was driving along the San Juan road. I noticed a woman standing by the roadside with a child in her arms, and after I had passed her, something in the recollection of her attitude caused me to stop and turn the car around. I found that her baby had fallen into the fire and was burned badly about the face. The mother had been waiting by the roadside, hoping for a vehicle headed toward Ibiza. I drove her in, questioning her and trying to decide how badly the baby was injured, and took her to the best doctor I knew. She tried, of course, to pay me and assured me that she had relatives in town who would see her safely home. More than a year later I was sitting in Cosmi's back room and Anna came in to say there was someone outside who wished to see me. I found in the outside room the mother, dressed in her best kerchief and shawl, a bashful man with huge red hands and wrists, and a baby. The man held the child and pointed to the face which had been burned, his eyes beaming with joy. Not a mark remained. Very diffidently the woman took a glossy black live rooster from beneath her shawl and held it toward me. Beside her on the table was a basket of eggs and another filled with dried black figs and almonds. Anna Cosmi, who is sensitive to social situations, nudged me lightly and indicated with the slightest imaginable movement of her alert black eyes that I must accept their gifts. The family had made the trip by donkey cart from Santa Gertrudis to find me, making inquiries on the way. A *forestero* with a beard? Ah! You mean Xumeu. In Santa Eulalia I had been given an Ibicenco name, Xumeu. They had been very busy on the farm or they would have come much sooner, they assured me.

The feeling of a live rooster's body is strange when the heart is beating between the palms of one's hands. Many times I think of the thousands of heartbeating kindnesses that have been done me and for which I have made no adequate return. To all of you, wherever you are, who have given me help and sympathy I should like to send a young Spanish mother, very bashful in bright colored clothes, and a red-necked stalwart farmer with a child in his arms. I should like to post outside your doorway a donkey and two-wheeled cart and lay on your table a basket of eggs, each one of which is stainless, and figs and almonds. I should like to leave you standing, thinking with a live black rooster in your hands.

Among the small shopkeepers, Mousson the butcher, whose place of business was between Cosmi's hotel and Andres' café on the side of the street that was sunny in the morning, was a lonely figure. He was a short man with a long face and a body slightly out of proportion to his legs. His house was small, rather dingy, and whenever the weather permitted a blind woman (probably an aunt) sat in a low chair, listening. On the other side of the doorway was a small tree which had been stripped of its leaves and branches and had died, and on this tree hung the carcasses of the sheep and goats Mousson had slaughtered and was offering for sale. He sold enough meat to maintain his family, but not so much as Francisco on the back street or Jaume on the *paseo*. The strange part of it was that he never seemed to establish anything but a distant relationship with his customers. All the other men on the street had friends and enemies. Mousson had neither. He dressed in faded clothes that fitted him into the general coloring and seemed to pass unnoticed in the crowd that gathered around the bus or in the post office at noon. His oldest daughter, Marguerita, had married Pedro of the Royalty, one of the most genial and voluble young men in town, and still it seemed as if Pedro took no notice of his father-in-law, and Mousson seldom spoke with Pedro. The blind woman sat in the sunshine, heard the bleat of the animals before and when they died, heard the customers come and go. The two younger children, Catalina and still another Marguerita, were both pretty but looked undernourished. No doubt the continuous butchering impaired their appetites. I never heard anyone speak ill of Mousson. No member of the family had disgraced his by committing crime. He had no political affiliations. He was neither rich nor poor, neither clever nor stupid. He was a shadow dimly clad in shirt and trousers, and whatever plane he had attained was uninhabited except for him.

I must record another scientific fact for what it is worth. I had organized a daily class in English for the young girls and boys. They were so eager and their parents so eager to have them learn. Each week I had a friendly oral and written examination and invariably undernourished shadow Catalina, thin ten-year-old daughter of shadow Mousson, knew more of the English words than any of the flesh-and-blood children, all of whom were smart and anxious to win. So whenever I passed the doorway the blind woman silently smiled.

The only man who actually joked with the blind woman, making her the butt of embarrassing remarks as if she were a young girl, was Pedro of the Royalty. He was the town's geniality and tact, the apostle of

glad words, late hours and the joy of progress. I want
you to understand a little of his spiritual kingdom,
built first with brick and inlaid with gold. It is best
to begin with Santa Eulalia's sidewalks, because
Pedro's footsteps were ringing on them in solo performance most often, so that where there was concrete they sounded out lustily, then were lost in
patches of soft dirt, resumed and lost again, ducked
into doors, returned. He stepped briskly on errands
when the sun had driven the others to cover. In the
section of the town near the *Cuartel* his whistling of a
tune, homeward bound at two, three or four in the
morning, his knock, knock, knock on the door in the
moonlight, his doorlatch (warm and soft from sleep
Marguerita opening, sometimes not remembering)
was *taps* as Ramon the bus driver's motorcycle bombardment was *reveille*. When it rained, Pedro was out
while others were in and he cleaned his black patent-
leather waiter's shoes fifty times a day.

"Pedro!" an habitué of the Royalty, or Juanito the
proprietor, or Juanito's anxious mother, would call.

"*Vengo*" (most joyfully) would sound from the
next room, or a store or café a hundred yards distant.
Pedro would come, swiftly, eagerly, but not in a
sweat. Most often his voice would reply from a vine-
covered plaster shack in the Royalty's superb backyard, where he secluded himself at odd moments in
order to post his numerous accounts. None of the
regulars paid cash for their drinks. Now and then
they got conscience-stricken and bothered Pedro for
a bill and he laboriously prepared it, forcing himself
to do well a task that was not the most natural for
him. He added his columns twice, or more if they did

not check, itemized everything carefully, used new pens and clear ink and otherwise kept himself up to the standards of professional pride. He had been the best mason's helper on the Balearic Islands. His ambition was to be the best waiter in the world.

"Who are you?" is asked of one of Gorki's derelict characters.

"A man, praise God," is the reply.

This attitude, this generous extension of membership in the human family, was Pedro's natural way of thinking, or rather, of acting. His young daughter, Señora Riquer and the blind one sitting by the sacrificial tree, all were women. A small boy crying because an older brother had run away from him was an injured man, brooding or weeping over untold wrongs and injustices.

In an astonishingly short time the old Arab house on the corner had been taken down, the stones that had formed its three-foot walls had been re-mixed with cement and a hideous modern structure had been put up, two stories high, with walls only six inches thick. The backyard had remained intact and did much to redeem the place. Pedro, on the evening before the opening festival, had put aside his workman's clothes, the overalls splashed with earth and mortar, the stained alpargatas. He had bathed himself carefully and devoted a long time to his hands, not from vanity, but because a waiter of the sort he aspired to be could not have bruised and calloused fingers. What the venture of the Royalty meant to Juanito, the young proprietor, or his mother Isabel, what it meant to Don Carlos Roman and Don Rafael Sainz, what it meant to Cosmi as competition, are different stories. To Pedro, it meant being born again. He had had one strong call in his earlier youth, the sea, and this had slipped away from him because of his impulsiveness with Marguerita. Now a profession he admired and whose possibilities he understood was opening for him. For weeks before the hotel was ready he consulted those of us who had lived in large cities as to how to serve. Innumerable details he had studied and considered and memorized. He knew his townsmen would not demand or expect too much, but he dreamed of a high standard, of strangers coming to the remote island and the small island town and receiving their *manzanilla* in exactly the right kind of glass, neither scant nor overflowing, free from bits of cork, at a proper temperature, placed where it should be placed. His reward was to be their appreciation of his efforts, not their tips. All Spaniards are comparatively indifferent to tips, and Pedro especially so.

The opening ceremony in connection with Santa Eulalia cafés or hotels was an impressive one. The proprietor proclaimed open house, the whole countryside knocked off work and the day was spent like an ordinary holiday, except more spontaneously. Cosmi, when he had opened his place, had sent printed invitations by the hundreds, to aristocrats, foreigners and neighbors alike. Juanito of the Royalty wanted as much as possible to keep his place for the rich and the visiting foreigners, without offending the rest of the town. That would have been no mean problem for Olivier of the Ritz in Paris. That it was solved, even partially, must be accredited to Pedro, whom we left trying to scrub the plaster from beneath his

broad finger nails. The morning of Juanito's opening
Pedro appeared in a spotless white linen coat, white
shirt with black bow tie, black trousers and black
patent-leather shoes. His black hair was well combed
but not slick with grease. He did not, like most of his
well-born customers, smell of stale bay rum. He laid
a napkin across his sleeve, and he was in no way
offended or even dampened in spirits when the whole
town roared with laughter. He knew that he did not
look as they had seen him since he was a boy and that
most of them cared not a hoot whether he served
them from the off or the near side. He was grateful to
a republican world for giving him his big chance.
Everyone expected that a day or two later the white
coat and the black tie would be discarded, but nothing of the sort took place. Pedro's stainless coat became as much a fixture of the main street of Santa
Eulalia as the eucalyptus tree in front of the Casa
Rosita. Cosmi, being a proprietor, did not feel the
need for keeping up such an unvaried sartorial standard. He was always neat, always distinguished, but
he wore no collar or tie. Pedro was the town's head
waiter and sooner would one see the sergeant of the
Guardia Civil parade the town in pyjamas than
Pedro out of character.

The Royalty got away to a good start. The blue
decorations, straw chairs and especially the prices
(the scale of which Juanito set higher than was customary in town) made the ordinary drinkers feel it
was not their place, and many of the men who had
avoided cafés since the (for them) catastrophic days
of April, 1931, crept out of their holes and foregath-
ered at noon for their *apéritif*. In the way republicans

felt safe at Cosmi's, the old guard began to breathe freely at the Royalty. Juanito was troubled by it, his mother Isabel even more so, because they both were afraid of politics. Nevertheless, the clients created their own atmosphere. A room containing Don Carlos and his boys, ex-Captain Nicolau, the Pilot, whose sister taught the girls' school as it had been taught in the days of the monarchy, the Catholic building contractors, the new young doctor Gonzalez, whose brother was a priest, Don Rafael Sainz the enormously fat Madrid banker, a former American bank clerk and his mother-in-law who looked like a Helen Hokinson and was the leader of Duluth's four hundred, a Baltimore woman who carried the blue book (open at the page containing her father's name) when she went swimming, Father Torres, the old doctor, who conducted the public clinic without having a basin of water on the premises, etc., etc.—such a room was not likely to exude a republican aroma or to buzz with a hint of progress. Juanito, having been advised by snobs, had formed an ideal that was in no way Ibicenco, while Cosmi had hoped to crystallize and improve the best Ibicenco tradition. Meanwhile they were good friends.

At noontime, when the bus returned and the mail was distributed, the crowd I have just described would be at the Royalty, indoors because the sidewalk would then be white hot. Next door, at Andres', old Vicent the mason would be having his absinthe and, goaded by Ramon or Mariano of Casa Rosita, would be upholding some reasonable proposition against their insincere arguments. The old man had few teeth and his step was not brisk. His clothes were fantastically patched. Nevertheless, he could do a terrific day's work, and he frequently did so.

You know who would be at Cosmi's, laughing and chatting around the mahogany bar: Ferrer, Guillermo, Pep Salvador if he was in town, Pep Torres, Vicente Cruz the mason (now fiancé of Cosmi's Catalina), Antonio the young barber, Bernardo the blacksmith's helper, Juan the captain of the fishermen, Mateo Rosa (dreading to go home to his fretful little wife), Pep des Horts from Arabie, Rigoberto Soler, Toniet Pardal all smiles, Marc Colomar and a group of boys about his age who were just beginning to work, Miguel Tur, Julian (the bus owner who chose his café by prices and disagreed with practically everything that was said to him anywhere), Edmundo and other gentlemen most useful in a tug of war.

At Can Xumeu the faces would be crafty, from the high dry hills. Masear, the Barberet, Sindik would be there. The fishermen who were not at Cosmi's would be in Antonia's. A morning's work done, a meal in prospect and then through the hottest hours a blissful sleep. They all went to their shops or stores or building jobs in the afternoon, but most of the work was done in the morning, and the rest of the day meant gradual relaxation and an evening in good company. At noon, the street was like a gamelong with cafés for gongs, so that by touching it here and there different tones of fellowship would sound. Lunching lightly in Santa Eulalia had never come in vogue. One ate heartily and one knew that in restaurants and houses all around one's friends were laying in a good store of nourishment, too, that the strong red wine was being passed from hand to hand and gurgled merrily. There

was no thought of saving one's energy for some unnatural use in the afternoon. One ate and drank, and
be damned to energy, and then, a long long sleep,
going down from the springboard of chicken rice and
quarts of Val de Peñas into caverns blue and topaz,
protected by a net from flies, and sinking, remembering dimly that at four would begin to be felt the Santa
Eulalia breeze, the sea wind from the skyline of Cala
Llonga.

9. *The Back Street*

AND now, in the damp blackness of the evening in the time of short days and mud, of rain against cracked window-panes that cracked last year or year before and never have been replaced, of floors mud-stained with red mud like Indian red from San Carlos way, with buff mud from the slopes to the south toward Cala Llonga and the darker street mud of the front street and the back street and the narrow alleys between. Of rain, air-cooled in the spaces where the darkness perhaps was less dense, slanting through paralleled air, sliding downward over glass and shutters, soaking into sodden straw and thatch of roofs, seeping through the walls of living masons and into the yard-thick walls of long-dead Moors, staining cracks between boards, wet Roman bridge, encroaching under doors, in gullies and drains and all the thousands of footstep pools, one two one two. Dampness, by mud out of rain, in the buildings of cheerful folk who think in building not of rain and December and March but of that other condition not now prevailing and which can be imperfectly remembered. These are the days of the drippings of pines, when the tall dateless palm in the Royalty's back yard has wet diamond crisscross of bark and aloft perpetual swaying.

In this early winter evening, so long time wet and

blanketed with the siftings of darkness, where feet are wet, sandals stained and between the toes mud and cool water over arches, let us who brought galoshes (making peasant women smile with fingers over mouth) start a pilgrimage on the back street, in doorways facing the backyards of those we know on the main bus road, and I find that I can pass no doorway.

Directly behind the blank wet brick back of the theatre is a small plaster house set thirty paces from the road and surrounded by the mud and for two months abandoned plant stalks of a vegetable garden. There, inside, squatting in a circle around a dustpan containing four pink coals, in low native chairs, are the members of the family Pedarcx. That is, if there were among them one who could write (except a little Modigliani-faced girl with a wide mouth) he or she would have spelled it in some such way. The father, an old seamed invalid in his low chair and bed half dressed for years, once caught fish, the gleaming absurd and mysterious basketloads whose gills worked in rows for not so much air and who knew the shell bottoms and the hidden sands, where forests and meadows swayed on rocks and ledges and a sea-water sky. He had drawn in his nets, mended them in salt sunshine spread upon his toes and his hands cut and stinging from spines. A short man, he had held up his end of the basket, and when he was sick he was through, but he lived a long time and was surprised when one spoke to him, and nodded and acknowledged pleasantly through a week's stubble beard. And once in a while he was shaved by the Barberet, pleased with the feel of the *sous* in his hand in his pocket, and his face was so small and so sore when he squinted in the glass, and everybody laughed on the way home.

Pedarcx played out too soon and (please, gentlemen, this is no poverty tale) his sturdy wife with arms and shoulders lovely after aeons of work was obliged to do what Ibicenco women dislike most, that is to go out daily or whenever she could to work in the houses of others. Señora Pedarcx disliked it less than any of her neighbors, for she was really Catalan and only a few generations in Santa Eulalia and still a little back from the back street and not strangers but nearly that way. Her words were always as if she were glad to use them, as if she had more things and friends and were spreading heirloom trinkets out on a clean wood table to be admired by her and by you. She enjoyed your "Good evening" as others love letters in the mail and hold them with both hands to their breast a while before opening them. This Señora was short but very trim and strong, and her forehead was as good as any that has been passed out small to girl babies to grow larger and contain inside what there is of life that cannot be seen outside. At the time of which I write, five years after her husband had been taken sick, she was forty-five and could walk a wonderful straight line, her skirts swinging Pavlova, with one hundred and fifty pounds of potatoes on her head, and thinking of pleasant things as she walked along. One daughter, taller by half a head, with a dangerous intensity and a clear olive skin and a list of attributes that poor girls in Spain or elsewhere have an instinct and necessity to guard, had left the island for Barcelona and her mother had

been told by a neighbor who had travelled that way
a few months before that this daughter was to be
married to a working man. Well, I said to myself, I
don't know how they do it, but the working men get
their share of fine-looking women, and, by God, I am
glad, and if he doesn't take care of Maria, she'll take
care of him, and if at forty-five she's the woman her
mother is, she will have the laugh on most women in
the large cosmopolitan telephone directories. Maria
came back to Santa Eulalia once for a summer vacation and a friend of mine painted her as a widow,
standing before a mirror in a black evening gown,
with her arms raised and her hands at the back of her
dark-brown hair, thinking that still there was disaster
to come and a little angry that it was not taking
shape so she could see and understand just what it
would be.

What if Maria, in her bare-shouldered loveliness
and apprehension should have had a vision, gazing
into that mirror, and had told me what she saw of
Spain? Then I could have said, in every doorway on
all the streets, "Pack up and let's go. . . . But where?"

Let be! We are all too stupid, and not at all fore-
sighted. And let no year but nineteen thirty-six be
proud of its death rate of working men (with or without handsome brides)! Let us all, safe in homes and
republics and hotels, smash every mirror in the place!

The Pedarcx boy was strong like his mother and in
fishing boats and lugging baskets by the shore grew
tall like his sister Maria and he was a fisherman
(knowing much of what the Captain knew about
those realms of up-and-down eyes, streaks, shapes,
colors, mud spots, reed zigzags, caverns—silences)

years before he was old enough to be deprived of his vote. He was a good-natured boy who swung his shoulders a bit from side to side as he walked, and he smiled and even blushed when you spoke to him, and if Juan the Captain who had taken him into a man's boat when he was only a kid, if Juan had softly asked him to spit in the eye of a Guardia Civil the Pedarcx boy would have done it. Otherwise he was as gentle as his little sister Catalina. Just now, in the evening mud and rain, they all are sitting around a pan of coals, waiting for their dinner. The old man, his hands mildly fumbling invisible nets finding holes and tangles, Señora with her eye on the stew pan and smiling, sweating a little, smelling stew of spined rock fishes and potatoes she had lugged and peeled, a large space of candle-lit air where the daughter widow Maria sat in Barcelona, the fisher boy with hands that could rip the back fin right out of a ten-pound *mero*, and dumpy smiling Catalina.

Had Maria, standing with arms upraised (La Argentina) before her glass, seen blood in the sun and blood red in the other red earth of her native town, would she have known, even then, I wonder, that her small sister Catalina would be the first in the town to plunge a knife in a beating human heart and draw the blade forth blood red.

When I first saw Catalina Pedarcx she always had a small child in her arms, her sister or some neighbor's baby. She was singing under her breath a semi-tone chant ah-a ah-a ah-a which had drifted to Ibiza from the African shore and she had a neat little dance step, swinging forward and back, other foot, forward and back, in front of doorways. Her face was round, not oval like her mother's, and her ankles were not slender like Maria's. One felt that she would not be pretty but very complacent and kind, also patient, long-suffering, meek and perpetually stepping forward and back singing ah-a hours at a time with babies. To such come adventure and romance, false whispered promises, bewildered thrustings of knives and damp prison walls.

When Catalina was fifteen years of age with a girl's naïveté and a woman's body, a young doctor came from Madrid to Santa Eulalia, was properly shocked by the filthiness and fastidiousness and general Tsar-like tone of Doctor Torres and decided to practise in the town. There was much coldness on the part of the old doctor (fifty-five, black coat, black tie) but young Doctor Gonzalez could not be ridden out by Matutes or Torres' aristocratic relatives because the young man had a brother who was a priest and an uncle who had often been asked for a cigarette by the ex-King Alfonso. The townspeople, even those who regretted the clerical and political affiliations of young Gon-zalez, soon found that he was an excellent and con-scientious doctor. He washed his hands a hundred times a day, he gave his most expensive medicines to the poor and told rich women there was nothing much wrong with them. In short, he had had splendid train-ing, liked his profession and the main street and the back street, and doors along the encircling hills and on hidden tortuous roads in the country were open to him. He rented an apartment, set up a modern office in the front room and to the delight of Señora Pedarcx offered a job (her first job) to Catalina because she was soft-spoken, poor and had her mother's instinct for cleanliness. Catalina prepared and served the doctor's breakfast, cleaned his office, kept hot water bubbling continuously on charcoal burners, and he taught her to receive the patients in an outer-room and usher them in in turn when he was ready for them. She bought a new dress, new silk stockings (her first pair), wore neat black shoes instead of cloth alpargatas and she was happy and proud to be working, and the whole family felt more secure and smiled. The doctor was content, for already he had sensed the advantage in employing a local girl instead of importing one from outside and keeping her under lock and key day and night.

Doctor Gonzalez built up his practice more quickly than he had hoped, and at odd times was lonesome, so he wrote the girl who was waiting for him in Albacete. They decided to get married sooner than they had planned. The doctor went away for two weeks (his wedding trip) and asked Catalina to sleep in his apartment and guard his instruments. Catalina, in her fresh new clothes, had stirred the thoughts of some of the young men, one of them a cousin of ex-Captain Nicolau, a young man of a family that would never think of uniting itself with the Pedarcx, but young Nicolau made skillful and violent love to little Catalina, promised her marriage and life-long happiness, and before the doctor's wedding trip was fairly under way the bed to which he had planned to bring his young bride was being ecstatically tested. Within forty-eight hours everyone on the island suspected what was going on and Señora Pedarcx, almost hysterical, hurried to the *Cuartel* and begged the Guardia Civil to interfere. Nicolau was warned away, Catalina (hardly understanding fully what she had done) was sent home and her mother guarded the doctor's office until he returned and then tearfully apologized. Catalina's brother got back from a fishing trip, started out to find Nicolau and was waylaid by Cosmi and Captain Juan. In Cosmi's back room they talked to the boy and explained a lot of things he didn't understand, that Nicolau's uncles were this and that, that years in jail and exile from the island afterward were a heavy price for what had already irrevocably occurred, that poor girls on the mainland were often misled by handling and promises. The boy blushed, then cried and gently Cosmi took his knife away and the Captain gave him a job in his own boat and insisted that he set out for Tagomago that night. As he walked down the road, the boy swung his shoulders not quite so strongly in the rhythm of waves and thought along the road and under stars and in the boat, on a coil of anchor rope, and felt as if something hitherto firm had slipped, and he wished it were firm again.

Catalina, crushed but still tingling with pleasure, sitting jobless in the plaster room with her fumbling father—this fifteen-year-old child, who the day before had rocked small children and sung ah-a ah-a, had thoughts go through her head and feelings course up and down and around. And what she did was to take a kitchen knife (her father not seeing), slip out of the house and wait in front of the dance hall where Nicolau was dancing. And when he came out, she stabbed him with the knife clean through the heart, and he died four minutes later.

The whole thing was a mistake, but remember

Catalina sitting in prison (they laughingly called the Ibiza jail the Hotel Naranjo) and watching the one small orange tree in the courtyard growing ever so slowly, and feeling inside and in the mornings and when she turned on the boards at night the beginnings of more forward and back in prison cells or doorways and the eternal Moorish chant ah-a ah-a. Remember her because her story is by no means finished, and her exit from prison was infinitely less banal than the events leading up to her incarceration there.

Forget her momentarily in the patter of rain, in the drive of chilling rain which does not cut, in the sucking of mud sounds by back-street footsteps and we come to a rain-soaked wall and a bit of concrete sidewalk, perilously high on the gutter side and obscured in the darkness until just ahead, in front of a baker's shop a dingy street lamp holds a tiny snake of grapefruit light which enables one to see what one already feels, namely, that it is raining, and little else. As the sidewalk's nearly ending strip is faintly visible, arises on one's right, behind a doorway, a chorus of barking, not of earthly dogs, no threat, no joy, no invitation, but assorted yips and yaps not of puppies but infirm, and as you knock upon the door (closed only because of the rain) a voice from an overstrained larynx implores the dogs to be quiet and you to come in and amid more undisciplined barking a smiling face, shaven head, steel-rimmed spectacles, alive pale-blue eyes, and behind him his wife in a knitted shawl and a parrot in a cage squawks "*Pa'amb oli.*" The man is ex-Sergeant Ortiz (years ago of the Guardia Civil), his good wife Carmen who speaks carefully with the manners of Madrid, and the parrot's cry means bread and oil, which is the Spanish equivalent for bread and butter, for the Scriptural daily bread and for that which was cast upon waters and is God knows where by now.

The dogs—they cannot be ignored. They bark, sniff at trousers legs, look at one another with their one good eye, turn their faces aloft, puff, wheeze and when they have done what they can, they amble back to baskets (rag-lined for their convenience), favorite chairs from which they are dumped as the chairs are offered to you, back rooms, corners, places by the fire. They are not like other dogs, and in the course of years the Sergeant (aged seventy-two) and his wife (sixty-nine) have collected them as one gathers misshapen stones for the borders of gravel paths in suburban gardens. Not one is a big dog, and none excessively small. They have a strain of pug or of spaniel, eyes worn dim, too fat and almost dropsical and perhaps because the Ortizs know that no one else on earth would be drawn to them, those dogs have too much food and all they can absorb of affectionate conversation. The Ortiz dogs and the parrot came from abandoned plush parlors of families respectable but now extinct.

Next to Admiral Platé, ex-Sergeant Ortiz is the best amateur fisherman in town. He has a dory moored at the mouth of Santa Eulalia's river, and early each morning he goes there, walking a mile in the morning air with fishing tackle in hand and a slice of bread and oil, and he thinks, sitting in his boat and pulling in now and then a good fish, of days and evenings in barracks, all the length and

breadth of Spain, of comrades, promotions, evenings
in Madrid. Of Carmen, how she was, and the pension coming in and, after all, although he had
doubted it faintly in his youth, how life goes on at
seventy and morning air smells of seaweed and the
red wine warms the gullet and the line of the hills one
could read like music as the current shifted the boat
and the Cala Llonga slopes wheeled gently to the left
and into the picture came the Santa Eulalia million-
years-ago cliff with the fortress-church, the priest's
house, the new hotel Buena Vista, and later the tiny
shrine on the highest mountain around which women
led sick donkeys who had recovered and within hung
broken off arms and legs and heads and even bellies
of porcelain dolls (which were parts of babies allowed
to get well). Swing boat, farther north, for the red-
streaked pine-covered hills, high hills, of San Carlos
and around to the east to the Tagomago cliff, and
what can a man, either twenty-seven or seventy-two,
find better with a fish tug in the morning? And Carmen caring for preposterous dogs and the parrot and
speaking to them the best woman's Castillano in the
town and probably on the island, keeping up the
manners of extinct parlor families from which such
ruins came and hoarsely barked. Not forgetting that
each afternoon Señora Ortiz put on a black-silk dress
and a mantilla and went to Cosmi's backyard, where
under a tree she taught to spell and to read and a
little to write the blue-eyed Can Cosmi's Catalina
who by now had jilted runt Francisco, the back-street
butcher, and was to marry Vicente Cruz, as good a
man and master mason as anywhere there is.

The Ortizs might have appeared to be futile people, with their yapping dogs (*Pa'amb oli* parrot cry) and a pension check each month, but my mind moves forward and I must hint to you of another time of war, when in the large port town of Ibiza, with formerly ten thousand inhabitants, when death was in the air and the crumbling walls and above Franco's airplanes seeking just such as they, only two of our human family were not taking shelter but were staying on the main street in a room marked Red Cross, not looking above when motors droned nor around them when iron fragments flew. Old Carmen, with her arms around distracted women standing behind carts of corpses looking for some specific and familiar corpse, and the ex-Sergeant (hoarse voice, blue eyes) pouring wine from jugs, tying bandages and all Ibiza in the hills, not cowardly but simply unaccustomed. And in the harbor, where accidentally bombs fell, were fish, belly up, and rowboats stove in, and day and night the Ortizs working.

In memory of Sergeant Ortiz and Carmen his wife I wish each and all of you seventy happy birthdays, as the Bible suggests, so that you may have a well-rounded life and sharp last recollections to take with you to the grave!

Meanwhile we pass along, although twice already urged to stay for supper, and crossing the muddy lane leading westward to Rigoberto's hill, we find attached to the dim street lamp what is known as *Es Forné Nau*, in other words the New Baker's Shop. There are two bakers in Santa Eulalia, one called Old, the other New, according to their length of service in the town. The New Baker is a big round-faced man, bare arms well muscled and a hearty laugh, and

his hair and clothes often dusted with flour. He has
a small straw-haired wife, sharp in repartee, an upstanding girl from the mainland, of a good tough
family. First came the baker, and Cosmi and Ferrer
and the others liked him and he decided to stay. Then
he ordered the oven from Barcelona and was in town
a few months waiting for that. There was a German
servant girl Anna he proposed to, but she had an
aluminum salesman somewhere, so he went to Alicante and brought back Manuela (who had the same
coloring as Anna but features sharper), and I never
knew a couple so pleased when the bride got pregnant
right away. They worked hard, built up a good trade,
made good bread which we smell as we stand in the
rain by the shop. And Manuela changed her shape
and outline until she looked like the third from the
left of the Cala Llonga hills, and when the child was
born dead, and joy for two weeks went from the New
Baker's round face, the fine little disappointed tough
girl was the first to say in front of Cosmi's bar: "*Ah,
fotre!* Ther we'll make another." So Anna Cosmi
smiled, and the crowd at the bar fairly roared and
the big baker put his arm over Manuela's shoulders
and at that moment snapped out of his mood—and
everything went on.

At this point in our pilgrimage, while we are standing in the mud beneath the street lamp to which the
baker's shop is attached by one of Guillermo's iron
scrolls, a change takes place, one which deepens the
darkness or removes in the lemon-orange pattern-
dotted lines of light in unison. Windows recede, then
fade. To be brief, the electric light plant has broken
down. In houses, women by charcoal fires and groups

of men in the cafés say "Ah" as the visibility lowers, and laugh and good-naturedly curse as the darkness takes its hold and prevails. There are scrambles for candle ends and matches, flickers, dancing shadows on white walls, and the town has made its readjustment from the white invisible current to the wax and string between the fingers, drops of oil in iron cups. It is as if one century, bowing slowly into the wings, and expected back, makes way for her mother whom the audience remembers. Ferrer, smiling profanely and chewing on his supper, sets a lantern in his door and waits. And as big fish glide on still nights when the Captain sets his flare, so come customers to Las Delicias, the lovable improvident ones who have not made ready—and *sous* and candles are exchanged.

In the early nineteen thirties, the light plant of Santa Eulalia was the town's hugest joke and got a laugh several times each week when the wind blew wires together, or belts broke, or for some reason unexplained the wabbly machinery in the mill house stopped twitching and lay still. On stormy nights, of which there were few except in the equinoctial seasons, the lights were sure to go out soon after dark. But more mysteriously when stars hung in the sky and the air bore the scent of the pepper trees, all windows and bulbs and cracks would never suddenly, but like Belmonte taking his time, swing back the gold side of the cape and let us touch bottom in starlight.

"*Ah, fotre! Carrai!*"

"*Attrecedre!*"

And the scramble for candles and matches and saucers would follow.

The first electric-light plant, in the building with the flour mill, was set up and directed by Mallorca Pete who, with sausage-stuffed wife and Brancusi baby Miguelito, lived on the ground floor of a quite new house facing the sea and next door across a vacant lot with hen houses and two goats to Can Xumeu and the telephone office. The Mallorquin, as Pete was always called, was a small man with a noncommittal face and freckles on his arms, not more than thirty-two years old, and not a relative of Matutes but nearly so. Matutes, for some reason he did not disclose, had wanted Pete to leave Mallorca and come to Santa Eulalia for the purpose of setting up a light plant, and no one like Pete ever thought of crossing Don Abel. So the short fat wife had faint pain of longing in her eyes when she sat on the doorstep and looked across the sea and saw steamers which reminded her of Mallorca boats.

Eventually Pete's dynamo began to turn, but all that resulted in the bulbs was a pitiful twisted red line that would have been outshone by two glow-worms under a tumbler. There was a fortnight of tinkering and at last the bulbs were coaxed into throwing forth a fair amount of light, and then after two hours the plant broke down completely and there was no light at all. Steadily, as the months succeeded each other, this condition was slightly improved, so that perhaps two nights a week there would be no interference with the service, and maybe only two nights there would be practically no light at all.

In the dwelling houses, still equipped with graceful iron lamps for burning olive oil or fish oil and where the women and children went early to bed or were

absent on holiday evenings, the failure of a light bulb
or two was not a grave inconvenience. To the owners
of cafés and the incredible cinema at Gork's, sudden
darkness so unexpectedly and so often was a nuisance,
and especially because no allowance was made in the
bill. Cosmi was the first to rebel. He warned the Mallorquin that if the service was not improved he would
disconnect the lights himself and depend upon candles
all the time instead of half the time. Matutes, Cosmi
said, had money enough to buy a good dynamo and
generator and instead had foisted on the town some
relic he had picked up for nothing in a Mallorquin
junk yard. Ferrer, Guillermo, Sindik and last of all
Juanito of the Royalty followed Cosmi's lead, and
within a few weeks the light plant folded up. Pete's
wife hoped in vain that her husband would be sent
back to Mallorca, for which island between feedings
of Miguelito she yearned, but Matutes seemed to
think he had given Pete his chance and straightway
abandoned him, probably to save the price of a couple
of third-class tickets on the boat he himself owned.
The Mallorquin was left strapped, an unconvincing
electrician in an anti-electric town. He got a job in
the mill, where the water wheel had turned faithfully
while his dynamo had been letting him down, and
walked rather lonely and dusty to the corner of the
road and back to his house three times each way each
day.

About a year after Santa Eulalia had turned back
to candlelight and kerosene, a Frenchman, Georges
Halbique, came to the town to spend his summer vacation. He was an electrical engineer, had a few thousand francs to invest, and decided to try his luck.

His principal assistant, who had worked with him a while in France, was a young Catalan named Primitivo. I liked Primitivo right away. He had irrepressible energy, playful like that of a cub panther, so that even in the heat of summer noons he made boxing motions with his hands and shoulders, smiled, waved boyishly and was always glad to see you. He had been lightweight boxing champion of Catalonia and seemed glad to be alive. Not long after he arrived in town, Cosmi told me one reason for Primitivo's joy of living. It seems that in a street fight resulting from a demonstration in Barcelona in favor of Catalan independence, Primitivo, having to pass through a group of Guardias who were swinging their sabres, had had the presence of mind (perhaps because of quick thinking in the ring) to cover his head and shoulders with the dead body of one of his friends, so that the body was badly cut and Primitivo was one of the few to get through and be alive.

Not less attractive was Primitivo's young wife and her mother, both Catalans, looking somewhat alike, with gracious manners and the calm aspect of those who have walked through worry like a bramble field and are on the road again. In Santa Eulalia all the native women walked well, but Primitivo's wife and mother walked superbly.

Halbique, being French and aloof by nature, and unable to forget by night the francs he had spent and was spending, took little part in the life of the town, but Primitivo, who could understand and speak Ibicenco and was incurably companionable, became a familiar figure on the main street without delay.

The new light plant was built on the north side of

town, two hundred yards beyond the theatre, at the intersection of the San Carlos and the Arabie roads. As soon as work started I detected a republican aroma. The contract to put up the building was given to Vicente Cruz, who had energy and youth and happiness like Primitivo and was to marry Cosmi's Catalina. Gleefully mounting a pole with borrowed climbers was Marc Colomar. Shipments of machinery and materials were more than usually delayed by Matutes. Customers who had been the first to abandon the Mallorquin signed up first with Halbique and tried to assuage his worrying. However, the dynamo and generator were finally delivered. They were new and shining, and the belt was new and in case one belt broke there was another in readiness. Guillermo, Gork and others were doubtful but willing to be convinced.

The new plant functioned quite well. Breakdowns were few and of brief duration, and when the days grew short and the equinoctial rains poured down the lights burned steadily until just before midnight, when three black winks gave warning, and in the cafés there was a rush for candles again. The other effects on the life of the town were as important. Guillermo, Pep Salvador and a man from San Carlos way, who in 1935 was to become republican mayor of Santa Eulalia, formed a company to bring talking pictures to the theatre once a week, and thereafter on Sunday evenings the farmers and their wives and children came streaming in from the hills, and in the horseshoe of boxes around the rim of the auditorium sat families gay in holiday clothes, and eager faces leaned forward in the balcony. Startled cries and exclamations, protests, encouragement were shouted as the picture progressed. On the stage in dimness, left of the screen, stood Pep Salvador piquantly translating the most important phrases from French or Spanish into Ibicenco, and when the film was an American (cowboy pictures the Ibicencos liked far best) Guillermo would come hurriedly to find me for the preview, and Pep Torres would supply Ibicenco words if I lacked certain ones and, braver because of the darkness, I would project my inadequate voice in nothing like Pep Salvador's style or aptitude, but it seemed to make the picture clear. I sometimes wonder if our Hollywood cowboys, riding their bronchos without pulling leather, shooting up saloons saving always the honest Western girl, were working at the time for breathless galleries and families so tense in boxes in Santa Eulalia, and if so, whether they did not think highly of themselves.

Primitivo, as soon as the plant was running, had a normal amount of time to himself, and with the young linesmen he had trained as a nucleus he formed an athletic club and taught all comers to box, until he could offer some hair-raising bouts on Thursday evenings.

Meanwhile, Primitivo's wife, an expert dressmaker, organized a sewing class to which came daily, chattering and watching every movement on the street as they sewed, Eulalia Colomar, Manuela (sister of Juanito of the Royalty), Odila the daughter of ex-Captain Nicolau, and a half dozen other girls between fourteen and eighteen years old. Soon in the Sunday afternoon parades up and down the main street, the modern dresses began to be less uniformly hideous.

Of the young girls of the town, who were to have lifted the island gaily on their upturned palms and revolved it, legs trippingly dancing, until it caught up with the clock I shall say no more just now. They deserve a chapter of their own. Only on the back street, across a vacant lot from *Es Forné Nau*, we reach the house of the family Noguera where lived Eulalia Noguera of whom I often think as an Ibicenco Joan of Arc. It is true that she led no armies, although she received one with infinite tact and grace, and to compare her to the peasant girl who had visions is not quite fair because Eulalia had no visions, but instead a crystalline sense of reality. Probably she will not be roasted at the stake but made to carry water jars over endless pathways through the graveyard of a broken dream, or if liberty flickers and holds its white light again she will smile and sing and be one who has never denied it.

The house has three rooms, the central one for sewing and eating and a bedroom on either side. It is one of the very few houses where, through troubled years, under monarchy, dictatorship, young republic, Lerroux and Robles, Azaña, no matter what or whom, each member of the family (women, too) has been united in the cause of freedom. Not even Cosmi had a wife who knew what political developments meant to him. Anna Cosmi was matter of fact and practical, and for her the sun did not shine except when she could see it. Noguera, lanky unprepossessing builder, had a wife who knew the source of his misfortunes and who was willing that they all should suffer for their good ideas. She had never set foot in the church, or given way to economic pressure. She was proud that her husband was a republican from birth and that contracts had been withheld from him by powerful groups on that account. She had remained aloof from cautious neighbors and had taken in sewing all her married life to augment the family income.

There were two daughters, Maria and Eulalia, and because Maria the older was pretty as a little girl and conventionally beautiful as an adolescent, Eulalia was considered rather plain and thought of herself that way. As a matter of fact she had a fine oval face like El Greco's daughter, except for a pert snub nose and humorous intelligent eyes. If there was a fault in her construction it was that her legs were a trifle heavy, or at least her ankles. When I first knew her she was sixteen years old and worked for Cosmi in the kitchen, and from the kitchen escaped snatches of song. The Ibicenco music, from ancient hymns and galley chants and nurtured and crossed in the hills through hundreds of harvests, was fast being forgotten. Old men and women remembered dozens of couplets and melodies, but the young ones disdained them, all except Eulalia. Her memory was prodigious, her voice flexible and clear, and to moods of weather, hen-plucking, cleaning of fishes that flopped all the way to the pan, thoughts of childhood, present, past and future, she sang in Cosmi's kitchen, and often Rigoberto, passing by, would hurry in, his face alight with pleasure.

"What was that, Eulalia? Please let's hear it again."

And Eulalia, never bold or bashful, would laugh and compose her face for singing, and, her eyes smiling or pensive, according to the song, she would repeat until Rigoberto's voice was heard too, and he would continue up the street with a new tune very old, and the small flame of that hill music would revive and be carried in two torches instead of one.

A chauffeur from Ibiza who came to Santa Eulalia each Sunday tried to induce her to elope, and Eulalia, genuinely astonished that anyone should notice her and not her beautiful sister Maria, started out with him, spent one night in the house of one of his relatives on the hill near the church, then thought better of the adventure and returned to her home. Her mother and father, who had been deeply distressed, made her give up her job at Cosmi's and kept her at home, sewing. After a year had passed and Eulalia had worked industriously, showing no further leanings toward romance, she was allowed to do part-time housework in the homes of certain persons her mother knew and trusted. Thus it was that she came to our house mornings, bringing jugs of cool water on her sturdy hip, conjuring sparks and then heat from charcoal, cooking joyful eggs and singing bits of Ibicenco song, telling what had happened the night before or several years ago and laughing, commenting always with clarity on world events, the reverberations of which had reached her, with malice toward none except those who soil all forgiveness, and always an indomitable spirit. Eulalia in the morning, the Cala Llonga breeze in the afternoon. Those elements, cool when the heat was simmering and when chill was encroaching, frank and warm. I wish your song and sound sense were everywhere, Eulalia, and I long this moment to kneel and receive cooked eggs from you and to hear all the things I am deathly afraid to know, to borrow your courage. And, please, how is my faithful dog I had to leave with you? And your father, re-sold into slavery, and your Uncle Mateo who took the helm of the schooner that bore some of the good men away, or Uncle Edmundo who was left behind?

On the rainy evening, Edmundo, whose house is next on the back street, is surely not at home. His second wife is cooking for his first wife's children and not fretting, knowing that Edmundo cannot fish when it rains, and that in cafés and peering near-sightedly through steel-rimmed spectacles he is plowing with seaman's walk through the mud between doorways, always near the crowds and somehow apart and alone, his voice gruff and his eyes near-sightedly smiling, black shirt, fingers castanets, dancing fiercely the *jota* or singing hoarsely as will be sung many times at Cosmi's and Can Xumeu and Antonia's this night:

Pescando la sangonisa
Salio un pes' gordo
Pescando la sangonisa
Salio un pes' gordo
Arrimé con el farole
Y era un mocoso
Asi de grande (hands outflung to indicate length)
Asi de gordo (fingers around circumference)

Wild fishermen's song about fishing for eels and catching something unspeakable (roars of laughter) "this long" (hands outflung) and "this big around." I wish I could convey to you the tune because it is a great tune for happy Spanish men to sing and its subjects rise with something like grandeur and its predicates recede and the music says "that long" as singers' arms are flung outward to extravagant dimensions and unmistakably "that big round" at the conclusion, for music is stronger than rain and always is sweet smoke, and men who sing with a will drunkenly go home like an arrow and tumble half stripped into bed and that sleep which for non-singers unexists and is never the sequel of tea or ice-cream soda.

I do not say that Fear, in peddling up and down the street, did not visit nearly all the houses, but the day he came around, Edmundo was out to sea and Eulalia, his niece, must have been far away. Of this you will be amply convinced.

10. Of Public Service

TO THE inhabitants of an island town the coming of the mail means more than it does on the mainland. The remoteness of a stretch of sea, wave surface bending as it falls away to a clear-cut horizon, memories of terrifying nights lying flat on soiled deck or in iron third-class bunks as women cried "*Mi Madre*" and "Maria" in blare of electric light with the steamer creaking, lurching, protesting and the sea dark demons, screech of wind. In other words, distance. The hazard of a journey, articles of clothing packed unskillfully in imitation-leather suit cases, bread and *sobresada* wrapped in handkerchiefs. The faintness as the bus set out, smell of oil and tar, fat pig prodded brutally from gutter mud and up the gangplank, clucking of crates of hens, the bottomless nausea. Through protracted night of fear the knowledge that the voyage must be retraced before earth shall stand firm, and food and children, smell of gardens. Truly, the women of Ibiza dreaded voyages. I remember that in Rockport, Mass., the women upstanding on land were wilted by the thoughts of the sea.

On the trans-Mediterranean steamers, arriving at Ibiza Tuesday morning from Barcelona, Friday morning from Valencia, Sunday evening from Alicante,

Wednesday evening and Friday evening from Palma; departing from Ibiza to Barcelona Tuesday evening, Wednesday evening to Valencia, Friday evening to Alicante, Friday morning and Sunday evening to Palma; on deck, in the soon unspeakable dungeons below where those who dared leave the sight of dark sky and hostile waves lay miserable, fully clothed and never in comforting darkness, the equality of the sexes so hopefully inscribed in the Constitution of Spain seemed a travesty on truth and never to be realized.

For the men, leaning easily on the rail and chatting, sitting thoughtfully in wind-sheltered nooks between bales or trunks or on dashboards of lashed autos, breathing sea air gladly and relieved to be looking upward at a swaying sky, pointing out each lighthouse as the boat passes the length of the island, awake and eager at dawn to see the first lights on the mainland shore, I doubt if as sailors those men could be improved upon anywhere. The men of Formentera claim the edge on those of Ibiza, and vice versa. The Basques laugh at the Gallegos and are ridiculed in turn. To have any one of them in a craft when suddenly bad moments arise is good fortune direct from Heaven. And meanwhile their mothers, wives and sisters, huddled and moaning, wailing for their mothers and the Virgin, expecting and inviting death. Not sure that the wrath of all the unseen powers, once enveloping them will ever release them again. From certain old races, engraved by shipwreck, fire and sword, plagues of locusts, boils and capacity to absorb punishment, lines of woe have been traced and

handed down, so that an Ibicenco woman, under
pressure of rough voyaging, may reflect in her gestures
and facial expression all the woes of the mothers of
humanity, birth pains, bereavements, massacres and
bondage. When the sea is calm and stars hang low,
the women seem to fare no better. They are lost before they set foot on the gangplank, crushed, demoralized. In view of this, a letter coming to them
from Mallorca or the mainland is precious. It has
accomplished a journey the thought of which makes
women turn pale. The men would travel oftener if
there were anything to impel them or if it were
simpler for them to get away. No matter how little
they do, they are conscious of tangling the skein of
family or community life if their easy routine is
abandoned. Letters, to them, are a reminder that the
rest of the world is accessible and the newspapers of
Barcelona and Madrid, some of which are not edited
by the bishops, bring a breath of freshness and hon-
esty that would give bronchitis to the Ibiza *Voz* or
the *Diario*.

Considering the importance of the mail service to
the people of the town, it is interesting to try to
fathom the processes of mind which led Matutes, by
means of his network of influence in the time of the
monarchy, to have appointed as postmaster of Santa
Eulalia a feeble-minded man of surly temper who not
only could not read and write, but was totally incapable of learning. Also sire of two idiot sons and
luckily two competent daughters. Although the postmaster did no work himself, except to potter in an
alfalfa field a mile up the San Carlos road, some dim
stirring of fear to be away caused him to insist on be-

ing present when his green-eyed from-long-before-Christ younger daughter Maria placed in a sack each morning letters which had been dropped through the slot to the floor of their living room, tied and sealed the sack and handed it carefully to Ramon the bus driver.

Immediately afterward, the postmaster, high and lanky on a small not-well-fed donkey, his long gnarled-toed feet in dirty sandals, ankles black with last week's dust, rode northward to his plot of ground. He had a gaunt hawk face, hair-nostriled beak, sunken cheeks and no teeth, wore a black felt hat indoors and out, and when it rained or the air was cool, a faded black shawl. All the doorways on the street he passed without seeing, and no words were flung out to him. His youngest idiot son was thirty, with the forehead and features of Philip IV, until the chin loosely slipped, and then long ape-like arms with hands much too large, knees always bent and shuffling broken feet. Pepe's arches must have given way when he was a small child and all his life he had walked laboriously, tilted forward, face vertical and peering ahead, huge hands clasped behind his back to help him keep his balance. Still his face was beatific and his smile was kindliness, he spoke softly pleased responses to greetings, always glad to feel the ray of a human glance and an "*Ola*, Pepe," and his family responsibility (not to be confused with his broader function as delivery man) was to care for his older brother Chicu, forty-two, whose eyes were nearly vacant, lower jaw dropped flytrap, head farther askew, whose arches were not broken but shattered and who leaned farther forward at an angle so perilous that he fell in dust and mud a dozen times or more each day.

Chicu got fewer greetings and his response was grotesque and fervent, for he could only speak a gibberish peculiar to himself, which Pepe and the green-eyed sister understood, but which to his neighbors was Choctaw. Let a crowd gather on the street and scatter laughter, if a boy touched off a firecracker or someone by an open door or window blew a few notes on the flute and beat the Ibicenco drum, Pepe first, broadly smiling, then Chicu stiffly staggering, would come catapulting from the post-office doorway and hurry to the scene of possible excitement. For labors within their weird range of ability they often were given *sous* and because all the café keepers in town knew it was best they should not taste alcohol, they drank inordinate amounts of coffee each day, which probably brought their innocent hearts to a state of flutter matching appropriately their inadequate brains. Had the younger brother chanced to be born near an advanced institution for the care of the mentally deficient, he might have been taught many things. Chicu, the older, could have been improved little if at all.

Before the hour when Ramon was due back with the bus the incredible postmaster would come riding down the street on his donkey, and straggling along behind, grunting, sweating, backs bent forward at precarious angles, Pepe and Chicu would follow, laden with sacks of alfalfa or *garobas*, making efforts of Hercules. In the shops the men would be knocking off work, children would be streaming from the school on the ground floor of the barracks of the Guardia

Civil, boys from the rear room at the side, girls from
under the front archways. The bus, obscured in dust,
would round the corner by the mill, and when it
reached the public square the crowd just beyond
would part to give Ramon a passageway to his stop-
ping place.

Ramon would have beneath the front seat packages he had bought for craftsmen and housewives,
telegrams in his leather cap. His first duty, however,
which he performed without variation, was to descend
with the mail sack and carry it to the post office where
Maria met him at the door. Back in dimness at the
table which later would serve for the family meal sat
old Anfita (hawk-beak) fingering in bony claws a
bottle of nearly dried ink which originally had the
color of permanganate of potash and a rusted pen in
a broken wooden penholder. The postmaster could
not sign his name himself, but he took a fanatic delight in making others sign theirs. He had learned
through years to recognize the printed slips which
indicated that Maria would find a registered letter,
on no account to be relinquished to its owner until
he had written his name on a certain line. Once a
registered letter came for Gwendolyn the Welsh girl,
and since it had been robbed of five one-pound notes
(in England) and stuffed with old newspaper, she,
having opened it, refused to sign. The old man was
restrained with difficulty by his daughter from attacking Gwendolyn. He nearly lost what was left of
his mind. He threatened, refused to eat, stormed into
places where Gwendolyn might be, and from that
time forth he sat on the registered letters, creasing
them with his odorous corduroy breeches, until he

had squinted at the wet imperfect signature of the addressee.

Behind the mail sack, citizens in shirtsleeves, women who had washed their arms and faces and tidied their hair, children from outlying houses, were drawn through the narrow doorway into the shadows of the postmaster's front room. Always Maria would open first the sack of Ibiza daily news sheets, the *Diario* and the *Voz,* and read out long lists of names (folded papers to hands outstretched, or relayed when one in a corner answered "Here") while half the town expecting letters, waited not quite patiently and wondered why the letters were not distributed first. Maria knew why but she never explained. She knew her father was annoyed and unsettled by crowds and that usually on Tuesdays, the heavy mail day on which the Barcelona boat arrived, he muttered and scarcely knew what he was doing half the afternoon. There were many in the crowd who got the paper every day but did not expect letters, so that by giving out the newspapers first she thinned the human pressure around her father at the table, inkpot in hand, and made a fairly tranquil afternoon more likely. For her mother, although not feeble-minded, was a vixen and replied sharply to all mumblings from the old man distrait. At such times the two idiot sons fared rather badly. They were never beaten or physically abused, but unkindness or domestic discord set their unprotected nerves twanging like the wires of wind harps, and Maria, so cool and competent and hoping to hold her fiancé (a young member of the powerful Guasch family to whom she was related but just beyond the church taboo) did not like through hot afternoons to be reminded that she sprang like Minerva from a loco family. Better she liked to sit under a small struggling tree (one of those finally planted by the Friends of Santa Eulalia) and watch her older sister's baby, whose forehead, eyes and nose were those of a lady Philip IV and whose chin did not slip, who learned brightly, sang like a bird and whose graceful small girl's legs moved spiritually in the children's dancing games.

Brave green-eyed girl from the gardens of Babylon, shapely anchor to which a faulty family was moored, you had not the luck you deserved with your fiancés! One sorrowing at a distance remembers the green of your pleated skirt and the sea-green of your eyes, the firmness of your hands sorting small-town newspapers and the neatness you by constant attention instilled in your flat-footed half-witted brothers. Their clothes, patched and faded, each day were clean. Their sandals were washed. I have seen infinite sadness pass like the shadow of a cloud over Pepe's face and when a mule fell have seen Chicu squawk with pain and fling his arms in a gesture of appeal to those more competent to help.

Boys, come have a cup of coffee, and I cannot say that you are not this day the Princes of Santa Eulalia, the only ones equipped to face the future as it lies before Spain. What you never will know will be enough to break down strong men who once thought they had an advantage over you. Or do you suffer more, jagged harp strings of nerves played endlessly by the winds of woe?

Back quickly to the post office at noon. The distribution of letters having been accomplished, the

crowd ambled away, opening, reading in the glare of
the sun and the dust, manoeuvring into bars, returning to sizzling kitchens or to pots in shadow by
the doorway. A few letters are left, at which old
Anfita glares malevolently. Some of these are for
foreigners, a few belonging to well-to-do families who
pay the idiots ten centimes for each delivery. So
starting flat-footedly out at their respective dangerous angles from the earth go stumbling Pepe north
and Chicu south, documents clutched in hand and a
singleness of purpose propelling them in a very straight
line from the imaginary continuance of which their
townsfolk instinctively stand aside. The arrangement is (a conception of the father) that they shall
not return to their chick-pea and dark-bread lunch
until someone has accepted all the letters in their
hands. So Chicu, the dullest, eyes and sagging mouth
like fish in window, halts his grotesque walk as best he
can (once achieving momentum it is hard to stop himself) on the approach of every stranger and barking
and gurgling non-existent words, holds out letters
beggingly and squeals with joy and wants to shake
hands if one is accepted. But Chicu has learned that
in certain recesses are men of golden hearts, and after
trying faithfully an hour or so in a blinding sun or
biting rain, he staggers toward Cosmi's and from
room to room until he finds Cosmi himself, knowing
that Cosmi has a hand which will reach for his left-
over letters and place them on a shelf weighted down
by a glass behind his bar, near a bottle of cherry-red
gazeosa, from which often is poured a glass to cool
the throat, no charge. Also strangers soon know that
wherever they are, Cosmi will promptly find them

and say almost blushing "*Rien*," "*De nada, nada*," or "Have a glass of cognac. It's good for the health."

Very often the postmaster's cross old wife, sitting with her back to the road and the passers-by, spins wool from local sheep into yarn with a rattling ancient spinning wheel and later knits white socks of the highest grade for her defective menfolks to wear.

11. Les Jeunes Filles en Fleur

FROM woodwind dawn force of brass pushes the sun across the horizontal waters, and air, washed by two days' rain, is breathed as whiskered Platé laughingly talking to himself and wooden saint-face old Antonia Masear, wrapped in shawl and kerchief over cactus fibre hat, stand at Cosmi's back gate. Cosmi's brother nods good morning, blue-eyed Wedgwood Catalina cocks her head *"Bon dia"* in a child's soul's voice. Old Juan, of Casa Rosita, in cowboy pants and invisible spurs, hitches up his belt to see the Barcelona boat clear Tagomago cliff. And up and down the street who sees it too? Ferrer, coffee-bound, Guillermo blue shirt on *paseo*, the women of the Royalty (Isabel, worried mother, Marietta, diminutive spinster, and Antonia the Chaste), in theatre doorway Sacristan Gork, and in houses and hotels, where masons and helpers sleep who weekdays work, are shouts *"Vols jaure tot es dia?"* (Do you want to sleep all day?), and the answer from the bedclothes is *"Si, Señor."* The sun clears itself and mounts as the steamer passes left to right, and after storm are puddles that quickly dry except in ruts and in the February calm, the slopes unearthly white with almond blossoms, the sea is smooth and still, transparent and motionless, a fortnight sometimes with scarcely the surface rough-ened. Those who have spent wet and toil-free days think of work again and drink coffee, eat their bread and oil and have cheer of clear weather to compensate for damp hours in bunks. The stormy weather rest has given them surplus strength for extra motions.

Ramon splashes mud as he dashes on motorcycle bike down the San Carlos road to get the bus. The Barberet comes bicycling in to unlock his barber shop. From beneath the tree on the *paseo*, where Jaume the white-haired butcher stands with sacrificial knife, arise bleats of unfortunate goat who soon will be roasts and chops, bladder blown for children, and from low branch very plumb a lights and liver with non-sacred heart suspended. In that tree, knowing scraps of lamb and goat, lives the butcher-shop owl who whistles F-sharp at night and his mate replies G-flat at regular intervals.

The back street dries as quickly as the front street, and next door to Edmundo, who will sleep as late as seven o'clock behind wooden panel with elaborate knocker, are a couple, old but not infirm, who speak to each other and to such of the townspeople as will understand (Cosmi, Pep Salvador, Guarapiñada, Platé, old back-street mason Vicent) in Algerian French. They were born in Santa Eulalia, plump well-fed woman and broad stoop-shouldered man, but having lived so long in Alger they forgot their native dialect, and Ibicencos laugh at them as Ibicencos who speak French. They are seldom outdoors, except in their commodious and highly walled backyard. They take no part, are never seen at shows or dances. The Sunday afternoon parade does not move them in its ranks. I do not know their names but there is one remarkable fact concerning them. Whenever there are no eggs to be had in any store or from any hen-fancying acquaintances, a knock on their knocker will produce the large plump woman speaking amazingly French and she in turn will open a cupboard and take fresh white eggs from a shelf, count three pairs or four pairs, whatever you want, and let you have them for the same price you would pay in the store if the store had eggs that day. Somewhere in Africa, where the Admiral learned the secrets of vegetables, shrubs and flowers, this almost hermit couple got the Indian sign on hens, and I, for one, said little about it, knowing how convenient it often was to buy eggs when eggs were scarce.

Directly behind Cosmi's backyard was the front yard and outdoor shop of Francisco the butcher, the gnome-like undersized man whom Cosmi's Catalina jilted, after months of indecision, some minutes after Vicente Cruz said shyly that he wanted her himself. Francisco hopped with rage, gritted teeth as he tore skins from lambs, cursed his inadequate stature and suddenly planned revenge. On a back road to San Carlos, near the house of a farmer from whom Francisco bought animals, lived an Ibicenco girl who dressed in the old-fashioned style and was nearly thirty years old without having a fiancé. She was bigger than the butcher, but not twice as big, and had another of those noble foreheads, hair parted flat and dark brown, calm restful eyes and smooth arms, folded quiet hands. She thought a moment, nodded calmly and said "Yes."

"You mean it?" asked Francisco.

Calmly nodded yes. So at once they were married. For that Francisco in black had to go to church and afterward come spiralling down again. The old crone, his widowed stepmother and also aunt, took the stool far in the corner and the calm good-sized woman cooked and swept and a year later produced a girl baby perfect but unbelievably small, and the day the child was born Francisco looked through the iron fence mockingly at blue-eyed Catalina, still unmarried and peeling spuds for Cosmi, and said: "Well, who's ahead now?" And at the bar he could only drink three or four himself, being small, but he urged others to drink all they wanted, and after each round planked down the *sous* and was pleased with his woman and himself. He was happy that the child was a girl because she was such a tiny one and he knew that small girls get along as well as large girls, or better sometimes, but that feet and inches off a man make him hop when laughter scorches him.

Of Catalina's home, a wide open door, across the narrow street the donkey's small shed, a brother somewhat dull who hauled seaweed and rocks, a silver-haired mother unwrinkled and handsome at eighty, having spent twenty-five years nearly still in a chair and lifted into bed, and a sturdy active little old maid aunt. Also a sister, exactly Catalina's stature, with honey-colored hair and thick braid to exactly the same spot below her waist, looking like Catalina's twin from behind, but with a different, piquant face in front, and the same childish voice and timid manner.

This was a quiet house where no loud words were spoken, where love and gentleness was a garden of phlox, and in carved wooden chests were colored clothes that would be gorgeous if ever there was a lapse in the period of mourning to wear them. When one spoke disparagingly of God the Father or of Jesus Christ His only Son, Catalina's child-blue eyes grew large and she chided, smiling and really near to being frightened. Vicente Cruz, intelligent, industrious, was pleased that she was learning A.B.C.'s, but he would never expect her to understand other than household affairs.

The sun has dried the branches and tendrils of Toniet Pardal's ancient grapevine, and on his doorstep are several of his children playing, his patient wife paring vegetables inside. Two days of rain have been somewhat of a strain for Toni, who is sleeping as deeply as Edmundo and will be late today, but some of the fish will surely wait for him.

I cannot leave the back street without a word about old Vicent the mason who lived with his sister in a small house almost opposite that of Francisco the butcher. He was a stocky old man with heavy, really saturnine eyebrows and not many teeth, and, having worked in Italy and Africa, he could speak Arab, French and Italian as well as Spanish and Ibicenco. There were many competent masons in the town, but each of them acknowledged that old Vicent could do the best day's work of any of them. He appeared in the morning at the exact hour, overalls patched but clean, standing with his arms at his side and in readiness. He worked steadily until the word was given to quit at noon. He knew the pace which would accomplish most, not too fast, not too slow. The young men would spurt and try to draw

him on, and in the long run he would pass them. At
noon he would have two drinks of absinthe before
his lunch, would sleep half an hour, and in the afternoon carry on again. His sister kept house for him
neatly, worried when he was ill (he suffered from
backache frequently), and when my English class
was organized they came to me with Vicent's grand-
daughter Angeles.

Which brings us to the *jeunes filles en fleur.*

It was in their eager faces that could be seen a new
and better Spain. Their poise and curiosity, their
dignity, the cut of their clothes placed a hedge between their era and the shawls, kerchiefs and thick
petticoats of their mothers, the simpering of farm
girls from the hills, the black silk and black mantilla
of Señora Nicolau and Señora Riquer. And as light
from a possible future was reflected on their faces, so
it has died there, and they have been deprived, not of
a life they had tasted and enjoyed, but of one they
had seen through the mist. If I speak of them as
children in one sentence and as women in the next,
that is as it should be, for the youngest was eleven in
1930, and the oldest was eighteen in 1936, and never
can they assemble in the same room again or look
forward to spring and summer.

Not one of them, whose faces I loved to see each
day, has not been seared with white-hot irons, had
friendships torn and replaced by feuds in which they
had no real concern, lost fathers, brothers, lovers
and seen their island and their country murdered before their eyes. Standing as they were on the thresh-
old of an epoch which was strangled, they have lost
more than their parents and grandparents, who had

only property and a tranquil old age to relinquish. Unlike their brothers, they are not allowed to die. There is no escape from Ibiza, no money or opportunity to take them to a distant land—if any remains that will receive them. Had I known what was coming, and one day when my class had assembled to learn English words, had I then unstoppered a cylinder of poison gas and seen them, Antonia, Catalina, Maruja, Angeles, Odila, Juana (oh, especially Juana), Mary, Maria the daughter of Mateo Rosa, and all the others, gasping and dying and lying in rows there quietly, I could have saved them much. When groups of men, in uniforms, frock-coats, cassocks, set out to steal governments and take crops from the fields, the customers and proprietors and goods from the shops, work and workers from factories, gold coins and paper notes from banks, and the young men are forced to fight against their will or defend themselves hopelessly, there still remain the *jeunes filles en fleur*. They are too old and too wise to believe that butchery is the order of the day and that the words of the master butchers justify it, too young to forget what they had hoped for and what they are forced to see. The burden of a ruined land falls upon them. Their young bodies, too soon older, must be twisted out of shape to bear sons for another bloody crop, and those who should lie with them are corpses, and the remaining ones from whom they must choose are cowards, for the most part. A race, by thieves and cravens out of stark disappointment (and tragically beautiful), for a land that is crusted with blood and whose ruins stink with indelible treachery. Young mothers bred shuddering to monsters of the past in the graveyard of

the future. German and Italian freebooters, bay-rum
traitorous generals unworthy to be called Spaniards,
leprous churchmen, fumbling senile England, miserly
small-souled France. Come and take these girls! They
are yours! You have won them in the manner con-
doned by neutrals! Priests, sprinkle holy water!
Newspaper publishers, change your names to Pansy
and Poppie and Rose and wear black silk stockings
and brassières as you wait around your mahogany
desks, and be sure to report these weddings. Some
day certain groups will be kicked out of the human
race, and for you printer's ink whoremasters, the
first turn!

Let us go back to the days when the town was
alive, forget if we can the waxworks now in its place,
and enjoy a moment with these young girls whose
flowering coincided with a world catastrophe. To see
them as children in the public square, on the raised
area behind the large fountain, playing a dancing
game to the accompaniment of their own sweet voices,
round and round the monument in memory of an act
of Edmundo, Captain Juan, Pep Salvador and several
other Santa Eulalia men (strong oarsmen) who rescued the crew of a Santander freighter which was
wrecked on the reef just north of the harbor. (And
happening in a storm, Edmundo drunk, Captain
Juan extremely happy and Pep Salvador roaring but
nevertheless the first to stagger into a dory and set
out on an angry sea.) To see the young girls dancing
and hear them singing a compelling song which ex-
horts an invisible wag not to set fire to their uncle's
shirttail, one could not guess that Antonia's father
was made cinders in a vat of molten steel in the

U.S.A., that Catalina was the daughter of shadow Mousson, Maruja the pride and joy of the Secretario (all things to all parties), Angeles the grand-daughter of a bricklayer, Odila the daughter of ex-Captain (and monarchist) Nicolau, Juana the only child of a decidedly fascist contractor, Maria the daughter of a republican fisherman. In that year and to that promising generation such facts were becoming unimportant.

The underfed Catalina Mousson, black-eyed Angeles and the undersized Antonia were extremely quick in learning, the Secretario's Maruja and the blue-eyed lisping Mary were surcharged with kindness and affection, Odila was a freckle-faced tomboy who could have made the football team had girls been permitted to play, Maria Rosa was dazzlingly beautiful and filled with music, and Juana must have been clairvoyant, for there was unmistakable tragedy in her eyes.

Juana was the daughter of Bonéd the *Picapedré* (that is, rockcracker or master mason), a benevolent-looking old man with blue eyes and silver-white hair and cheeks slightly sunken, and his fat but solid Catalan wife Teresa, who, in spite of her bulk, could dance better than most of the light-footed girls of the town. Bonéd had been a sergeant in the Guardia Civil, and one who had caught the spirit of that relentless institution in the days of Primo de Rivera. Unable to accept the fact of the Republic he had retired on a generous pension, had brought the savings from several years of good pay to Ibiza and had gone into contracting. His wife, although never letting fall a word that could have been construed as disloyal to him, had divergent ideas, and throughout her girl-hood and young womanhood in Barcelona had kept alive the *sardana* and other Catalan dances and songs forbidden by Primo because of their patriotic effect upon performers and spectators. She was one who could be fat without being unsightly, and in dancing with her one soon learned that her flesh was firm and solid and her energy inexhaustible. Two opposed and contradictory traditions met in Bonéd and his wife, and their only child, Juana, feeling so much more than she understood, was aloof, almost sullen. She danced with the others, but always in her dark eyes, almost orientally slanted like those of her mother, was a reservation, and a cautious lack of abandon marked the movements of her shapely legs. It was as if she were thinking, "Ah, yes, you dance with me now, you stretch out your hands to take mine, but are you really friendly, have you found nothing in my face or frock or in my parents (having come so recently to Santa Eulalia) to ridicule and despise? Perhaps you will hurt me, and if you do I am fire and my hate can flare up in a moment—so beware."

Her mother Teresa seemed glad to stop and talk with me, as if then she were talking freely and was sure I would understand what not to repeat. When she brought this long-legged daughter whose eyes looked blackly into mine, not turning away, but de-fiantly, I was not at all sure Juana and I would ever be friends. Vicent's quick-witted Angeles and neat little Maria Sabio would spring from their seats in their eagerness to answer a question promptly. Juana would fix one with her fathomless eyes and after a pause the answer would come deliberately from their

converging tunnels. She moved through the town like
a cat who senses that her house will soon catch fire.
Nothing astonished me more, after three months of
seeing Juana every weekday and noticing no change,
than when one day, moving as if there were no one
else in the room, she placed a peony on the table near
my hand before she took her seat. I suspected that
Teresa had ordered her to do so, and so I sought out
the mother, on the slope a hundred yards behind
Cosmi's where for want of other employment Bonéd
was building himself a new house.

"*No pod se!*" (Impossible!) Juana's mother ex-
claimed with such genuine surprise, her face suffused
with relief and pride, that I had no further doubt
that Juana was the author of her own idea. The fact
that Juana had been able to unbend and to give me
a flower formed a bond between us. I never asked her
questions unless I was sure she could answer, and in
the dark pupils of her eyes I noticed a flicker of rich
warm brown when she looked so straight at me. Of
course, the day after Juana brought the peony, Maria
Sabio came in with a huge bouquet from her mother's
home in Santa Gertrudis, and Angeles, her eyes flashing jealously, had an armful of wildflowers she had
gathered at Arabie the afternoon before.

Odila had no age. She was freckled, cool, well-
formed and sensible. In action she looked boyish and
athletic. In moments of repose she appeared to be the
most maturely feminine young woman in the town.
I am sure she brooded from time to time because she
was not a man, or perhaps because her womanhood
caused so many doors to be closed to her. In 1934,
two Catalan young women, smart and sightly,

opened a pharmacy on the back street south of the *plaza* (between Ramon's house and the shop of Francisco the barber and shoemaker). Odila could not stay away from them, and they liked her. She would glance admiringly at their framed certificates on the wall, her grey eyes would follow them as they compounded prescriptions or suggested simple remedies to customers. A dark-eyed slim brother, who was supposed to help his sisters but seldom did, tried to turn Odila's head to thoughts of love. She danced with him competently, walked in the moonlight now and then, but the affair came to nothing, for the boy was aglow with Latin indirectness and sentimentality while Odila was honest and matter of fact. Had she felt anything that even remotely matched his ardent words she would have said, "Sure, why not?" As it was, the boy got nowhere, and the friendship with the sisters became an important factor in Odila's development. Not for her a small house and a husband only there for meals and to roll into bed, nor a large house in which to walk restlessly from room to room. She was determined to have a professional career and to that end was patiently opposing her black-silk-mantilla mother, step by step, each hint, gesture or sigh. Her brother, just two years older, had been sent to a military school and her small brother Justo undoubtedly would follow. Odila had the best brain in the family, a strange product of her military father who spoke to his dogs as if he were commanding a regiment and her snobbish mother to whom progress and impropriety were synonymous. Be assured that in the time of trial by fire and sword Odila was one of the dignified ones.

The Secretario's daughter, Maruja, should have been ill-tempered and sour, for her mother was partial to boys and had five of them between twelve and twenty years of age, and what little attention or justice Maruja enjoyed in the house was due to her grandmother. This remarkable old woman, peeling potatoes, cleaning fish, listening sardonically to neighbors' gossip but never joining in except to end the conversation, kept herself mindful that Maruja if not in range of her sight was somewhere else and should by no means be neglected or accused of misdeeds her brothers had performed. The mother, not essentially mean but blinded by her partiality, could rant and now and then slap, but just in time for Maruja the grandmother called a halt, and when the old woman said halt, the Secretario's wife shed her woman's garments and became a child again. To much of this, strumming his guitar in spite of his missing finger, the Secretario paid little attention. He was more impervious to household squabbles than political changes. Infrequently and perfunctorily he would shout a relayed command to one of the larger boys, as if he had suddenly been reminded what was expected of him. For the most part he played as best he could his guitar, or sat looking at the calendars on the wall in the mayor's office (just across from his house on the ground floor of the *Cuartel*) or tilted back in a chair in front of Antonia's café. I suppose Maruja got much of her good nature from the spectacled Secretario, the four-fingered smiling man who played the guitar just as well or badly whether Alfonso or Primo or Don Niceto was in Madrid.

Maruja's classmates were jealous, aggressive, even

spiteful at times. They had promise of more spec-
tacular beauty and allure. They had quicker ears,
more responsive brains. Words clicked from them
more easily. I don't mean that Maruja was stupid or
plain. I do mean that she never uttered a word that
was barbed to a classmate, or failed to smile ruefully
when the others laughed at her for saying a *mono*
was a donkey, when she should have said "monkey."
Could I have chosen one of the girls for a daughter,
it would have been Maruja, for calm and comfort will
be diffused from her like the fragrance of great beds
of petunias. Or she will grow pale and be consumed
by her own amiability.

White middle-sized casket now standing upright
and waiting in the rear of Sindik's shop from which
inner box is taken in churchyard, the casket brought
down hill again and stood on end in corner near pile of
two by fours.

What can one say of Angeles? That all the other
girls looked a little like someone one might have
known or who might have existed and that Angeles
was unique, from the turn of her long young legs to
the shape of her head revealed by black hair neatly
parted and bangs on her forehead. One might have
been abashed by the force of her competitive spirit
unless one knew how badly, as a strikingly handsome
grand-daughter of a hard-working mason, she would
need it in Spain. Angeles did not dream of having
children, as did Mary, or expect to get a degree in
pharmacy or medicine, as Odila was determined to
do. She knew Vicent was getting old and that all the
years of her life he had given her everything the
other girls had. Her plan was to get a job, in an office

or store, and when Vicent was unable to work to send him a part of her pay, so he and her great-aunt could eat and drink as usual. This she explained to me at the age of twelve. When she was seventeen she did it, and at the parting at the bus, the great-aunt (streaked grey hair and grey dress with white apron) shed tears her hands at her side did not rise to wipe away, and near by, pipe in hand, stood toothless patched Vicent who would do his usual work that day and say, not crossly, at noon and at night:

"Mallorca is bigger than Ibiza. What could she do here?"

Affirmative nodding of streaked grey head, and Vicent turning to the doorway to go and get his absinthe and wishing that women could be still about what they felt and what couldn't be helped. And often when one passed the doorway the great-aunt would like to stand, arms on hips, and talk hopefully of Angeles far away.

It is needless to say that if Vicent had had a surplus of savings from his steady days of work in many lands, Angeles would have been taught to be a stenographer or dressmaker and could have earned more pay.

The girl with the most diverse gifts was Maria Rosa, Mateo Rosa's daughter. She was as beautiful as Eulalia des Puig, in the class of thin Catalina Mousson and Angeles with her quick logical mind and retentive memory. Her gentleness of character was like Maruja's and her musical talent on a par with little Antonia's. I was surprised to learn when I began to get acquainted with the family that her father, staunch and active in the vanguard of liberal politics, resisted any tendency of Maria's to advance herself beyond the sphere of the Ibicenco women of yesterday, and that her backward mother, hysterical, superstitious and afraid of life and the hereafter, secretly encouraged her daughter to learn new accomplishments and to dream of a career as a music teacher or even on the stage. Mateo wanted Maria to sort and pack apricots, learn plain sewing and dress unbecomingly. The light-headed nervous mother risked daily her tall husband's displeasure by finding time for Maria to practise singing and the mandolin, and when Mateo was away on fishing trips took her to the dances and followed her progress proudly as she moved with her partner through the maze of graceful couples on the floor.

In the light of subsequent events, I cannot say whether Mateo Rosa, brave man with clean convictions and acquaintance with the principal ports of the world, foresaw a possible turn of events which would send him into exile and his wife and daughter back to her family's quiet farm near the Cala Llonga divide. He and other Spanish fathers were aware that, in the scheme of things favored by Gil Robles, the late San Jurco (whose understudy Franco found himself in large-sized boots because of San Jurco's sudden accidental death), and such churchmen dressed like mandarins as one sees in the movies flinging holy water over the heads of ten-*peseta* Moors, the handsome daughters of poor men were destined to become prostitutes and the plain daughters household and factory drudges, with a few of each for the convents to acquire the complexions and odor of uncooked pork sausages and the mentalities of hand-wound music boxes having six tunes apiece. It is remotely possible that Mateo Rosa dreaded to have his promising daughter become conspicuously attractive, and if that is so, as usual he was right and his pitiful black-shawled woman was wrong.

One of the girls who had no time for the study of languages or for evening dances, and still one of the finest, was Julia who tended the fishermen's bar. Her older sister Maria was tubercular and could work very little. Her mother, Santa Eulalia's business-woman pioneer, was laid up half the time with rheumatism and financial worries. Julia, dark eyes, white skin, dark wavy hair, was busy at the bar from early in the morning until late at night. At the age of fifteen she could keep a roomful of hearty drinking men within the bounds of propriety. She knew all the words that filtered through their speech, their vagaries and lusty desires, their inherent decency. The purity of mind of Eulalia des Puig, living high on the hillside with her small sisters and a kind and helpful father, had the quality of alabaster, let us say. That of Julia, nourished in the tobacco mist of a company of fishermen in drink, was of silver. When other young girls passed by she could wish she had more freedom of movement and that her legs did not ache with continual standing without being sulky or unhappy. Julia was not vain, but the fact that she knew she was comely and desirable kept her smiling through days and weeks of work that had no break. Also, on two occasions, she saved the police much trouble by stepping between two boys, insane with rage, and severely, with pursed lips like a schoolmarm, telling them to put their knives away and behave themselves.

Very often, if arguments got too loud, she would step into them and dogmatically announce who was right and who was wrong. A silence would follow, and a change of subject.

For all of these, Juana, Angeles, Catalina, Odila, Maruja, Maria Rosa, Antonia, Julia and Mary, wounds incurable, hopes in cinders, and beneath their white feet a dead land and the shadows of vultures wheeling!

12. The Guardia Civil

THE *Cuartel*, which with its lanes on either side formed one side of the plaza or public square, was a roomy box-like building two stories in height, white-washed inside and out, with a concave roof almost flat to catch the rain for the cistern below. The back and sides were plain oblongs, with two rows of small windows. The front was a series of archways on the ground floor and had small iron-railed balconies in front of each second story window. Surely the building was unpretentious and had been put up with utility in mind. Nonetheless its proportions were not unpleasing, and with Guardias in grey-green uniform (a touch of red braid) informally grouped in the covered area behind the archways and their wives and daughters dressed in the brilliant colors only Spanish women successfully can wear leaning comfortably against the balcony rails, the plain white walls came to life and the green of the trees near by was intensified.

Those women, somewhat restricted because of the rule that neither the Guardias nor their families must become too intimate with the people of the town they were policing, enjoyed a vista that did much to relieve their boredom. Directly beneath them was a space for hitching mules or parking automobiles for the use of those who had official business. Since this area was so seldom in demand for its original purpose, a few soccer enthusiasts practised there each afternoon, and in the days of the sergeant with the handsome daughter they often got the ball in the nose because of inattention to the game. Just beyond was a level quadrangle raised three feet above the street on the downhill side, a playground on which the small girls played their dancing games. The town fountain with a pool of running water bordered the playground just opposite the enormous tree under which the fishermen sold their fish and where, on hot noons, Ramon parked the bus in the generous spot of shade. From there, the broad *paseo*, its central walk lined with pepper trees, its outer boundaries marked by rows of plane trees twice as tall, led all the way to the sea, and at the water's edge was the white-hooded entrance to the public well. The water of this well was sweet and cold and lay at the foot of broad concrete steps which descended far below the level of the sea near by.

The mayor's office, in which the Secretario car idly, occupied the northeastern corner of the *Cuartel*. In the brief period of Spanish freedom two mayors were elected in turn. The republican mayor was chosen just after the 1931 revolution, then defeated and replaced by a farmer churchman in the days of Gil Robles (1934). The first mayor was a genial soft-spoken man who had been a republican in the dangerous days. The fact that technically he lived across the San Carlos border and was not a citizen of the town did not prevent the liberals of Santa Eulalia

from electing him nor deter him from accepting the
office. The Spaniards have a way of cutting across
such formalities. The mayor did not enter his office
oftener than once a month. He trusted the Secretario
to do the necessary office work and he was right in
doing so, for the Secretario when he was working
under a republican regime was scrupulously republican and knew well whom to please. When in 1934
under Gil Robles and the figure-head Lerroux the
plot that resulted in civil war and the practical destruction of Spain was set in motion, a fascist mayor
was in office in Santa Eulalia and the Secretario was
giving him satisfaction. This man, one of the Guasch
family, had a farm on the slopes west of the church,
and each Sunday morning sat with his black felt hat
on his knees on the altar platform while the mass
was said. The nearest I ever saw him approach his
office was the sidewalk in front of Antonia's café.

The rest of the municipal force consisted of a bug-
eyed moon-faced man who under Alfonso had been
guardian of the fields. He was a relation of the postmaster Anfita and was noteworthy for two reasons.
First, he spoke the most ancient meticulous and dis-
tinct Ibicenco on the island, in a sort of Homeric
rhythm which seemed to cause his sentences to fall
into verse. Second, because he would walk enormous
distances each day without seeming to hurry. His job
was that of *portero*, or doorkeeper to the mayor, but
since in the days of the king he had formed the habit
of tramping the highways and byways he continued
to do so when his title was changed, perhaps in the
spirit of loyalty to his exiled sovereign. In town he
had no friends, although no one disliked him violently

but often he chatted familiarly in country houses, and once in a while bought a drink at Gork's. Also he played the Ibicenco flute and drum, and in the capacity of musician and raconteur attended many country weddings and pig-killing feasts.

Courage is found in strange corners. I shall only say now that this man who in many ways appeared grotesque, speaking the language of two centuries ago in the tempo of a clock running down, was the one and only fascist official who did not run when the town was approached by the soldiers of the other side. The *portero*, who in peace times was never at his post, found it consistent with his dignity to be there completely alone when an overwhelmingly superior force tried to enter the empty barren room on the *Cuartel's* northeastern corner. For the lonely act, and the tunes of his now silent flute and the verses he recited to rhythmic drumbeats at the country weddings, for the fields that knew his footsteps and the love he bore the Ibiza countryside, let all traffic cease today for five minutes, beginning at twelve o'clock noon.

I have forgotten a clerk, perhaps the Secretario's assistant, whose place in the scheme of things I never discovered.

The second story of the *Cuartel* was broken up in small apartments, in which lived the Guardias and their families. The Guardia Civil, the national police, were trained as antagonists of the un-uniformed population, not as servants of the public, but as masters, obedient only to their own commander. They were taught not to be brutal, except in cases of unauthorized meetings, gatherings or public demonstrations, but to be mechanically relentless. Frequently on the mainland they shot prisoners dead if the latter resisted, but to beat a man up was unthinkable. It was against their orders. Their uniforms were calculated to inspire terror—black patent-leather headgear, three-cornered with the broadside back, automatics in holsters, short high-powered rifles slung by clean strap over their shoulders, sweeping cloaks for the darkness and rain. Always they patrolled in pairs, fully accoutered, not a button missing. Under Primo and Alfonso they strode and rode roughshod on the lid of popular discontent, alert for the faintest sign of non-conformity. I have never seen a force more perfectly trained. The Light Brigade would have seemed like a company of Hamlets compared with them.

This much for the Civil Guard as a whole. In Santa Eulalia the Guardias were simply a company of men, of stalwart individuals to whom the friendliness and well-being of that favored town had restored such humanity as they had lost as recruits in distant barracks. Again and again it had been feared by higher officials that the Guardias there were lax because of the scarcity of crime, and several sergeants had been transferred for that reason. In each case except one, the result was the same. The sergeant became a man again. In the final catastrophe the most ardent republicans were sorry for their friends the Guardias, considering them rightly to be the victims who had the least chance of surviving.

The first sergeant in charge of the Santa Eulalia barracks after the 1931 revolution was a tall handsome man from Albacete named Gutierrez (which is

like being named Smith in England). Having little
else for his men to do, he kept them busy cleaning
their uniforms and polishing their arms. He loved
display, not of force, but of regalia. On any day that
might by the stretch of his imagination be termed a
holiday, he and his men would appear in dress uniform, rich navy-blue capes lined with scarlet and
trimmed with gold, scarlet stripes down the trousers
legs, black velvet-covered tri-cornered hat with white
braid. It was he who had the beautiful daughter almost as tall as he was, with a flush of natural red on
her cheeks, full red lips, inviting eyes and elegance
of arms and ankles. He could not resist having his
daughter put on gay stylish clothes and walk with
him when he had his dress uniform on, and the pair
of them would cause each head to turn and men and
women alike to sigh with admiration. Once I saw old
Antonia Masear (who had been a beauty of the opposite school, *petite*) wipe her eyes with her apron,
so touched was she by the spectacle. Only one in the
town did not relish the performance, the sergeant's
rather homely wife, who glared through a narrow
slit in her shutter, grinding her teeth with jealousy.
With the townspeople, Gutierrez could not be severe.
He liked them, ate up their appreciation of his
daughter's winning points, and soon he was calling
them by name. The friction of his home life made him
long for cafés, and place was made for him at Cosmi's
bar, and the Guardias and citizens were mutually
content. (The Royalty was too near the *Cuartel*, and
Gutierrez had come to believe that his wife could see
through walls.)

In 1934, when Gil Robles and the disloyal generals

and the archbishops decided to do away with elections and new freedom and let the army rule, and Hitler and Mussolini had promised them support and funds, it was feared by Gutierrez's superiors that he would not be the man for the place. The Balearic Islands lie directly between France and the French colonies in Africa and their strategic importance in the Mediterranean can scarcely be overestimated. It is known that Alfonso at the time he was dethroned was considering an offer to sell them to Italy. Italians control them as I write today.

In preparation for the plot against the people of Spain there was much to be done, and since powerful government leaders were in league with the other traitors, the plot progressed swiftly. One of the details involved the transfer of Gutierrez and the assignment to Santa Eulalia of a sergeant who looked like Woodrow Wilson in his Princeton days. The sergeant's first move was to call in all firearms in the possession of the citizens, and in the cases of men known to be republicans, their premises were searched for knives as well. No hunting licenses that year were issued unless the licensee was known to be Right. On the pretext of army manœuvres, six hundred soldiers were transported to Ibiza in order that arms and ammunition shipments might be made and stored away secretly in convenient places all over the island. In Santa Eulalia, it was discovered later, the principal arsenal was a tunnel which led from Father Torres' house on the hill to the church, and which had been walled up and unused for years. Small stores of rifles, machine-guns and cartridges were also placed in Nicolau's house, in the home of Francisco Guasch (next door to the town house of Ignacio Riquer) and in the cement shed of the mason Bonéd, who resealed the priest's tunnel after it had been filled with arms. Of course the fortress in Ibiza was thoroughly stocked and several houses in San Antonio, the town on the western shore of the island, a little larger than Santa Eulalia. A Catholic society of young men in Ibiza, coached by a similar and larger organization in Palma de Mallorca, built up cautiously a force of fascist volunteers, secretly armed and ready to answer call at any moment.

The Woodrow Wilson sergeant in Santa Eulalia began to enforce neglected ordinances and issued a few of his own. For instance, he ruled that if a weapon was found on a boy under twenty-one years of age, the boy's father (or nearest male adult relation if the father was dead) was to serve thirty days in jail. It was soon apparent that no member of a conservative family was to be molested and that the new restrictions applied only to republicans. Cosmi was ordered to close his café at midnight. The Royalty and Can Xumeu were permitted to stay open as long as the proprietors liked. Naturally, Cosmi did not obey. Just before twelve each night he looked up and down the street to see if any other café was open. Nearly always there was light streaming from the windows of his competitors. In that case, when the sergeant came in, Cosmi listened to his remarks and said, quietly and positively, that he would close when the others did. On the infrequent occasions when the others had lowered their shutters before twelve, Cosmi would pull down the shutter on the café door and leave the hotel door ajar. There was a communi-

cating corridor, and behind the shutters the late
customers lingered as usual. The Leftist victory in
the general election of September, 1935, put an end
to the sergeant's rule. The results had scarcely been
announced before Cosmi, with a long paper prepared
by Miguel Tur and signed by every liberal in town,
made a voyage to Valencia. By the time he returned
the sergeant had been transferred to some distant
point. The fascist mayor, however, did not lose his
job, for nobody in Santa Eulalia cared much who was
mayor. The change in the face of the town was striking. The timid men who were liberal in their sympathies but afraid to be identified with one party or
another began coming to Cosmi's again. The gatherings at the Royalty lost half of their membership and
all of that submerged air of triumph that had charac-
terized them throughout the year. Most important
of all, the new sergeant was a likable easy-going young
man who saw at once what a marvellous town he had
drawn in the lottery of reassignments. Spontaneously
the town responded in like manner.

"The sergeant is a good fellow," one man said
happily to another.

There was no more nonsense about knives or guns.
Cafés were opened or closed at will. Guardias were
admitted into groups for conversation, dominoes,
drinks. They paused in their night vigils to stand in
the wings of the theatre and watch the boxing
matches or listen to the music. Two men who were
serving a term in jail because of misdeeds of their
sons were released and that evening were given a
rousing *fiesta* that began on Cosmi's sidewalk and
swelled up and down the street, with song and public

dancing in the plaza. I am sure that young Sergeant Gomez knew nothing of the treasonable tasks he would be ordered to perform, for his face was frank and open and there was nothing like bravado or despair reflected in it as he passed along or lingered, receiving and returning friendly greetings, enjoying that Santa Eulalia fellowship that has perished from the earth. He was not aware of the rifles and machineguns in the annex of the House on the hill that God had taken from the Moors, nor of the secret fascist organization in readiness to strike. Good men like the late Sergeant Gomez are not to be trusted in such matters.

I first heard the term *duro Sevillano* one day when I was standing in the main street talking with Edmundo. Ferrer, the most popular of the Guardias, approached us and paused to pass the time of day. Edmundo winked and whispered in my ear, loud enough for Ferrer to hear: "*Un duro Sevillano.*" Ferrer somewhat sheepishly smiled.

It is necessary to explain that many years ago in Seville were issued a quantity of *duros* (the Spanish coin about the size and weight of an old-fashioned American silver dollar and with formerly the same value) that were not up to standard in the content of silver. These counterfeit coins are still in general circulation but are passed and accepted only when the recipient is either tipsy or preoccupied. To the members of the Guardia Civil the people of Spain had affixed this derisive term, implying that what they did for their pay and lodging could hardly be termed a man's work. Like all similar terms *duro Sevillano*

could be applied either contemptuously or affectionately.

No one in Santa Eulalia would have wanted to be
unkind to Guardia Ferrer. He had a jolly freckled
face, quite boyish in expression, and a talent for
avoiding unpleasant duties. While sergeants had been
removed and sent here and there he had stayed in the
same *Cuartel*. His wife had many friends: the wife of
the man who owned the Royalty building, Ramon
the bus-driver's wife, several others who lived near
the plaza. Ferrer spent his hours off duty playing
cards (his uniform blouse unbuttoned) in Cosmi's
back room or playing dominoes in the front room (his
blouse buttoned carefully). His temperament was
suited to an easy life. He had found one and was
content.

The Guardia who patrolled the roads most often
with Ferrer was a quiet man of very different character but equally likable. He had luxuriant black
moustaches and was always seen standing on the edge
of the crowd, as if some voice from the clouds had
said "Tableau" and he was aware of his importance
in the picture, a trifle self-conscious but detached. A
very thoughtful man. His name was Jimenez, and as
he walked, side by side with Ferrer, the latter smiling,
watching lizards or the flight of birds, Jimenez was
deep in thought about the whys and wherefores of it
all. There was something in the angle of his patent-
leather headgear that disclosed, even from behind,
that round and round in his mind certain questions
were revolving at a moderate pace. Long before I first
saw them, these two officers had said to each other
nearly all they had to say, and their communication

was "Yea, yea" or "Nay, nay" with slight nods of
the head, and Ferrer's ready smile, miles and miles
along the road toward San Carlos in the dust and
wild artichoke blossoms, in lanes between pink flowering shrubs, purple thyme, fragrant laurel and young
pines, on stormy nights in greased boots and water-
proof capes, on starlit evenings under drifting con-
stellations. Tramp, tramp, side by side in measured
tread, the one smiling, the other thinking—and
Guardias had read nothing in their manual of arms
about thinking or smiling. They moved in grey-green
with a touch of red braid and patent-leather hats
among farmers stooped in nearby fields, the masons
mixing concrete, slapping plaster on walls. At night
deep silent slumber in white houses, creak of waterwheels turned by blind-folded mules, chorus of frogs
and night insects and the breathing of patient animals in sheds. Ferrer, to himself: "Oh, surely this can
never end." Jimenez, to the wheel of his mind: "Can
this go on?" A pair of Guardias, two friends, two
men.

There was another, somewhat heavy in his movements, onion eyes. His name was Bravo. He sat
blinking like a frog, not stupidly but never threaten-
ingly, and his uniform was not as sleek as those of his
companions. Bravo did not like to be alone. He enjoyed having men around him but was not expansive
like Ferrer. He listened, was amused, but contributed
little to conversations. One night in Cosmi's, when
the light plant was out of order and Cosmi had hung
up a capricious contrivance known as a Petromax
lamp, the lamp exploded, and Bravo, sitting beneath

it, caught fire. I have never seen a large man move so quickly. He shot through the back door, flames streaming behind, and raced in a panic around the garden destroying thousands of plants and flowers. It took Cosmi and me at least a minute to catch him, tackling football fashion, and wrap him in our coats to smother the flames. Bravo's neck was burned badly and for weeks afterward he wore a grotesque bandage and carried his well-meaning head on a slant.

How it pleases me to say, in the midst of things so painful to relate, that Bravo later proved himself to be a hero, nothing less. There was that in his Albert Fratellini headpiece which could not be perverted, and he, when the time came, knew exactly where duty led, that first came mankind, next his countrymen, and third his superior officer.

And one must not forget the young Guardia, so youthful that when he started out with a veteran like Bravo or Ferrer he looked like a nickel rolling along beside a half dollar. This Guardia was in love and didn't care who knew it, and his fiancée was the daughter of Jaume, the white-haired butcher on the *paseo*. So he sat in the doorway of the butcher shop, his arm around the girl, gazing into her eyes and she gazing happily. Up to the time the young Guardia came to town I had thought of Jaume's daughter as comparatively plain. Then afterward I saw that the young man was right, and that I had been wrong. Her light-brown hair caught the glints of the sun, her grey-blue eyes were mischievous like those of her father. She was nimble, gentle-mannered, looked well in white (which almost none of the other girls wore). The young Guardia had never known the days of Primo de Rivera and San Jurco, and I doubt if he would have shot his grandmother point-blank if a sergeant yelled "Fire," as the older ones very likely would have done.

13. Communists, Fascists, and the Others

THE first communist in Santa Eulalia was the potter, Mousson, a small man, round face, pale blue wide-open eyes, thin white hair, somewhat stooped but in no way incapacitated by his sixty-odd years. He always wore black (slightly modified by dust) and was never seen without a coat and string tie except at home. To find him, one sets out on a delightful walk, due south from the plaza, across the river on natural stepping stones, and follows a pathway which leads to a pass between the Cala Llonga hills. Looking back, the church and its precipitous cliff and familiar hill have for a background Rigoberto's house, small white spot, and scattered dwellings on the farms farther north, among them that of Pere des Puig. One mounts, the vista shifts and changes, and then on the other side of the divide one looks far down into a narrow sheltered cove, converging cliffs joined by perfect crescent beach, green-yellow depths of water over sand, impenetrable blue. At the foot of the steep ascent are a house and several sheds and a rectangle of dull green clay, cut in squares and drying in the sun. Against the hillside, dug in like a cave, is the large kiln or oven. In another cave always cool and shady is the ancient potter's wheel, revolved by the potter's feet on a circular platform as he sits on a stool and gives shape to water jars, *paellas*, crocks and pitchers, bowls and other earthen objects, damp and consistent, never twice precisely the same. One tiptoes, led by Mousson this time in faded blue shirtsleeves, avoiding tile warmly baking in the sun, and peers down into the clay pit fifty yards from the shore, deep like a well. Mousson lets down on a rope a jar of his own making and brings it up filled with water, cool, clear and miraculously refreshing.

The man who turns the wheel and shapes the vessels is an auburn-haired Irish-looking man from Galicia, who works in a mad rapid rhythm, gets bellowing drunk each Saturday night and sings as he staggers up the hillside pathway and tumbles down. There is a shed with a cot and bed-clothes for him, but only when it rains he sleeps indoors. Other nights find him stretched on the beach beneath the stars, near a rock whose shadow keeps the morning sun from waking him too soon. Saturday night, very drunk, he rolls nearer the rock than usual so that his sun alarm will not shine in his face until a later hour on Sunday. Another man, who seldom talks and never sings, shapes tiles and picks them up and stacks them when the sun has cooked them to a turn. Mousson's wife is busy in the kitchen. His rowboat is moored near the ramp at the water's edge.

In this secluded cove, remote and beautiful, the rule is share and share alike. There are four members of the colony, Mousson, his wife, the red-headed Gallego and the taciturn tile man. To each, one-quarter exactly of the matchless blue sky, so many measures of amber-colored water over sand, so many gallons of water of impenetrable blue, a segment each of fine white sand, equal numbers of jewel-colored fishes (brown and zigzag scarlet, pale with violet thumbprints, pink and brick-streaked monsters, sea butterflies with peacock wings), cubic meters of air to breathe, calories of sunshine. Mousson sells the product and buys the food and clothing, his wife does the cooking and sewing, the red-head turns the wheel, the wordless one bakes tiles. In each *peseta*, four *reals*. One worker, one *real*.

Where Mousson got his ideas, it is impossible to say. They were dangerously simple and will cost him his life at the hands of Mussolini. It seems that the small house, the oven and clay pit and the land and beach bordering the Cala Llonga shore fell to Mousson by inheritance. He had not worked for them, in fact had spent his youth on sailing vessels away from his parents who disapproved of him. Consequently, when he found himself in possession of the property he felt that it belonged no more to him than to his wife and the men who worked with him. The receipts from the sale of pots and jars were not enormous but, divided in four parts, were slightly above the prevailing rate of wages. When Mousson learned that there were others in the world who were following his idea on a larger scale he was happy and wished them the best of luck. The neighbors called him a communist, in the mildly derisive way they called Guardias *duros Sevillanos*. Mousson read a little, learned as much as he could of what a communist might be, and accepted the designation. He had no Red credentials signed by Lenin or Stalin but felt himself to be a part of a sensible world movement and was content with that.

It was not the Pope or Hitler or Mussolini or even

the Premier of Japan who dealt the first blow at the Golden Rule quartette in Cala Llonga. A Hand more capricious intervened. Señora Mousson, although emancipated from capitalistic economics, was still bound by the rules of Ibicenco dress. She wore half a dozen petticoats, a shawl pinned tightly around her shoulders, a black kerchief over her hat and tied beneath her chin. One day when the three men had decided to take the dory and go fishing she went to the shore to clean some fish, leaning over from a sheer rock above deep water. She leaned too far and was drowned, weighted down by her heavy clothes, and the men returning saw her sunken body as they were putting up the boat. Mousson's grief was so deep that he shunned his friends and wandered alone and miserable on the outskirts of the town, unable for many days to return to the cove. The red-head, unable to bear the weight of such unfair disaster, got violently drunk, so that it took five or six men to subdue him. It was memorable to see him standing, blood streaming down his face, his eyes flashing murder, swinging chairs as primitive clubs, pitting his rage and strength against a world that had made him feel so badly. He spent a few days in the Hotel Naranjo and wordlessly took a boat for the mainland, leaving only Mousson, small face distorted with misery, and the taciturn man who sat by his tiles (some baked, some moist) and munched his bread and *sobresada* out of doors. From that time until the end of the Cala Llonga world, the work there had a long up-hill convalescence with relapses in which it was never pronounced quite dead.

Communist Number 2 belonged to Santa Eulalia

only because he was engaged to an orphan niece of Isabel at the Royalty. He was a school teacher who taught the boys' school on Formentera, the long low island a few miles east of Ibiza. Over week-ends and during vacation periods he was to be seen at the Royalty, decidedly not preoccupied with Party affairs, although he was a full-fledged member and knew what it was all about. School teacher Fernando was tall with light-brown wavy hair, and talked for hours in corners with Marguerita, his adoring fiancée, a fat girl of a type not seen on fashion plates but which has always proved alluring to sensitive men. Marguerita had been well cared for by her relatives, but she had no money and had not expected that life would be so kind as to send her the one man she could worship, and make him want to marry her. As they sat at a small corner table, leaning across until their heads almost touched, the talk around them was never the sort that would be comforting to young communists, for, as I have said, the Royalty's clientele was composed of the rich and their hangers-on. The teacher never seemed to hear it, neither did Marguerita.

Had Fernando taught the Santa Eulalia school he would have been in trouble the moment it was known that he had communist ideas. Formentera, however, was a radical community and the parents there were glad to have their children brought up in a Left tradition, the farther Left the better.

As far as I know, Fernando's only convert in Santa Eulalia was his older sister, unmarried, who looked very much like him and was famous for her Ibicenco pastry called *oriettas* (little ears). This erect and capable spinster had told her brother what to do when he was small, and at some precise moment, having sensed that his mind had outgrown hers, she began following his slightest wishes as if they were commands. She was a pushover for the Third Internationale, but never joined the Party formally. The old father, who had a big farm down San Carlos way and was shaved in Santa Eulalia once a week, was not hostile to his son's development. He was proud of the boy and his fluent talk, and saw no prospect that such theories would be put into practice.

Fernando had a cousin named Carlos, shorter and stockier, more alert and active, also more gay. He taught the school in San Carlos and often on Sundays would come to Santa Eulalia to see Fernando and Marguerita. The three would walk down the *paseo* and along the shore, Fernando and Carlos exchanging political gossip, and the fat girl, between them in Sunday black, inattentive except to the pressure of Fernando's hand upon hers. Carlos had a more precarious post than Fernando, for San Carlos contained the wildest anti-clericals as well as the most bigoted Catholics on the island. Whenever the churchmen would have a procession, carrying saints or palm branches around the churchyard, the infidels would parody the ceremony in plain sight of the faithful, carrying wine-casks and brooms and chanting lustily in true Gregorian style:

> *Un cura*
> *Dos curas*
> *Formen una cora*
> *Hacen las mismas cosas que un cura sola.*

One priest
Two priests
Form a choir
And do the same things as one priest by himself.

Cosmi, Pep Salvador, Juan the Captain, Mateo
Rosa, Ferrer, Primitivo, Edmundo, none of the men
who formed the backbone of the liberal movement in
Santa Eulalia were communists, or even sympathizers. They knew well that their opponents were anxious to place a communist label on their moderate
reforms and thus antagonize the body of the voters
who were afraid of sudden change and had been
frightened by anti-Russian propaganda. All these
men were Socialists, and their aims I have stated but
will summarize here again: Restraint of the Church
from political activities; redistribution of large unused estates; equality of citizens before the law;
local police, responsible to their townsmen; civil
service reform; state control of natural resources;
(and most pressing) to free the commerce of Ibiza
from its two liege lords, Matutes and the notorious
Juan March.

I must say again that Santa Eulalia patriots did
not choose their wives and families because of the
women's political views or breadth of mental outlook.
Costa's wife, and the sister of Mayor Serra, was a
tory of the first water, her comely face set in lines of
disapproval. She would have attended church if her
husband had not forbidden her. Eulalia Noguera and
her mother, the restless Maria on the farm near Can
Josepi, Cosmi's Catalina's old-maid aunt, the Formentera schoolmaster's sister, and another statuesque

Eulalia who worked for Yvonne Rogers and whose
mother did ironing (*Olé*) of a neatness never to be forgotten were about the only women in town who
would have laid down their lives for their country.
They were given no opportunity, under no matter
what regime. Observers who were elsewhere will tell
you no doubt what they saw, but I assure you that
in Ibiza no one made war on women. One can see that
this policy, shared by fascists and government men
alike, would create a problem—numerous women forlorn and unattached, wandering here and there for
shelter after their men were safely underground. But
the women are not lined up and shot, and neither are
they raped. It will not be pretty to see them slowly
distorted by privation. I suggest to the women of
America, the forward-looking ones who have worked
in the interest of their sex and secured in the happiest
of all lands a long list of advantages, that they raise
a huge fund for the purchase of pearl-handled revolvers and neat little cartridges and dress themselves in appropriate uniforms with a cross of some
sort on their sleeves and distribute in ruined towns
small firearms wrapped in cellophane (strictly un-
transferable and on no account to be refilled) for the
use of unshot Spanish women who are desperately in
need of suicide. "If Franco won't, America will"—
something of that sort for a slogan.

A young man from San Carlos, who had worked as
a stevedore on the mainland (Valencia and Barcelona),
completes the roll of communists on our end of the
island. He was not the talkative kind, but the one
who would be selected when drastic action was needed
and who would stop at nothing. You will make his

acquaintance later, when he is working in the interest of law and order, for previous to the outbreak of the war he was completely obscure and unknown to any of our friends except Pep Salvador. There may have been thirty pre-war communists on the rest of the island, to add to our five. Each week they held secret committee meetings in Ibiza and elsewhere, the hour and place of which (with a complete list of those in attendance) was known to everybody on the island.

"I have not even told Anna," Cosmi said to me in one crisis. "There is no need of the radio on Ibiza. News spreads itself."

The members of the fascist organization in Santa Eulalia did not outnumber the orthodox communists. First among them was Francisco Guasch. He was not the richest and, because of his unpopularity, his influence with the passive population was nil. His value lay in his zealous hatred of all liberals, of anyone who would wrench from the tight fists of the Guasch and other dominant families the control of Ibiza's wealth and trend of thought. He was the traditional mean man who was a pillar of the church, the Pharisee. Francisco smiled, his voice was jovial. He was tall, broad-shouldered, walked with an easy stride without swinging his arms.

"Hello, Señor Paul. How are you today?" he would shout, when he was near enough to me to shatter my eardrums. He waved his hand at hillside cronies, grinned and tapped his foot in time when the Ibicenco drums and flutes broke loose in church. Altogether a man who was pleased with himself and the way the world was going; and the reasons for his increasing gaiety are known to us now, as then they were concealed by him. He talked a great deal and loudly, but never about the things in his heart. His wife was a pretty brown-eyed little woman, soft-spoken, gentle-mannered, but, according to my friends in town, she was sharper in a business deal than her husband. It was Señora Guasch who was credited with persuading Platé in a drunken and befuddled moment to sign away for five hundred *pesetas* the remainder of his property, a lot of land on the hill between the town and Rigoberto's property, worth more than ten times the amount she paid. She had known how much Platé owed, how he was worrying, and offered him an amount that covered his debts. He had laughed, wept, and said, "All right. I'll sign."

The Guasches' house was on the main street, just south of the plaza, adjacent to the town house of Ignacio Riquer. An unused stable rented by Guasch as a garage opened on the back street opposite the shop of Francisco the shoemaker. Guasch built a modern house, which, however, conformed to the principles of Ibicenco architecture, on the lot his wife had wheedled from Platé. This house was rented by foreigners, one after another, but Guasch reserved for himself a plot of land right under the front windows and so annoyed his tenants by shouting there at five o'clock in the morning that Gwendolyn, the Welsh girl, during her occupancy, once lost her temper to the extent of throwing him bodily off the porch. He was bigger and stronger than Gwendolyn, but she took him by surprise. No woman had ever attacked him before. No officers in the pay of any government had ever asked him if they could use his sheds as a secret arsenal before, either. He was gleeful that so much confidence had been placed in him and that he seemed to be awakening from a nightmare of republicanism to find himself safe in a soft four-posted feudal bed. Guasch liked feeling important, on the platform of the church, on the porch of his newly built house. His two sons, good healthy boys, were brought up with their mother's good manners and their father's belief that the Guasches and others even slightly more important were to re-inherit the earth.

Francisco's neighbor, ex-Captain Nicolau, had many friends. He had never cheated anyone. He was included in the week-end excursions of Ferrer, Guillermo and the others. In all my time in Santa Eulalia I never heard a man say a good word for Guasch. Knowing his neighbors did not admire him he kept within range of his family, where he was unquestionably master.

Fascist Number 2 was also named Guasch. He was probably a second cousin to Francisco, but had no traffic with him and did not resemble him at all. Joachim Guasch was a reckless young man with a romantic longing for dangerous adventure. Toiling impatiently on his father's large farm (westward near the Santa Gertrudis border), he thought of the desperadoes of whom he had read and wanted something violent to happen. For such a boy, the drifting of the seasons, the almonds, then strawberries, oranges, figs, pomegranates, apricots, pig killings, then almonds again, was like paper on a small bedroom wall, a pattern going up and down, round and round, repeating itself in a way that became increasingly annoying. He was tall but not handsome, rangy and energetic and when drunk was always seeking some pretext to be unafraid. Maria, the green-eyed daughter of Anfita the postmaster, was his fiancée, and when he spoke boastfully, sitting beside her in her doorway, she looked at him appraisingly and thought of the day when she should be distant from the feeble-minded family, the care of which had made her character so firm. She was not fond of him, in the way that plump Marguerite loved her schoolmaster Fernando, or the butcher's suddenly attractive daughter admired the young Guardia Civil, but she was thoroughly enthusiastic about marrying a rich and healthy young man, and after her years with her father and unfortunate brothers, young Guasch's talk, foolish as it was, seemed an improvement over that to which she had grown accustomed. She felt that she could modify Joachim when she had a better chance. She knew that he was infatuated and he made no attempt to resist. His impulse toward her was strong, and he followed it unquestioningly. Whatever murmurs reached his ears about the risk of marrying a girl whose relatives were mostly *loco* served to strengthen his desire.

Joachim did many foolish things. He frequently got drunk, after having been admitted to the fascist society, and at times when firearms were forbidden and men of the other party were being arrested and fined for carrying them, he brandished revolvers and made drunken threats in cafés. Once at Gork's he tried the patience of Pep Torres to the point that Pep challenged him to fight then and there. Their friends interfered. Fights were rare in Ibiza. But resentment lingered in young Guasch's mind, and also in Pep's, and there was an uncomfortable strain in the air whenever they were in the same room or near each other on the street. Pep knew that in case of trouble, Guasch would have all the force of law on his side, but Pep was obstinate, too, and his anger smouldered more bitterly because of the official set-up against him.

Then there was Xumeu Ribas, and again I feel the relief and sadness that comes to me as I write of a familiar friend. Xumeu, with your weary smile, that wistful look as if to be gay was unwise and something one should sigh about and think "Now you have caught me again." I think you were the wisest of your party, Xumeu, for you knew that politics had the odor of death and you wished every day that your neighbors would simply go on with their meals and their dominoes, that fruit and vegetables should grow upon farms, that fish should be brought in baskets to the doorways, that men would cease to play with laws and guns and let those who liked the church go there and the others stay in town. I remember you with the dice box, old friend, how the lines deepened in your forehead and the crow's feet around your eyes (so capable of mirth or indefinite sadness but never of hope), how you took each die in your hand and dropped it in, sighing, so sure you were to lose again, or at least that somebody must lose.

"*La penultima,*" someone would say. No one in Spain ever refers to the "last drink." It is always the next to the last.

"Oh, no more," you would reply, but your reluctant fingers would be feeling for the dice, and you would woefully incline your head and roll them out again.

Xumeu Ribas was "director" of the public telephone, that is, the switchboard was in his house. He drew a small salary for receiving and relaying messages. As a matter of fact, his sallow daughter tended the switchboard and his son Francisco, an eighteen-year-old student who was quite lame, delivered the messages. Xumeu occupied himself with his café, which was next in importance to Cosmi's and the Royalty. His family were all royalists and practising Catholics and the thought of offending or hurting his parents would have been enough to keep him from acquiring any contrary opinions. I never heard Xumeu say a word about politics. Should political matters be discussed in his café, he would look up nervously, then down at his feet, and be busy washing glasses or refilling bottles until the subject was changed. There was a splendid flower garden in the patio behind the café, and Xumeu's wife and daughter tended it carefully and kept their house neat and clean. The well was one of the best in town and women came with jars from other houses near by to draw water and chat a while. There were pigs in a pen and a sleek contented goat and a big yellow tomcat named Simon that knew he was invisible when he slept in beds of nasturtiums and when awake was a match for any of the dogs. This race of yellow cats, quite superior creatures, was bred by Cosmi's mother-in-law, the terrible Señora Colomar. One of them was the pride of the Casa Rosita, another prowled through the jungle of chair legs in the empty theatre. Simon, of Can Xumeu, was the king of them all.

Some men are naturally progressive, others fearful of change. Xumeu was typical of the latter group. He was friendly and tolerant, pleasantly lax in his religious observations, fond of fun and good living, neither lazy nor over-zealous about work. He was not greedy, never unsociable. What he wanted was peace. It seemed to him that men everywhere were unappreciative of the blessings of life as they had it and unaware how much worse things could be. Watch Xumeu closely when the hurly-burly gets under way and see what can happen to moderate lovable men who are used to further the plans of others more ambitious. If you think that grief and worry cannot tear the tissues and destroy, if you imagine it takes cancer or shrapnel or the consciousness of sin, step right up and be enlightened. Put him on the scales, before and after. It will make you adore class war and cheer those who (knowing all wars as rearrangements of the letters of the alphabet) advocate alphabet bloodshed and drinking of the blood. Little good it will do Xumeu to know that I have shed as many tears over him as for the best republican in the land.

Half dozen communists, half dozen fascists, three thousand men and women of Santa Eulalia who wanted the extremists and traitors to let be. Ghosts and live men, for a moment take your places in the town as once it was. Distracted women, find your partners. Masons, your trowels, fishermen, your nets. Pose first in sunlight, scintillating green of foliage, dazzling white of plaster houses, fruits, flowers, gardens, cornfields, birds and bees. The sea, deep blue, reflecting stream of sunshine, small dories moored in the cove, and passing right to left a two-masted schooner, and farther, on the horizon, the thinning smoke of a tramp steamer lost to sight. Group yourselves as in the days when the bus at noon brought news from outside, when friends met for *apéritifs* when hearty meals were eaten after work well done. Remember when you could reach toward your memories as if they were fruits in a basket, and choose them carefully or at random, from long ago or recently, and find them without blemishes. At what figure would you have begun to consider an offer for your island, the land that was yours and your fathers', the sea and sky and air, the olive trees, almonds, eucalyptus, evergreens and palms. The laurel, thyme and sage. White houses festooned with scarlet peppers, open doorways, sharp shadows, sea birds, shore birds, lizards, bees. Old people (in pairs or singly), parents, husbands, wives and children. Life, liberty, pursuit of happiness. Goods, chattels, commodities and merchandise.

To FRANCISCO FRANCO
AND OTHER TRAITORS, Dr.

One town, complete with inhabitants
and accessories

————*pesetas*
————*centimos*

One must not fix the price too high, for in each morning's mail through all eternity, countless similar statements of indebtedness will be placed in those neat wire baskets.

I cannot help calling you back from exile and graves for a final hour in the moonlight, old friends! Stones, to your place. Dust of mortar, bind them as

of old. I can see you smiling and hear your songs.
Dear friend Cosmi and your little son, Pep Salvador,
Jaume, Ferrer, your hand. Tune up Guillermo, Pep
Torres, sound your A. On the edge of the crowd is old
Platé, José from Can Josepi. I'm glad you were not
too exhausted to come. Mousson, cheer up and smile,
Pardal, stop talking. Come out, Edmundo, Rigoberto,
lead the singing!

Pep nods his head, his bow is poised. The signal to
start. Together. This is the final recording. . . .
Chorus.

Dos cigarros ting
Tres qui vol fumá
Dos y tres fon cinq
Y cinq fon dao
Y dao fon vint
In unfathomable light years distance
Dos y tres — ——
Y cinq —— ——
Y — — ——

PART TWO

July 14 *to* September 15, 1936

14. The Barcelona Boat

WE DESCENDED the gangplank from the friendly and not too elaborate *Ciudad de Barcelona* to the port of Ibiza on the fourteenth of July, my wife, her five-year-old son hereinafter known as Peanut, our grave and much-travelled boxer named Moritz, and I. We had passed through Paris on the way, in fact had left there on Sunday evening (the fourteenth being Tuesday) and although a few of my friends among the newspapermen there had suspected that there might be trouble in Spain, none of them had mentioned the matter to me, believing erroneously that I knew about the situation in Spain as well or better than they did. Indeed one of the best informed of them, Dick Glenn of the *Herald Tribune*, had promised to join me in Santa Eulalia the following week and spend his vacation with us.

The last stage of the journey from Paris to Barcelona is a harrowing one, especially in the heat of July. One is obliged, between trains at Port Bou, to pass with one's baggage through the Spanish customs house, surely one of the least efficient in Europe, and then run the gauntlet of officials whose duties are ominously described by the Spanish word *vigilancia* and whose temperaments range from benevolent indifference to zealous distrust.

In Barcelona we had just time for a bath and lunch at the Hotel de la Marina. We saw little of the city and what we saw gave us no cause for alarm.

There were few passengers on the *Ciudad de Barcelona*, but I knew the officers, the members of the crew and the stewards, and I am sure none of them suspected that the boat which for years had plodded between the mainland and the islands was embarking on its last round trip. Our journey's end was near, and as I watched the waterfront and the buildings and towers of the city recede, the excitement that took hold of me whenever I was approaching my chosen island began to stir my brain and I knew I should not sleep that night, and was glad. I saw the buoys that traced the channels in the harbor, the lighthouses marking rocks and promontories of the shore and after dinner (begun by a morsel of months untasted *sobresada*) I stood at the rail hearing snatches of the dialects of Mallorca, Ibiza and Formentera, and at last the sea was all around and diagrams of stars were where they should be and for some time had not been and I thought, "Here at last is peace. This is the old old wisdom that men so long have been seeking for. I have attained a zone of contemplation where the voices of sea and land say 'You may rest. You may now re-assort your memories, dimming some of them, burnishing others. We offer you centuries and civilizations to which you bring a new and amorphous one to be clarified.'"

Do not smile. I lay down very calmly, and long before dawn I was up again, this time in the bow, my eyes fixed upon darkness from which (the sea being also excited but calm) would emerge the first glimmer of lanterns from the fishing fleet, Captain Juan and his partners, the tall Mateo Rosa, very possibly Edmundo in his motor boat alone. And it happened. Things were happening regularly then. I saw those lanterns dimly, then rising and falling, glowing more brightly, winking out of sight as the swell interposed, and much later I passed between them, seeing figures of men who could not see my wave of greeting but were pausing, looking at the boat that marked an early hour of Tuesday morning and thinking there might be someone there who knew them and many who did not. I had always preferred not to let my friends know when I was returning to Ibiza, and none of them expected me that day.

What were they catching then, I wondered. What patterns of stripes and spots, huge gasping gills, fixed eyes, would meet me later beneath the tree in the plaza at Santa Eulalia? Cirviolas, dentuls, meros were in season. From brine a glistening harvest. Then persistently straight impact from an unseen headland to the bridge, the Tagomago light, dead ahead and unwavering. And (unaware of tired legs and muscles strained from waiting) the first dim outline of the island, starlight thinning, perceptible smudge of dawn. Close up to the lighthouse, San Vicente to the north, the sandstone cliffs of Estañol. Slowly in review three distant beaches and San Carlos' line of hills. The coral sands, the steep white dunes, a scrubby woodland and the sweeping crescent of Escanat. Around the small islands, fishermen in dories —Toniet Pardal with his lobster trap, Carlos whose baby I hope is well in Jaume's alley. A slight change in the course and the *Vei Isglesi* re-exists, and high and white the church on Santa Eulalia's hill. We are passing the Punta Blanca, are abreast of Arabie and Cosmi's pebbled cove. The town is in place and all the houses, with a few sprung up while I was gone. I know, a mile distant, who is watching from the street —Antonio Cosmi, Juan of Casa Rosita, Ramon tuning up his engine, Platé with his feet in cool water and his breakfast nearing his hook, the women of the Royalty, Sacristan Gork.

We are rounding Cala Llonga (the potters' shacks far back in the narrow cove) and soon the old walled city of Ibiza, compact roofs and angles on the hill.

The first man I recognized in the early morning crowd that had gathered to see the boat come in was Ferrer of Las Delicias. There he was, delightedly smiling, shouting "*Ola*, Xumeu," holding aloft his sturdy blacksmith's arm. We shook hands, others pressed around. "Where have you been? Welcome back." El Gordo (the fat man), head porter of the waterfront, extended his hand, then hurried up the plank in search of my baggage. As an afterthought he shouted from the deck, "Any new ones?" I assured him that he had seen all the suitcases before, and no further instructions were necessary. We stopped a few moments, which in Ibiza meant at least three-quarters of an hour, for coffee and *ensaimadas*, Ferrer sitting happily with us and chuckling to think of the surprise in store for the men and women along Santa Eulalia's main street. He had something else up his sleeve which at first was not clear to me. When I mentioned getting a taxi to take us and our baggage to Santa Eulalia, he made mysterious signs to El Gordo who perspiringly nodded

and started away with our bags in his pushcart. I
asked no questions, feeling grateful that at any time
among my friends I could let go of the reins and
things would just naturally take care of themselves.
After breakfast Ferrer led us into a shaded narrow
street behind the row of buildings along the waterfront and there, with Ferrer's older son in the driver's
seat, was a dented automobile which at one time had
been blue.

"There it is," said Ferrer with pride. He had taken
another step forward, from the short quick steps
neat feet of Napoleon the donkey to the chugging
of a motor and complaining of gears. Without reading
and writing Ferrer had progressed from an iron-
worker's helper at forty cents a day to grocer and
now was one of the few who could ride to the port
when he liked and be back before a mule got fairly
started. With his quick instinct for business, he had
made the practice of meeting all the early morning
boats and could offer a lower rate to Santa Eulalia
than the Ibiza taxis which must return nine miles to
town. We piled in, six in all, with complacent Moritz,
and all our hand baggage and set out for Santa
Eulalia. By that time it must have been six thirty
and the sun was getting strong.

The road from Ibiza to Santa Eulalia describes first
a half circle around the western rim of the inner harbor, passing first the brewery and ice plant on the
left and fishing vessels from Alicante and Valencia
moored side by side on the right. A long tangent
lined with middle-sized plane trees led through flat
fertile farms, rose slightly, then past the fork of the
San Miguel road turned snakelike and mounted until

Ibiza and the harbor, compact walled hill with
Picasso white violet-shadowed houses and the lower
buildings on the waterfront obscured by tangle of
masts and spars, was well back and low. I did not
mention on a bare lot the smallest almond tree which
some other time would have a dozen blossoms, nor a
sharp red-covered window where one expected woodwork to be wagon blue. There is an unexpected patch
of cane, rising twelve feet high on either side. Don
Ignacio's famous well, and the road (cut steep on the
right) is approached by the river on the left, the water
deep and slow-moving behind a small dam, then shal-
low and ungreedily active, and at that point, just
before I knew I should see the church high ahead and
soon the sea beyond the river's mouth, our dog Moritz
raised himself very rigid on his haunches, sniffed the
air and turned his head (nose high) very slowly, exactly as Gabrilowitsch used to turn when from the
piano increasingly pressed upward the volume of a
Beethoven crescendo. In a moment the dog relaxed
and sighed. No more trains, hotels and boats. Sighed
contentment. Dog peace, which lets well enough
alone and likes finding things where they usually are
and no hysterics in the family and a well-known town.
So much for animal presentiment.

Because Cosmi's hotel was filled with several families of vacationing Catalans and some out-of-town
workmen, we went to the Royalty, and were overwhelmed with welcome by Juanito, the young proprietor, his mother Isabel, and Pedro, the best waiter
in the world. They had never had us before, except
for occasional meals and drinks, and Juanito had
known that I found something there not exactly to

my liking, and he and all the staff made every effort
to please us. The other guests in the hotel at the time
were Alice Frankfurter, American humorist, Colonel
and Mrs. Fairchilds and their son (the colonel being
a retired American army physician with many tales
of the Philippines), a wonderful middle-aged Spanish
woman from Madrid, called Doña Guillermina, who
was spending a few years in the town in connection with getting a divorce, two French Jews (man
and wife) with a child who made one bite nails and
think kindly of Herod, a Swedish nursemaid who was
as gentle as her employers were uncouth, a young
Mallorquin veterinarian, and an exiled German Jew
with much to worry him.

That evening an impromptu *fiesta* of welcome was
organized by Pedro, Ferrer, Guillermo the blacksmith and others among my friends along the street.
Pep Torres had for several months been staying on
the family farm in Santa Gertrudis, but an auto was
sent to fetch him and he arrived with his violin and
trumpet in the late afternoon. The local stores brought
out their stock of fireworks and shot them away, the
orchestra (which had not assembled during my absence) got together on Cosmi's terrace. There was
much music and singing and serving of drinks by
Cosmi and several of his relatives, much dancing in
the street. One thing, even in my excitement of being
guest of honor and orchestra leader at the same time,
struck me as unusual. When some of us sang *"Un
cura, dos curas, formen una cora"* I saw discomfort
and quite noticeable fright on the outskirts of the
crowd and some men who had come in from the country moved quietly away. Sitting in front of her door-

step, not many feet away and facing me directly was Maria Anfita, of the post office, whose green eyes and cool competent manner I had so long admired. It seemed to me that definitely she wished I would discontinue that particular song. Since it had been a favorite and I knew that no one near by had acquired in my absence a love for the priests, I could only conclude that in some way their power had increased. Knowing that the last election had gone triumphantly Left, I was puzzled. The degree of openness with which one speaks or sings about the clergy has for centuries been the best political barometer in Spain.

The next morning at bus time I met for the first time Sergeant Gomez of the Guardia Civil. Juanito of the Royalty introduced us, and the sergeant was cordial and content. The town had been gay the evening before and he liked it that way.

"The sergeant's a good fellow," Juanito said, after Gomez had started back toward the *Cuartel*. Ramon blew the horn, the occupants of the bus huddled closer together to make room for the tardy ones and, gaining momentum as the dust rose, the bus rolled through the square, past the row of villas with resplendent gardens on the right and turned the corner by the mill. It was then I remembered that I must find a house in which to live.

Can Pedro es Mallorqui', the house we immediately selected, was on the main street just below Can Xumeu and the telephone office. Mateo Rosa the fisherman, Paja his timid wife, Maria their talented daughter (who played the mandolin in our orchestra), and their son who was runner-up in the lightweight class of Santa Eulalia occupied the second floor. The well in the backyard was used also by the Rosas, and the pulley creaked pleasantly as they pulled the bucket to the second-floor level. Thursday afternoon we were comfortably settled there, with all necessary furniture and utensils. Pep Torres, who acted as tutor of Peanut, taught my wife and me what he could of languages and was adviser, companion and family friend, occupied the lower berth, with Peanut in the upper. My wife and I had a back bedroom, and a third bedroom we were reserving for a friend from America who was to join us for a long visit beginning August 14. Moritz slept in the large central living room, his nose near the door, restraining himself through the long night hours from barking at the passers-by.

On Saturday evening just after the dinner hour I entered the Royalty's back yard and found Juanito, his mother Isabel and Pedro the head waiter sitting silently around a table under the arbor of night-closed morning glories, their food almost untouched. Around me was moonlight, fragrance of sea and flowers, shadows of leaves and the tall quiescent palm, and unmistakably in the arbor an atmosphere of dread. I asked no questions. They all roused themselves to greet me wearily. Not understanding, I passed into the dining room where the guests were drinking coffee and chatting as usual. Imperfectly from the radio came the strains of *Maria de la O.*

A few minutes later I saw Juanito standing alone and dejectedly on the sidewalk, facing the public fountain. I approached him, stood near him a mo-

ment, then asked him what was the matter. He did
not reply, but his manner seemed to indicate that he
wanted to explain to me and could not find the words.
Had there been death in the family I should have
known it long before.

"Cheer up," I said. "Shall we have some music?"

"This is a grave moment for Spain," he replied.

We walked together down the road toward the mill,
turned and started back again, Juanito still wordless.
"No one knows what will happen," he said.

A little later I sought out Cosmi. He was busy at
the bar, but evidently troubled. "What's wrong with
everybody?" I asked. The anxiety on his face deepened and he made a gesture, a thumb on each ear and
his fingers extended upward. It meant "the priests."
There was going to be trouble on the mainland, he
said. No one knew exactly what would happen.

Sunday evening Pep Torres, who played trumpet
in the Ibiza municipal band, returned on his bicycle
just before midnight in a mood of black despondency.
We sat up until nearly dawn, and at long intervals he
would speak briefly and resentfully. Armed fascist
volunteers had paraded the streets of Ibiza that evening, their first public appearance. The Casa del Pueblo
(House of the People, or socialist headquarters) had
been closed by the Guardia Civil.

On Monday, the military commander of the fortress in Ibiza, Commandant Mestres (a cousin of Ignacio Riquer) proclaimed martial law and took over
the powers of the civil authorities. Workmen were
forbidden to strike, to hold meetings, or to refrain
from their usual work on pain of imprisonment or
death. There were few men on the streets of Santa

Eulalia that evening—the attendance in cafés had dwindled by half. The Royalty had its group of foreigners chatting as usual, but no Spaniards were there. In Cosmi's, grim, with eyes hard and strained, were those who could not be intimidated and whose temporary helplessness drew them closer together. There were Cosmi, Captain Juan, Ferrer, Mateo Rosa, Pep Salvador, the former mayor, Edmundo, Vincente Cruz the mason, old Miguel Tur, Primitivo. When my wife and I entered and sat at a corner table, each one of them at odd times would reassure us.

"Nothing will happen here," they said.

I told Ferrer that we were expecting two friends from Paris (Dick Glenn and his wife) on the Barcelona boat next morning and asked him if he would take me in to meet the boat.

"Yes," he said doubtfully.

Cosmi, standing near our table, tried so hard to look hopeful that I suddenly grew doubtful myself. "The boat will come, I think," he said.

Rigoberto entered, grey with apprehension and sadness.

"Any news?" he was asked.

"*Nada*," he replied. "The radio has been censored."

The next morning I got up at five o'clock and went to find Ferrer. He was having coffee at Cosmi's as usual, and we went out into the street and stood watching, our eyes fixed on the sea in the direction of the Tagomago cliff. I saw that all up and down the street, standing silently in doorways, were men and women watching, too. Not only the usual early risers, but others who ordinarily did not appear until later.

"It will come," said some of them.

"It should be here. It's not coming," said others.

The steamer from Barcelona did not appear.

15. An Airplane

THE way of life in Santa Eulalia involved so little that could be dispensed with that each interference with it, however slight, was felt at once. The sea, by day and night, was unstirred by the movement of a sail. No trails of smoke showed on the horizon. One could almost see the flowers bloom and the fruits and melons ripen, so warm was the sun, so refreshing the afternoon breeze, so mellow the mid-summer starlight.

"We might as well be on Pitcairn's Island," Pep den Horto said to me. Then as an afterthought, "Come to think of it, they have a regular mail service there now. They have the advantage of us."

Ramon shattered the morning air with the backfire of his motorcycle each day, but few of the townspeople were awakened by it. They were standing in their doorways, looking unhopefully toward Tagomago, thinking that perhaps the trouble was over and the mail boat would come. The bus went to Ibiza twice each day, but there were few passengers. It dawned on Ramon that the number of gallons of gasoline on the island was dwindling unnecessarily, so the afternoon trip was abandoned on Friday of the first week. Guillermo the blacksmith gave up thoughts of work right away, and few of the fishermen went

out. The local demand could be supplied by the
dories near the shore, and big catches of fish would
have gone to waste for lack of shipping facilities. The
stores did some desultory business, but the farmers
from the hills already had begun to cling to their
supply of *pesetas*. For some reason, the peasants got
nervous about paper money immediately and tried
to change it for metal coins, some of which were
buried. Costa, Vicente Cruz and some of the other
masons continued work with their few remaining bags
of cement.

"When it's gone, we'll stop," Vicente said to me,
lifting his eyebrows.

Along the main street, at bus time, the crowd was
larger and more animated, and all morning groups of
men went from café to café trying to guess what was
happening. The two daily news-sheets of Ibiza published nothing but successes of the *Movimiento* (as
the rebellion was called), but Rigoberto, aided by
Primitivo, had contrived to catch a few reports on his
radio which had been overlooked in the cursory
search for instruments made by the local Guardias
and told a few of his friends that Madrid was announcing that the rebellion had been put down within
a few hours in Madrid, Barcelona, Valencia and Alicante, and that San Jurco, the exiled leader of the
Guardia Civil, had been killed in an airplane crash
on his way into Spain to take command of the disloyal forces. The slightest rumor took wings and was
strengthened by long series of imaginings. But out
of it all, an opinion began to crystallize and was heard
up and down the street and in the houses, namely,
that the people of Ibiza must be patient and would

be forced to be guided by whatever decisions were reached on the peninsula.

"Here, we shall not begin killing one another," I heard men and women say, again and again.

The republicans were indignant at the action of Commandant Mestres, who had betrayed their government and the one to which he had sworn to be loyal, but it seemed to be his policy during those first few days to interfere with their normal course of life as little as possible. Everyone who could, it was thought, should go on working and conduct his business as always. There were whispered complaints because the citizens were deprived of their news sources, but no one believed the isolation would continue many days.

Cosmi, Juanito of the Royalty, the storekeepers, taximen and others who derived a large part of their summer income from visitors already knew that their season had been ruined, that the news in foreign countries of an insurrection in Spain would keep tourists away and that Spaniards on the Levantine coast would not come to Ibiza for their vacations. The cost of the fascist adventure to them was immediately oppressive. To Juanito it was likely to be ruinous.

The rich men of Santa Eulalia, landowners like Ignacio Riquer and Don Carlos Roman, Don Rafael Sainz, the millionaire banker who was spending the summer in his Santa Eulalia residence, the pilot, old Dr. Torres and their intimates stayed at home behind closed doors. Young Dr. Gonzalez spent his time going from house to house all over the countryside, telling peasants that the *Movimiento* was a patriotic one and that, under the dictatorship of

General Franco (of whom almost no one had heard
before) Spain would prosper and the Church be restored its proper rights and privileges. Bonéd the
mason talked fervently, but slyly, with all the young
workmen, in a similar strain. Whenever a priest made
a trip to Ibiza, he was escorted by a member of the
Guardia Civil.

While the Royalty was empty, Cosmi's was filled
with republicans who refrained from provocative
acts, but secretly comforted one another. It was not
until Friday afternoon that Mestres, increasingly
nervous because of the incredible smoothness with
which he had taken possession of the island, and disturbed particularly because in Santa Eulalia and San
Carlos his own supporters appeared to be badly
frightened while the government party seemed confident and orderly to an ominous degree, decided that
Santa Eulalia must be made to feel that a state of
war existed. Sergeant Gomez, in charge of the local
garrison of Guardias, shamefacedly made the rounds
of cafés and posted on the wall of Antonia's fishermen's café and the door of the Teatro de España an
order, signed by Mestres as Military Commander of
Ibiza, that cafés must be closed and that everyone
must be in his house with the doors closed after half
past ten each evening. As far as the cafés were concerned, the order was aimed directly at Cosmi and
his loyal clientele.

Before dark, Edmundo, squinting through his
rimmed spectacles, read the order and then and there
abandoned passive resistance. He went from café to
café, the whole length of the street, announcing belligerently that he would see himself in hell before

anybody would put him to bed until he got ready to go. Cosmi, his brother Mateo, Captain Juan, all his friends tried to reason with him and restrain him. Their cautious words made him angrier and more de-termined. Also he got increasingly drunk. At half past ten, Cosmi told him he could stay and drink as long as he liked, that he would close the front shut-ters and the café door, leave unlocked the communicat-ing door to the hotel, and all would be cozy. This did not satisfy Edmundo at all. His face grim with rage and his step uncertain he broke away from his well-wishers, charged out of doors and started walking up and down the now deserted street, so beautifully marked by shadows and cool moonlight, yelling at the top of his voice as he shook his fists in the air:

"I want to be locked up. Come and get me, damned *Duros Sevillanos*. I want to be locked up." (In Ibi-cenco most expressively *tankat*.)

I hurried after him, thinking perhaps he would listen to me, and as I did so I saw the Guardias Ferrer and Jimenez coming toward us from the direc-tion of Cork's. At the alley on which Carlos the fisherman and Jaume the carpenter lived I saw them hesitate in a non-military fashion and disappear into the narrow side street. It was impossible that they had not seen and heard, and their efforts to be decent stirred me to redoubled activities on Edmundo's part. I asked him to come to my house and drink with the door wide open, and for a few hours there-after the sleep of the Rosa family above us was made difficult if not impossible. The drinks I poured for Edmundo would have staggered a rhinoceros, and eventually they made him drowsy. Pep Torres and I saw him safely home.

Sindik the carpenter and the men in his shop seemed less affected by the military confiscation of the island than any of his neighbors. The whine of his lathe, the soft mewing of his planes, the tapping of hammers continued all day long in his shop. Sindik himself was at his bench before the hour of opening, his sons and two apprentices were obliged to forsake the excitement of the street and start work at the exact moment they had before the proclamation. Fortunately Sindik had a fairly large stock of wood, and when he needed nails or drift pins (which carpenters in Spain do not have on hand) Guillermo good-naturedly consented to open his blacksmith shop next door for a few moments to find or make what his industrious neighbor needed. The fact that many of the other men in the street had abandoned their habitually mild activities for the time spurred Sindik to more concentrated effort. He set a furious pace for his men to follow, was more severe about conversation during working hours, would allow no one to go out for a drink. His sons and his two apprentices responded as best they could. It was hard for all of them to remain diligently at work while their friends were passing up and down the street, spearing bits of news from empty air, discussing how long the trouble would last (no one then called it war), how long the food supply would hold out, whether the news in the *Diario* and *La Voz* was true or false, a hundred new questions. For Juan, the older son, it was harder to work as if nothing outside were happening than it was for the others. Juan had spent his life in the carpenter shop, had played with tools before he could walk. He was an excellent carpenter, but his mind had developed in no other direction. In all respects, aside from his strength and stature and the stiffness of his beard, he was a child. He liked to spear fish by lantern light, to swing long sticks of cane through the air at dusk in the hope of killing bats, and especially he loved to hunt. His father had a rifle and a shotgun and before the firearms had been taken away by the former sergeant of the Guardias, Juan had used them Sundays and holidays, hunting pheasants and rabbits. The sound of music or any undue commotion on the street brought him running to the scene, almost as promptly as the half-witted brothers Anfita, the postmaster's sons. Juan was twenty-four years old.

In the house behind the shop and in the walled backyard (two beehives, a well, orange, lemon trees and flower garden) the women of the Sindik household kept themselves occupied as steadily as did the men. The second wife, a tall rangy woman from the hills, took scrupulous care of the first wife's children. The older daughter, taller than Juan and with a well-shaped head and sloping shoulders, drew water, cleaned vegetables, kneeled hours at a time by the Moorish ditch behind the house on the back street, washing clothes in the cool running water. Governments might rise and fall without interrupting Sindik's labors. There had always been demand for carpenter work. He was convinced there always would be, and because an inner force impelled him to work from morning until night at rapid pace, keeping his thoughts within his broad sloping forehead and focused upon the lumber and the tools before him, he looked upon idleness as anti-social and sinful.

Guillermo's first thought had been that in a short time, with the island isolated, no one would have money to pay. So why work? Was it not better to keep what iron he had? At any rate, with so much gossip and conjecture in the air, he could not have put his mind to his work if he had wanted to.

Neither Sindik nor Guillermo took sides in the conflict. The carpenter's religion and his political creed was work. Guillermo knew that whenever somebody wins, somebody else loses. He was not sure, in spite of false news reports and proclamations, that the fascists would triumph. He could not be certain that the government would defeat them. He thought it safer to be a non-partisan, friendly with Cosmi, friendly with Bonéd. Always he had been outspokenly anti-clerical, but after the trouble began he was less so. He did not mention the priests at all. So the most industrious man in town and the laziest man in town were emphatically *m'en-furikistas*, or believers in letting well enough alone.

The first of the civilian fascists of Santa Eulalia to show his colors was ex-Captain Nicolau. He went to Ibiza at once, was enrolled as an aide to Commandant Mestres, given the rank of Captain and, being an expert marksman, was given the job of teaching the fascist volunteers to shoot. His wife was not far behind him in aggressiveness. Before the first week was out, she began warning her neighbors what would become of republican families and sympathizers. Odila, their daughter, sat silently in the pharmacy with her republican friends, pale beneath her freckles.

She had always admired her father, rather than her mother, but her ambitions conflicted with her strong filial love. Her father, she knew, was fighting to keep her in black lace and a mantilla; her father's enemies (her republican friends) wanted to open the doors of progress for her. As is the case with so many robust and athletic girls, her worry and uncertainties made Odila ill. She forced herself to move around, but some vital force had been cut off. She lost weight and grew more silent daily.

The Tuesday after the first failure of the Barcelona boat to appear there were a large number of people on the street at five-thirty in the morning, and they were disappointed. The familiar shape of the *Ciudad de Barcelona* did not come out from behind the Tagomago headland. The women went sadly back to their houses, listless and uneasy. A few of the men made a pretense of going to work. About seven o'clock I saw to my astonishment, a large steamer nosing past the lighthouse. I called out to Toni Ferrer, who was standing near me. The sun was shining in our eyes, and he shouted: "*Es correo*" (the mailboat). The word flew up and down the street, and groups of men and women gathered in places where the view was unobstructed.

"It's not the *Ciudad de Barcelona*," said one.

"I think it's the old *Jaime Segundo*," another said.

"It's a Spanish battleship," a third one said, and the women showed signs of fright.

"Has no one a telescope?" I asked Ferrer.

"Costa has one," he replied. We set out across the street for Costa's house, next door to the theatre.

His wife was standing in the doorway, scowling and clasping her hands.

"Is it a warship?" she asked.

"The devil knows," said Ferrer.

We asked for her telescope and she brought it out, after a few minutes of searching. It was an old-fashioned spy glass, two feet long when stretched to its full length. Something was wrong with the screw-piece by which the lenses were adjusted. We carried it across the street to the crowd we had left, and one after another of us tried to adjust it and train it on the vessel which now was a third the distance across the open water toward Cala Llonga. No one could see what the flag was, but the speed with which the boat was travelling convinced us all that it could not be one of the passenger steamers of the Trans-Mediterraneo.

Cosmi was on the roof of his hotel, with a pair of opera glasses Dona Guillermina had produced. I joined him there. He said, "They've come to talk to the bishop," expressing his fondest hope, that is, that a loyal Spanish warship had come to demand the surrender of the island. We listened together on the roof, long after the vessel had disappeared behind the Cala Llonga hills and, hearing no sound of guns, we went down stairs, disappointed.

At the same time Commandant Mestres had ordered all citizens to bed at ten-thirty. He forbade the use of the telephone or telegraph except for military purposes, so that each town on the island was cut off from the others. Consequently, it was impossible for any of us to telephone Ibiza and inquire about the mysterious craft. Mallorca Pete, however, had been detailed by the fascists to assist in operating the radio station near the church on Santa Eulalia's hill, and we all saw him go to Can Xumeu, where the telephone office was situated, undoubtedly for the purpose of putting in a call. I believed that Xumeu Ribas, if he found out about the warship or whatever it was, would tell me privately. With this in mind I went to his place alone. Xumeu had left the bar in the hands of his son Francisco, the lame student, who was talking in hushed tones with Guillermo and the Barberet, both of whom had stayed away from Cosmi's place since Mestres had taken over the island. They did not wish to be considered partisans in any controversy, or at least they wanted to balance the effect of their former outspokenness against the priests and the Guardia Civil by drinking in a café the owner of which had family connections with the clergy and was acting under orders of the man who was then in control of Ibiza.

I found Xumeu in a dim room at the back of the courtyard, sitting alone and in silence with the door just ajar. He face when he greeted me was grey with misery and apprehension. I asked him about the warship that had passed. He groaned, covered his face with his hands.

"I know nothing about it," he said. His wife and daughter were standing side by side in the kitchen doorway, sick with sadness. They knew they were involved in something frightful, and their ignorance of its nature or significance made them more anxious and hopeless. Francisco was the only member of the family who seemed pleased and excited. All his friends in the college in Ibiza were Catholics and reactionaries, his relatives had always looked with suspicion on the republic. Better things were in view, he believed, and he reproved his parents and his sister for their fears and their timidity. His education indicated without question that the fascists would win, but he said nothing about it and took no active part. He only tried to make his folks stop worrying, and meanwhile tended bar.

Xumeu was not to be consoled. I told him I thought nothing would happen on the island, that Ibiza would naturally have to accept whatever government ruled the mainland. Nothing I said eased his mind. He was aware that Mestres did not represent the government under which he had accepted the custody of the public telephone and that in obeying the orders of the military commander to close the office to the public he was committing a breach of trust. The alternative was imprisonment in the fortress of Ibiza under conditions his delicate health could not long withstand, the arrest of his son, dispossession of his family. His natural tendencies were reactionary but entirely passive. He saw nothing but disaster ahead.

Perhaps some innate historical sense warned Xumeu and the conservative peasants (whom he resembled although he was a café keeper) that clocks seldom are turned backward. For notwithstanding that the faction they favored held the island and the news they read each day assured them the fascists were winning all Spain, their attitude was of fear and distress, while that of the helpless republicans was defiant and tinged with hope they expressed with their eyes and with words they left unsaid. Eulalia Noguera, in whose judgment I had more confidence than in that of most of the adults, said grimly:

"*Es derets van gañá.*" (The Rights will win.) But she added in a whisper, "There will be another time." Until then, ruin for her family, the members of which were fanatically devoted to one another.

A few minutes after I had left Xumeu Ribas, I entered Cosmi's from the back street. Antonia Masear was peeling vegetables with nervous haste, her head nodding mournfully from side to side. Blue-eyed Catalina was as frightened when I mentioned the battleship as if I had spoken disrespectfully of God. In the kitchen, Antonio Cosmi was working in his effortless way, his smouldering eyes fixed on the bench and the ingredients before him. He was enveloped in the stillness of his deafness. But Anna entered just then, her dark eyes snapping, and said positively that the warship was English. It had come to take Englishmen away, she declared.

"Was I going?" she asked.

For the thousandth time I explained that I was not English but American.

"*Es igual,*" she said.

Where Anna got her information I cannot say. She was vague when I asked her about it. The fact remains that what she said was true and accurate and was confirmed when Ramon returned at noontime with the bus. Cosmi had often told me, and I had observed myself, that news flew around the island without need of wires or radio. This was another instance.

One of the first men I met, after having been informed by Anna that the British navy had arrived, was Derek Rogers, a young English painter who had been in town two years, an excellent and interesting man. When I told him what Anna had told me he went post-haste to the *Cuartel* and demanded of the sergeant that he be allowed to telephone to the port and get in touch with the British commander. The sergeant was regretful but could not disobey his orders. Rogers grew indignant and told the sergeant that his government would stand no nonsense. (The young painter at that time did not have the slightest idea of leaving Ibiza, not being opulent enough to live anywhere else on his small income. He was determined, however, to learn what he could about what was going on outside.)

Sergeant Gomez agreed finally to telephone the military officials himself and reported later to Rogers that a fascist officer had promised he would tell the British officers that there was an Englishman in Santa Eulalia. This, it transpired later, was not done. In the middle of the afternoon Rogers decided to walk to the port, but when he got there the British light cruiser had gone, taking with it a half dozen British subjects who were eager to get away. No doubt the British navy had so much pressing work on hand that the officers of that cruiser could not wait to scour the island for Englishmen in distress. Their casual attitude is understandable because they saw no one except Mestres and his trusted lieutenants. No republican was allowed to go near them or to communicate with them. British subjects who did not happen to be in sight of the port that morning did not know until too late that their rescuers had called. The next day, however, Rogers heard over the radio from London that Ibiza and Mallorca were tranquil and the populations were enthusiastically in support of the *Movimiento Patriotico.* Up to that time Rogers had kept very quite about having a radio set, and the Guardias had not searched the homes of foreigners. The refusal of the rebel government to allow him to talk with his country's representatives stirred his British spunk and thereafter he became the principal news source of the republicans. He was a liberal in politics and his sympathies were strongly with the Spanish government. The first few days he had been cautious in order that his contact with the outside might not be broken by zealous fascist officials. The telephone incident caused him to throw his lot openly with the then weaker side.

None of the stores in Santa Eulalia kept a large stock of staples on hand, and it became evident that in a few more days there would be a shortage of coffee, white flour and sugar. The awareness of this, which spread quickly through the countryside, brought peasants to town to buy as much as they could of these provisions and Miguel Tur, Guarapiñada, Ferrer and the family at Casa Rosita decided to sell only small amounts, except to their intimate friends. In the town of Ibiza there was a larger supply, but it was sold only to storekeepers who were staunchly fascist in the outlying towns, and Santa Eulalia had none of these. Miguel Tur had been exiled under Primo de Rivera; Guarapiñada had deserted the Guardia Civil rather than shoot two republican aviators; Ferrer would have broken anyone's neck who suggested he was not republican from birth. Old Cowboy Juan, of the Casa Rosita, was reactionary

enough and his calm daughter-in-law, Vicenta, was
a sister of one of the rebel lieutenants in the Ibiza
garrison. Mariano, Juan's son and Vicenta's husband,
was not of the flock, however, and had never concealed his mild leanings toward the Left. Consequently,
Santa Eulalia could hope for little when scant supplies were distributed. The reactionary inland towns
were served first.

So now in the stillness of the air and the unbroken
sea and sky we could hear not only the grain ripening
and the soft forays of pink oleander blossoms, rows
of corn and sweet potatoes, circus-tent shadows of
fig trees and on the road near Can Josepi the twelve-
foot stalks of two century plants bursting high clusters
of yellow once-for-always flowers. In the vibrant
chorus of these summer sights and sounds we could
hear also the trickle of sugar and flour from the sacks.
Before bus time, when the smoke of rosemary twigs
rose from hotels and ovens, the pungent odor of coffee
grew fainter, day by day. It was useless to point out
that honey could be used for sweetening, that corn
was magnificent food and no lack of that could occur,
that there were fish in the sea and tons of sweet and
white potatoes, and that the dark peasant bread tasted
better and was more nourishing than the product of
the bakers in town. The women were pessimistic and
afraid. They had been accustomed to having certain
supplies for their kitchens—their fixed habits were
threatened. Those who were able bought all the coffee,
flour and sugar they could get, and the others complained that they were being discriminated against.
No one except a few of the men I have mentioned in
the town had had any political experience. The ques-

tion was not: "What theory of government shall survive?" but "When shall we see the *Isabel Matutes* bringing in a cargo of white flour?" That their acquiescence in Commandant Mestres' theft of the island in the name of some rebel generals made them guilty of treason they did not suspect of course, nor that such men as ex-Captain Nicolau and Francisco Guasch were in the plot and acted with malice aforethought.

The bus made one trip each day and continued to bring back ice for the use of Cosmi's hotel, the Royalty and a few of the foreign families. The café keepers began hiding away their cognac and other liquor that came from the mainland and served whenever possible the local brands distilled in Ibiza by Mari Pol and Mari Mayans, both protégés of Matutes. All the banks in Ibiza, Matutes' bank, the Credito Balear, and a bank operated by Juan March (the Staviski of Spain) stopped paying out money and tried to collect what they could, which was practically nothing. Pep des Horts began to wear a worried look because he was under treatment for a dangerous disease he had contracted on the Amazon years before, and Dr. Gonzalez was nearly out of the necessary drugs to continue his cure. And all this occurred in the most heavenly weather one of earth's most favored regions could display.

Vicente Cruz and Cosmi's Catalina were victims in a special way. They had postponed their wedding over a period of two years, he in order to be sure he had money enough to start a household safely, she because of her reluctance to leave her invalid mother. The week before the island was cut off from com-

munication, he had gone to Palma, ordered the furniture for their apartment (on the back street next
to ex-Sergeant Ortiz and his flock of defective dogs).
Vicente had returned by the last boat from Palma.
The furniture was to follow. So the wedding had to
wait. In the beginning, Vicente had held out for a
civil wedding, but long ago he had decided that a few
moments with the priests did not matter and had
promised that one time to climb the rocky hill.
Among the masons, Vicente was the only one who
had risen to the rank of contractor and builder without borrowing from Matutes or calling on his relatives for aid. He was a strong and amiable young
man, intelligence shining from his sharp grey eyes,
his broad shoulders and capable hands quite eloquent.
Men liked to work with him. He did not get large
contracts but he fulfilled many small ones faithfully
and well. His bed was in a small room in the theatre
building, over Gork's café. He ate with other workers
in a small dining room Cosmi had set aside for them
and where the food was as good as that served the
foresteros (front room, orange-bordered napkins and
tablecloths). The workmen paid less, ate at one large
table with the hotel staff and Cosmi's family, and for
an hour after the noon meal they slept in the shade of
the trees. There were other workmen on the island
who looked forward to very lean times, when the
small supply of cement would be gone and their daily
wage (about seventy cents) would cease, but that
group who ate at Cosmi's knew that as long as Cosmi
had one chunk of bread and a slice of *sobresada* they
would be welcomed at mealtimes by greetings which
had no thoughts of *pesetas* and *centimos* to dilute

their heartiness. So around their long table they sat and joked about their predicament and forced the apprehensive women to smile. It was evident all through the town that the men who had been republicans were still republicans and that, although they believed resistance was impractical at the time, they did not consider themselves as subjects of Commandant Mestres or any former general named Franco. Watchful waiting expressed it perfectly, and the strain was too great for the Commandant's nerves. He decided that Santa Eulalia and San Carlos should be impressed with his permanence and power.

The second Friday evening after the proclamation of the state of war, the Guardias, acting on Mestres' express orders, searched Primitivo's house (in which Primitivo's wife conducted her sewing class) and found some parts of an obsolete radio set. Primitivo was taken to the *Cuartel*, kept in the guardroom that night and the next morning was sent to Ibiza, escorted by the sergeant, and imprisoned in the fortress there. The result in Santa Eulalia was instantaneous and ominous. Not only the active republicans, but men and women who formerly had been indifferent protested and complained. They all knew Primitivo had been innocent, in so far as his actions were concerned, and their sense of justice was outraged. Instead of striking at Cosmi, whose resources and family connections and following would have enabled him to make a strong defense, the rebel officials selected Primitivo, who had no relatives on the island and no money outside of his wages at the electric-light plant.

The psychological effect of that first arrest was heightened and the indignation it caused was multiplied because of the fact that Primitivo was the only one in Santa Eulalia who knew how to operate the light plant, excepting the Frenchman, Georges Halbique, who that same day was taken sick and could not work. Thus by a single stroke, Mestres threw the town into darkness, and the wavering candles in windows and doorways and grotesque shadows on the white walls enhanced the feeling that disaster was in the air. Halbique, who had invested all his money in the light plant, was probably ill from worry. He knew that as long as the island was incommunicado no one could pay his bills, and he had been made to believe that the government faction on the peninsula consisted of rabid communists and anarchists who would take his property in case they were victorious.

The next afternoon, Fernando the schoolmaster from Formentera and Carlos, teacher in the San Carlos school, were arrested, without formal charges being made against them. They were talking on the terrace of the Royalty when the sergeant and Guardia Ferrer came to get them. Edmundo, the moment he heard about it, strode up and down the street, bellowing and demanding that he be arrested, too, that the Guardias were *ladrones*. Apparently the fascists did not want such a troublesome man on their hands. Sunday evening, Pep Torres did not return from Ibiza at the usual hour and when he got back to Santa Eulalia the next morning he was fighting mad. The Guardias in Ibiza had prevented the band from giving their Sunday evening concert, on the ground that the assembly of the musicians was a public meeting. The real reason was that a fascist volunteer had overheard the bandsmen talking indignantly about the unjust arrests that had been made. On the same evening, a large fascist meeting was held in the Catholic seminary on the hill. When Pep had tried to return to Santa Eulalia on his bicycle (the hour being later than half past ten) he was stopped by a fascist volunteer who inexpertly threatened him with a loaded gun and ordered him to go back to Ibiza and stay there until morning. That same morning I was passing Andres' café, between the Royalty and post office, and saw Magdalena, the *patrone*, in tears. I asked her what was the matter and her husband, cross but equally worried, said she was afraid her son Andres (the talented young painter) would be the next to be thrown into prison. Everyone knew he was a socialist, and he was disliked thoroughly by ex-Captain Nicolau. I lost my temper and became less restrained than was wise.

"Andres will be here, alive and well, long after Commandant Mestres has been hanged," I said. Seeing the alarm on their faces I turned and saw in the doorway not four feet distant not only Rigoberto, who looked as troubled as they did, but the Pilot, one of the slyest of the fascists and an intimate friend of the officer I had just condemned to the gallows. The Pilot pretended not to have heard, but we all knew he had, and the moment he went away Rigoberto took me aside and implored me to be more careful.

"There are some people here who would take personal vengeance," he said, as if that were unthinkable. It was, in a candid mind like Rigoberto's. I promised to be discreet.

One evening, Derek Rogers reported that an American vice-consul had been on the air for a moment, speaking from Barcelona, and had inquired about numerous Americans in Spain, among them a Mrs. Emma Gramkow, an American woman who was on the register as living on Ibiza. The Fairchilds told Mrs. Gramkow, who then with her two sons occupied part of Can Josepi. They all held a consultation and decided that Mrs. Gramkow, having been named by the vice-consul, should apply to the military authorities and demand permission to send a message to the American Consulate in Barcelona, asking that an American warship be sent to Ibiza. Ex-Commandant Mestres would only permit her to send two words.

After the first wave of indignation about the arrests of Primitivo, Fernando and Carlos had subsided and the *Voz* and the *Diario* for days had assured their readers that the *Movimiento* was victorious all over Spain, the rich men and their followers took courage, and some of them ventured out of doors. July 26th was the first day on which ex-General Franco announced that he would take Madrid on the morrow. As I write, seven months later, he is still repeating the same announcement, with very slight variation, and those who wish to take it seriously are doing so, as they did last July. Don Rafael Sainz was such a one. Since the nineteenth of July he had been cooped up in his tremendous house just north of town on the San Carlos road, and a rich Spaniard had no facilities in his own house for amusing himself. Secora, his wife, was drenched with tears and piety. She prayed for the success of the rebels night and day, kept priests scurrying back and forth between her mansion and the hill. Each of his seven children had a nurse who was praying also. In all his jolly life Don Rafael had never put in such a ghastly time. One day I saw heading toward the Royalty Don Rafael and a young man I think was his bodyguard, at least I could never find out what else, if anything, he did. The millionaire banker was one of the widest men I ever saw. His paunch was commodious but was put to shame by his colossal bottom. His face was round, flat and flushed (alert and smiling) and his voice was squeaky and always cordial. In Madrid he sat in the front row, section 10, at every good bullfight. Headwaiters, men about town and the swankiest of the Madrid prostitutes called him by name and offered him the best they had. In Santa Eulalia he had treated the workmen well when they were engaged in building his huge ungainly house. He was a popular man, wherever he went, and took a healthy joy in living, ate well, drank deeply, and I have been told was a talented financier.

The long days with his wife Secora had shaken him deeply. His five-foot belt was a trifle loose and the ends of his trousers legs scraped the dust as he walked along the sunny street bound for Juanito's. His manner was self-conscious, his greetings a bit overdone. But there still was ice in Juanito's ice-box and Don Rafael refreshed himself and calmed his jagged nerves with numerous mugs of cold beer. The next day at the noontime *apéritif* hour, young Dr. Gonzalez, the Pilot, Don Carlos Roman and three of his boys joined Don Rafael and his bodyguard. The Royalty's corner regained its animation, and Pedro, the headwaiter, darted here and there in his spotless white coat, happy to be working again. The bus brought a bundle of Ibiza news-sheets which were perused at each table with chuckles and satisfaction. Rebel gains in the Guadaramas, in Aragon, in the north, triumphs in Seville and Granada. Largo Caballero had fled to France, so had Azaña. Prieto had quit Madrid for Valencia, and Franco was at the gates of the capital.

And among those stage-whispering revellers, seated in a small musty cabinet of death or leaning, looking southward, against one of the posts of the grape arbor near the ancient majestic palm, was Marguerita, plump and haggard in her black lace dress, her grief too deep for tears or the bounds of her own comprehension. Now and then the Pilot, who liked to be reassuring to everyone (and who might have been the one who had reported that Fernando's conversation was dangerous) would smile at the heartbroken girl and say that nothing would happen.

While beer flowed and canned clams were being eaten in the Royalty, and the news was passed around with gay comments and relief, a few of the *Diarios* found their way to Cosmi's, where men looked at them silently, said they contained nothing but lies and let them slide to the floor. Captain Juan was listless because of idleness. Mateo Rosa did not dare to talk, his feelings were so strong. Edmundo growled and drank harder. Ferrer laughed loudly and rode astride his disappointment. Only Cosmi was as always. His movements were sure, his pronouncements restrained. He derived comfort wherever he could, but did not manufacture false hopes. The day Mrs. Gramkow and the other Americans were refused their reasonable request, Cosmi was much heartened.

"If everything were going as *they* say it is" (meaning Mestres and his crowd), "they would not be afraid to send a telegram like that," he said, and the men around him nodded and took courage.

Then suddenly, on the morning of July 29, in an instant the situation was transformed. The town and the island were no longer adrift in blue sea and space. The outside world reached over and touched them, gently and mysteriously from the sky.

16. The Manifesto

THE morning of July 29 was fair and cool, an ideal
one for the vacation period which the fascist plot had
marked off the books. The sea was mildly choppy
and the air was filled with summer fragrance. An
electrician had been sent out from Ibiza to operate
Halbique's light plant the night before. Primitivo's
wife and her mother had proudly, very unostenta-
tiously, taken the bus to the port in order to see
Primitivo through the fortress bars and assure him
with calm eyes that he was where all honest young
men should be. Postmaster Anfita and his feeble-
minded sons had ridden and stumbled to the alfalfa
patch north of town, their minds declouded by ten
days' absence of mail (blankness and work with
alfalfa), but by habit at noon returned to receive
nothing from Ramon and before lunching not to
distribute it.

Santa Eulalia, after ten days of outer nothingness
and inner fermentation, had its glistening white
houses in rank along the front street, the back street,
the small street still farther behind, the dwellings
scattered on the slope, the white fortress-church with
spiral road, high very high shrine on back mountain.
Nearly all its people were there, more men idle,
women nearly the same. And can anyone forget those

major trees, the tall palm across the narrow street from the Estanco, the slender eucalyptus by Casa Rosita, the tallest broadest spreading tree at the head of the *paseo* where the fishermen no longer sold their wares, and on the Arabie road the twin mariner's pines from the time of the Moors?

Pep Torres and I had pooled our enthusiasm about Ibicenco music and had busied ourselves collecting it and committing it to paper in various forms, a labor that seemed to remove us another degree from the town's mild hysteria. The island adrift from the month and the season, the music detached from the century. At ten o'clock that morning Pep was at the beach by the mouth of the river, teaching Peanut how to swim and I was listening to Eulalia Noguera singing an intensely beautiful song, *Quand yo era petitet.*

> "When I was very small
> My mother took me to mass (*missa*)
> In a cloak she had made
> Of baby lamb's wool . . ." (*pelissa*)

Like so many of the old songs of Ibiza, Eulalia's offering that morning ended on the dominant, leaving the perfect summer morning (island, sea and sky) to lift one silently to the level of the tonic again. Instead we heard a strange humming in the air, not of summer sounds, but a deeper more compelling tune. At the doorway, faces upturned and squinting against the sun, we listened, and doorways sprouted faces, on street upturned necks of lounging men until Ferrer by Las Delicias exultantly saw a speck not too high in air and not far distant, and he pointed.

"An airplane," each one said to others who were saying it to him, and hearts long waiting for something to happen, almost anything, leaped and the ones who had been winning, and had seemed most afraid, tried not to look alarmed and murmured, "It is nothing." But nothing it emphatically was not. It followed the coast line, not curving horizontally for each little cove and ledge, but approximating smoothly the map from Ibiza city past Jesus, Cala Llonga and then breath-takingly to Santa Eulalia, by evident choice like an arrow to the town. The motor was roaring and the plane (two helmeted occupants) dipped low and passed above the main street, from the curve by the mill to the plaza, Cosmi's Can Xumeu, the theatre and out over Arabie. We, below, could read only non-commital figures and initials on the plane's newly painted belly. No national colors we could identify, no whence or wherefore, but no longer an island forgotten, remote and unreachable in blue sea. Two men with helmets in a plane, and not only the island but for some reason Santa Eulalia, the town least favored—and with reason—by Commandant Mestres and his fascist volunteers.

An airplane, even in ordinary times in Santa Eulalia, was a sight no one would miss seeing, for although a few had passed that way of sky (and once Herr Doktor Eckener and his *Graf Zeppelin* in a miracle of silver), a plane was a rare sight. This one, by its behavior, stirred conjectures that flew faster than the fastest plane. Having flown over Arabie, with me wondering if from its height pink oleanders in creek beds were visible, the plane turned seaward, looped back and followed the coast line again as far as Cala

Llonga, then made a bee-line over the main street again, headed northward, and lower, lower, yes, surely not landing, yes, landing neatly in the cove near Cosmi's pebble beach.

A few of the men and boys started on the hotfoot to see what the airmen would do next. I thought I could do better by going to Cosmi's roof with Doña Guillermina's opera glasses, and in heading that way I nearly collided with Sergeant Gomez, self-consciously adjusting his rifle strap, and beside him, more pop-eyed than ever, the Homeric *portero* of the mayor's office, a strange uniform cap on his head and in his hands a carbine. Side by side they marched in the direction of the plane now bobbing on the waves, and I could not help thinking that the two airmen sitting in a plane not more than fifty yards from shore would make an easy target for trained marksmen concealed among the rocks.

We watchers from the housetops waited what seemed to me an interminable time. Probably it was about ten minutes. Nothing happened at all. The sergeant and the diligent *portero* continued, not hurrying, along the Arabie road, then cut across the fields toward the cove. The plane bobbed and its occupants made no attempt to land. Cosmi was beside me, and at the same moment we saw a man who could only be his brother Pep Salvador lugging oars to a dory and rowing out to the plane.

"The damn fool," said Cosmi, admiringly. Pep rowed steadily on and, before the sergeant and the *portero* were within shooting distance, came alongside. After a few minutes, Pep Salvador rowed away, to my intense relief. Cosmi watched, inscrutable. Nothing, for some time. Then I saw Mrs. Fairchilds and her son start out for Arabie, it being evident from a distance that she was more eager than he to approach the zone of action. I thought I heard a rifle shot. Cosmi nodded. Then the plane started moving in the water, got slowly under way, turned its nose to Punta Blanca and came to rest again derisively across the small bay. I was enjoying Cosmi's face, and I knew that he would rather be himself than anyone else just then.

"They're not fascists," I said, but we both turned, aroused by the commotion of a laboring motor on the road behind us and saw in a thick cloud of dust an automobile tearing past the mill toward the plaza at its highest speed. As it passed through the town, where many pedestrians and dogs came close to losing their lives, I saw that it contained a squad of soldiers from the garrison of Ibiza. At the fork of the Arabie road, although that road was passable, the auto stopped abruptly, the four soldiers and an officer got out, and, leaving their vehicle nearly two miles from the enemy, proceeded raggedly on foot with darts of unheard laughter behind them. There was no more shooting, and in less than half an hour the plane described another arc on the waters of the bay, rose steadily and headed eastward out of sight. The whole countryside was seething with explanations. The soldiers, returning with Sergeant Gomez, the *portero* olive-green, and waddling Don Rafael Sainz (his face lobster-red and white shirt hugely soaked with perspiration) had been coached to say that the plane was an Italian commercial craft that had lost its way, but a corporal, native of Ibiza and

a friend of Pep Torres, conveyed silently to him and
to me, by winking one eye slowly, that his words were
not true. We had felt sure of that before, but were
glad to have confirmation.

The gathering at the Royalty that noon was almost
pitiful. Don Rafael had fear written all over his broad
red face, and his high squeaky voice, repeating reassuring platitudes, did not cover the fact that he could
not swallow his beer. In a corner, with dejected boys
around him, Don Carlos Roman sat stoically. He had
not been well. Cognac lately had not been agreeing
with him. He looked tired and ready for anything he
could accept without exertion. Young Dr. Gonzalez
was not voluble and smiling, as he had been the day
before. He was wishing fervently that he had talked
about politics less and medicine more, and that he had
not made it so evident which side he wanted to win.

The news about the plane, with even more fantastic explanations, had spread to Ibiza and every town
on the island. Soldiers had been rushed to the scene
in varying numbers, increasing numbers of shots and
volleys had been exchanged. If a plane could fly low,
right over the main street of Santa Eulalia, what was
to prevent another dropping bombs? The active pes-
simists expected disastrous action, the passive ones
accepted the story that the plane was a stray and
declared that neither airplanes nor ships would be
seen near Ibiza again.

That afternoon Francisco Guasch stood in front of
the *Cuartel*, a long rifle over his arm, looking defiantly and often shamefacedly at the sky. He had
been made an officer of Mestres' law, with a loaded
gun and discretionary powers, and the murmuring

that arose was not confined to republicans. No one trusted him, no one had been his friend. His soft-eyed wife, who had kept aloof from most of the women because their men were not friendly with Francisco, stepped contentedly like a cat and wrapped her shawl more closely around her shapely shoulders. One could see who was master now. Young Joachim Guasch, the fiancé of Maria at the post office, went belligerently from one republican café to another, automatic in his holster, dagger in his belt, looking for trouble.

After dinner that night I entered Cosmi's and was struck right away by the lack of familiar faces, and hardly had I tasted my coffee before Sergeant Gomez, Guardia Ferrer and an officer from the Ibiza garrison entered. Marc Colomar was tending bar, assisted by Anna and her old father. In answer to a question from the sergeant, he said, "How should I know?" and Anna talked indignantly and rapidly. "He doesn't tell me where he's going," she said. The search party entered the kitchen and could hardly get Antonio to look at them, let alone tell where Cosmi was. They looked in the dining rooms, upstairs, and for hours all through the town. Another party consisting of Francisco Guasch, Guardia Jimenez and another officer from the garrison returned crestfallen from Arabie. Cosmi, Pep Salvador, Captain Juan and a half dozen others who were active republicans had disappeared, an hour before they were to have been arrested. Those remaining, Ferrer of Las Delicias, Edmundo, Pep Torres, Vicente Cruz and all the mason's helpers laughed and chuckled, and I remembered suddenly the hasty words exchanged between Cosmi and the Guardia Ferrer early in the day and was sure the officer had tipped off Cosmi, telling him who was listed for arrest and when the search would be made.

To any of his friends who inquired for Cosmi, Anna or Antonio said that he had gone to Formentera in a rowboat to sell potatoes and onions. Pep Salvador's wife and children worked steadily on the farm, Pep's favorite daughter in a corner where she could watch the road and the pathways through the field. Mixed parties of Guardias, soldiers and fascist volunteers walked through miles of thickets and hid themselves in caves to watch the shore and the sea.

The day after the visit of the mysterious plane and the disappearance of Cosmi and Pep Salvador, I was on the street a half hour before bus time at noon in the strong heat of the sun. A dull reaction seemed to follow the excitement of the day before. Everyone had grown tired of guessing, and the town moved listlessly. No breeze was stirring and dust hung heavily in the air. In all the heat and stillness I saw a young girl coming down the hill, neither walking nor running, but ominously straight and purposeful and in mortal despair. Juana. It was Juana, Teresa's daughter. I hurried to intercept her at the corner of the lane.

"What is it, Juana? What's the matter?" I asked. Her agate eyes blazed out at me.

"Come," she said.

She led me at the same swift pace back up the hill to the house of a neighbor who lived near her new home, opened brusquely a door and pointed, just one accusing gesture. No fright, no tears. A girl's untrembling finger pointing and dull hatred in her eyes for all the world. I glanced in the direction she indicated and saw through the mouth of an open cistern a wire exactly taut and plumb and with dead face perpetually choking and distorted, dirty thin grey hair, an old man's head and (as I leaned farther forward, restrained from gasping by Juana's fierce control) a stringy old man's neck awry and patched clothes hanging limp beneath it into cistern dimness. Old man Serra had hanged himself. He was an old man who had lived alone, neither rich nor poor, taking trouble to cook infrequently and somewhere on the mainland having a son who was in the Guardia Civil. His hanging was simple and workmanlike, and because old men were the same to Juana as young men and she had often done errands for old Serra before noon, she had come face to face with suicide.

I had never seen Santa Eulalia plunged suddenly into such black depression. Ordinary deaths were received there with Oriental wailing and demonstrations of grief. In no one's memory had a neighbor taken his own life. Ramon, his eyes sick with misery, forgot his lunch and walked to Serra's house, as if the sight of the dead old man were a treatment, heatless rays of death to penetrate the vitals and cool the living tissues for the death to come. Guillermo, shaking his unruly mop of black curly hair (face unshaven, blue-striped shirt) and thinking that to kill oneself, choking alone in empty cistern with wire gripping neck, is an exaggeration, that woes and hurts of the necessary come to or from those who exaggerate. Guillermo unable to weep or to feel through absinthe deeply what it could have been like for Serra-Guillermo then, at that precise moment of descending, for how could a man (not really tidy old man) do ununderstandable thing with such precise result? In the shade, Ramon, Guillermo and the new baker, standing inside a dead man's doorway and around them, on trees and scrub bushes and patches of grass in pathways worn thin, the sun, the noontime heat, no beat, no warning, as when at midnight the lights are about to go dark. An old man dies without winking the sun, and Teresa next door is weeping, her daughter Juana angry at her mother's tears. Old Bonéd, her father, fascist mason, standing almost corpselike in patched linen suit, cheeks sagging, thinking of implements of death beneath cement sacks in shed, and old man Serra, not the man or men the ones wish to have dead. A few women are coming, Anna Cosmi and her dogs, not knowing where her husband is hiding, Costa's tory wife accusing her husband's sacrilegious friends. Is the old man her cousin? No (lips pursed annoyed), her second cousin. Blue-eyed Catalina's stalwart old aunt, to lay down law in the old man's favor. Whose business is it, if a man wants to die? To the devil with the priests . . . Oh, don't say that. Women frightened. Ramon and the men undecided. Why not, half thinking the new baker, happy to be father, to give life? It's unnatural, Guillermo. One cannot put oneself in dead man's place, still hanging taut, clothes limp.

Sometime late in the afternoon Ferrer cut him down and lifted him with loving blacksmith arm. He was buried without ceremony. But in houses, kitchens, under fig trees, old man strangled spread like mildew, over the slopes to San Carlos, San Miguel, Santa Geritrudis, southward to Jesus and

Ibiza, across the island to San Antonio, ghostly over salt marshes and pyramids of drying salt where idle workmen sat on rusted narrow-gauge rail and shivered in the sun. Never was dead old man spread so thinly on the crust of an island.

That was an evening in which one rose slowly to the surface of the waters of death, rising for the first time to struggle in moonlight a while and to match one's breath and strength against the second sinking and as air from lungs so bubbled thoughts expelled from mind concerning that third time down, from which no man ascends on rope or wire.

I thought for several hours that old man Serra had accomplished what Commandant Mestres had failed thus far in doing, and that Santa Eulalia had lost its spirit and its power of recovery. Not so. An afternoon of burial, an evening of moonlight, the familiar morning sounds, strong sun over smiling sea, and the next day when an old woman who lived near Pere Des Puig was found dead, dressed in her holiday clothes (clean petticoats and stockings), hanging from the branches of a fig tree, box kicked away and spread near by a clean never-slept-upon mattress the wool for which she had picked and sorted in the last days of her life—when this neatly dressed corpse was discovered by Pere's lovely daughter Eulalia in search of stray goat, many more men and women went to see the body, and it was cut down sooner, and there was not the terrifying impact felt the day before. Ibiza, the adaptable, survivor of so many conquering people, had in twenty-four hours made the grade. Old folks' suicide was an occurrence which now would be accepted.

Just after the *siesta* hour on July 31, a droning. No ?
A droning, unmistakably, and again the heads, shaking off deep sleep, cocked upward from the doorways, and sleepers springing out from under trees to see. I was playing checkers with Juanito in the then deserted Royalty, and about to win. We hurried to the sidewalk and saw, running like foolish hens to the *Cuartel*, Francisco Guasch and a young fascist who looked like Harpo Marx and who owned a black Arabian mare much too good for him. Both Francisco and Harpo had guns which nearly tripped them up, and from behind the pillars under the archway they peered skyward.

"There it is." A speck far beyond Cala Llonga, not approaching, not passing. The plane ignored Santa Eulalia and the northern end of the island but circled over the port city, and after half an hour disappeared. Those of us who watched from Santa Eulalia could only imagine the flight over Ibiza, being shut off from view by the Cala Llonga hills. Mystery, but now surely not forgotten and alone. Of course there must be some connection between the visit of our mystery plane and that speck in the afternoon two days later. Invigorating leapfrog of events, plane hopping death of man and woman, bridging them. Ferrer waving and smiling from Las Delicias, Mariano smiling in the doorway of Casa Rosita (amid scowls of old-fashioned father, Cowboy Juan) and approaching gleefully, head with topknot held high, Catalina's sturdy aunt.

"*Viva la Republica*," she said, and looked around defiantly. "*Viva!*" Looking right and left, particularly to the left toward Francisco Guasch and rifle, Guasch scowling, amateurish. Blank of knowing what to do.

"For God's sake, be careful," said Juanito.

"*Viva!*" And smiling. Drinking breeze and face toward the sky, looking at plane behind Cala Llonga's hill.

By that time I had learned the technique of keeping abreast with events. I went straight home and waited for Eulalia Noguera to appear. After her family, we came first whenever she had information. There was a swish outside and the tap of feet. Pep Torres, streaked with sweat and dust, had dismounted from his bicycle. I had forgotten that he was in Ibiza that afternoon, doing with his customary method some domestic errands. Once inside the door he jumped, waved his arms, and whooped silent.

"Wait," he said, as I started to ask. He motioned me to an inside room. "Lock the door," he said. My wife complied. He hastily and clumsily drew forth a pin from one of his wide belt straps, explored with finger, and out fell a bit of paper, tightly rolled. He looked cautiously around him.

"From the plane?" I asked excitedly.

"Listen." Pep unrolled and unfolded the paper and read gleefully in a whisper:

"To Commandant Mestres and the garrison of Ibiza!"

Knock! A rap on the front door startled us.

"*Quin es?*" I asked.

"Eulalia," in a hoarse whisper. I rushed to the door and opened it.

"Lock the door," she said, and from under her hatband drew a folded bit of paper. Pep laughed, waved his own. Eulalia, delightedly, "You have one, too." My arms around their shoulders, dancing. Oh, no. Not forgotten, Ibiza. Not done for, exactly, our friends in the woods. Cosmi, where are you, that you may read? We composed ourselves.

"TO COMMANDANT MESTRES AND THE GARRISON OF IBIZA," Pep reading.

"From the plane," Eulalia whispered. Slapped her on the shoulder. Yes, go on!

"The fighting planes of your government are above you. Abandon your abominable project which can bring you only disgrace and disaster. Come out with a white flag in token of surrender to the gunboat that is waiting off Formentera . . .

" . . . TO THE INHABITANTS OF IBIZA

"If Commandant Mestres fails to obey this summons and surrender, EVACUATE YOUR CITY.

(signed) "Your Countryman
"JUAN TORRES,
"Sergeant of Aviation."

17. The Fleet

LEAVING my wife and Eulalia Noguera laughing and chatting, new gales of laughter when one or the other would mention how the news might affect so and so, Pep Torres and I started down the street. We were changed, enjoying breathing and the motions of walking, bearing something very precious for all our friends. Still I could not ignore, having passed but a single vacant lot on which goat and small black hens searched the ground, that in his backyard stood Xumeu Ribas and that for him the garden had become a vast desert on which he stumbled sick with thirst. Had he heard? Pep and I paused at his doorway, looked at each other and passed on, momentarily dampened. Also, because we knew that possession of the bit of paper or dissemination of its contents was a punishable crime, we passed up the loquacious Barberet, owner of acres, goldfish and sweet potatoes. Sindik was working hard with a spoke-shave, pulling it, clearing it of shavings, sensitive calloused thumb exploring fragrant board, pulling harder.

"*Bon dia, compañeros*" (a word I want on my tombstone).

Large hand wipes forehead, deeply wrinkled, and shavings in broad black head of hair. He had not heard, and sadness paled his eyes.

"It's not right," he said. "Mestres won't surrender, and who will be blamed?" To honest Sindik,
carpenter and bonesetter who had never locked the
door of his house, to be unfair was a two-headed calf
seen stuffed in Sunday papers from Barcelona. We
left him working and saw his adult son Juan hurrying
with small-boy excitement also to tell him that the
plane had dropped a message, not knowing exactly
what it was.

Guillermo's shop was empty and the forge was cold,
so we went on to Coomi's and there we saw faces
smiling that had not smiled in many days, but the
women out back were silent, and were doubtfully
wagging their heads. Too many days of news print,
worry about Cosmi and Pep Salvador which they had
been obliged to conceal, had shaken their confidence.
They believed the rebels were winning, that the government was powerless and had forgotten them. But
Anna stirred herself and marshalled the others to
efforts I did not at first understand.

"We must make up all the beds," she said. "We
won't have room for everyone tonight."

Sure enough, as we were standing there, the first
auto from Ibiza came to rest in dust and squealing
brakes near the hotel door. Another and another were
behind it, each one laden with large women in black
and packed with children. They had passed a long
procession of mule and donkey carts which would
appear two hours later. Every taxi in Ibiza had been
hired, some families with relatives in San Antonio
had gone there, most of them were headed for Santa
Eulalia. As soon as the autos were emptied and the
pesetas counted and exchanged, the chauffeurs started

noisily, turned in whirls of dust and went full speed toward town again.

In front of Mousson's the blind woman sat, the sightless look of peace she habitually wore somewhat modified. The vibration of unusual happenings was in the air and dust all around her and the butcher stood in neutral coloring in his perpetual attitude of having missed a bus. The Royalty was absolutely clean, almost without flies, and whispering in the arbor, stood Isabel, Juanito's anxious mother, Marietta the diminutive old maid and in black, apart, the plump Marguerita, whose fiancé was imprisoned in the target for all planes, at the mercy of men whom fear would make vindictive and thirsty for his blood. Nevertheless came smiling in his white coat the matchless waiter Pedro, and gladly he brought beer and one for himself, and as we raised mugs, the three of us, no words were uttered that might add to the fright of the women near by, but a silent toast was offered. Shall you snicker if I tell you that three fools thought of liberty, and that "Long live the Republic, any republic if there can be more than one" was our unanimous and spontaneous thought?

The first man I told on the back street was old Vicent, the mason. His granddaughter Angeles was in Mallorca, and he had heard nothing. It was hardly necessary for him to hear. Angeles had had a small government job, clerk in some insignificant office, and she lived with relatives who worked hard for a living and were republicans. Vicent knew she must have lost her job, and that all her cousins had lost theirs and that eight of them had no money and were cursed with appetites. As he laid aside his pipe when it was smoked to ashes, so he placed on his wooden table his personal problem (Angeles being vitally himself) and nodded grimly and with honest satisfaction.

"Now we'll see what happens to men who want to shoot their neighbors," he said in his loud husky voice, with a wave of the hand toward the *Cuartel*, where no longer stood Guasch with rifle.

Francisco the cobbler, barber, musician and mechanic, old-time republican and exile under Primo was sitting happily in his shop. Not optimistically. All his life (except for a while in 1931 and at election time in 1935) his side had been getting it in the neck and to remain sane he had had to believe that progress was a slow, almost imperceptible process. "Juan Torres," he said, and smiled. The "countryman and sergeant of aviation" Juan Torres had been a boy in Las Salinas (the salt mines) who many years before had listened to Francisco in the noon hour and while unhurriedly shovelling salt, and clandestinely had taken in that grand old stuff set to music in the Marseillaise. "Juanito Torres," said Francisco lovingly, as he rose with his spectacles for wings and for the first time flew in spaces of the air. He sighed. No one knew better than Francisco that perhaps he had got Juan Torres in a peck of trouble, but he smiled and wished he were young again.

The pharmacy, with two blonde Catalan girl-republicans—but as I entered impetuously, in a corner was sitting Odila Nicolau, pale with faded freckles, staring without seeing at a framed certificate of registration in pharmacy, and instead of speaking of airplanes or republics I stammered and bought some medicine I needed not at all. Although I greeted Odila and she smiled bravely at me I did not try to comfort her, for I knew she would last as long as the stuff of which she was made and which daily was being consumed.

The message from the air had been countersigned by a major of aviation and the trade-mark of a printer in Mahon, Menorca, was stamped on the paper. Its effect on the Royalty clientele would have been ludicrous had there not been so much death in the air. The crowd of landowners and millionaires, the tight-faced contractors and relatives of men who had always been important, livid Dr. Torres (not white with fear but with loathing), soft-footed Dr. Gonzalez and a few resident foreigners who enjoyed hobnobbing with men they liked to consider their betters stayed behind closed shutters in their houses again, more emphatically invisible than they had been in the first days after the proclamation. In Can Xumeu a scattered few of the unprosperous reactionaries sat with heads propped up by hands and elbows, expecting the worst. The young cousins of the Ibiza aristocracy and their young fascist friends who had prospects with Don Abel Matutes, and a very few who were stirred by religious zeal, were filled with hysterical determination.

Mestres seemed to lose all sense of reality, or rather tried to stamp out reality and substitute his faked press reports. I cannot say how far he deceived himself and to what degree he was hoodwinked by his superiors in Palma and Seville. His first act was to forbid the civil population leaving the port town, as the government order had directed, and to station fascist volunteers on all the roads leading in and out

of the town with instructions to levy on each in-
habitant who had fled and tried to return a fine of
fifty *pesetas*. The escape of the leading republicans in
Santa Eulalia and San Carlos had not worried him
much in the beginning because he expected to have
plenty of time to hunt them down, and so many of
his followers were hunters. The advent of the message
from the air prompted him to organize large searching parties at once and send them into the woods and
the deserted mining region north of Santa Eulalia
and San Carlos, the two towns he could not subdue.
I saw Cosmi for a moment on Sunday, August 2,
when he had slipped into town to have a comfortable
shave in his apartment, that being a Sunday habit
he did not care to abandon. He was thoroughly alive.
The woods and high hills and rocky shore line (three
silent beaches between the cliffs) in which he and his
companions were hiding had been their haunts from
boyhood. He knew every man, woman and child who
was safe, and those to be avoided. I learned later that
Ferrer and Guarapiñada, storekeepers *par excellence*,
were improving their shining hours in manufacturing
ingenious grenades made of tin cans, dynamite caps,
black powder and scraps of iron. Pep Salvador's
daughter was having pleasant chats with loyal women
all through the dangerous area, and each of them,
working in the fields, wore a green petticoat and a
bright pink one. If there were Guardias and fascist
hunters within a mile or so the pink petticoat was
exposed as they worked. Captain Juan, suave smiles
and gentle syllables, was catching the choicest of fish,
large flaky sea bass and pike, and at certain hours

there were hot meals and cool wine to be had at convenient points near the Estañol shore.

Monday morning was a tense one in Santa Eulalia. Some of the men and women from Ibiza who had spent the week-end there, intimidated by threats and orders from Mestres, returned to the port city and were admonished and fined. The main street, before bus time, was almost deserted and in the Royalty, increasingly impatient, sat Colonel Fairchilds, the French couple with the unruly child, the Swedish nursemaid, and the very worried German Jew.

That afternoon about four o'clock two planes appeared and, after circling over Ibiza, flew over Santa Eulalia and streaming downward at an angle which carried them toward the hills to the westward came flocks of high white papers gleaming in the sun. Twenty minutes later Eulalia Noguera was at our house, excited and breathless, with a folded slip of paper in her hand. This second message was addressed to the population, and was long and eloquent. The government, it set forth, was humane and benevolent. The people of Ibiza were implored not to make it necessary to kill innocent persons, destroy their houses or lay waste their orchards and fields. They were asked to insist that the garrison surrender without resistance, in order that the people might be saved from suffering on account of the action of a few misguided and selfish men. At the end was another warning to noncombatants to evacuate the towns immediately if Mestres did not display the white flag on the fortress.

Primitivo's wife and Fernando's proud sister, suspecting that the fortress would be bombarded that day, had gone to Ibiza in order to be near their husband and brother, respectively, and share whatever scraps of stone and metal might be flying around. They returned in a donkey cart a few hours later, saying that the people of Ibiza were murmuring and protesting and that many had escaped, but that the fascists had posted guards and were restraining the people so far as possible from obeying the second warning. Also they said that the diet of the prisoners had been reduced to one piece of soggy bread each day and that the officers of the garrison had ordered the soldiers to sprinkle gunpowder all around the cells in which the prisoners were locked, in preparation for a possible attack from the air. What they did not tell, because neither Primitivo nor Fernando had mentioned the matter to them, was that both men had been informed that they were to be shot the next day.

All along the front street and the back street, hasty preparations for flight were being made. Women packed loaves of bread, meat, whatever food was portable into straw baskets. Rolls of quilts and blankets were bundled together and, amid scowls on the part of the Guardias and the very few armed fascists who did not know what action if any they should take, many families departed for the hills to spend the night beneath the trees. I should say that one-third of the families slept in the woods or with relatives in the country that night.

Sergeant Gomez made the rounds of the cafés with a proclamation from Commandant Mestres, announcing that Valencia and Barcelona were safely in the hands of the *Movimiento,* that all statements in the government pamphlets were false, and forbidding all citizens to act in accordance with the false messages "or to give credence to them in any way." The "enemy" planes had no ammunition, he stated, and no "enemy warships" were in Mediterranean waters. The navy, he announced, had placed itself heroically at General Franco's disposal.

One's memory of events is often confused, but in each life there are stillnesses into which one may re-enter long afterward to enjoy a familiar and brief eternity. Such an epoch was the night of August third-into-fourth in which external happenings were suspended. Santa Eulalia, living dream in which, with the effortless development of dream-scenario, we had reached the Royalty's flat roof, in chairs by small tables lounging—a company of quiet-seeking friends in a world a pot still cool and about to boil. My wife, Pep Torres, Francisco the patriot-shoemaker, old Miguel Tur (another longer peace to his thoughtful methodical soul) and a stray (not then but always) Dutch poet with a divine accomplishment. He could turn on or off, like switch with Yale lock (single key), his good sense and wide thinking and instruction, and substitute mild insanity. Deliberately he became for the benefit of Santa Eulalia the volatile buffoon, and shouted with eyes protruding and vacant smile "*'Dios*" to everyone he passed on the long main street. To individuals, one *'Dios*, for small groups two, for larger gatherings four, and small boys and adults shouted "*'Dios*" in reply. So the greeting and the name of the Most High God made running volleys up and down whenever he passed through the town. He elected to be outwardly crazy. And at table he ate daintily with forks (quite alone) and turned to right and left politely to speak social nothings to imaginary guests and offer plates and condiments to air companions.

That night Pietr chose to be sane and silent, and the plant of all our friendships flourished. Beneath the Royalty's roof in bedrooms the foreigners slumbered, and farther down, the café and kitchen were resoundingly empty. Juanito, his mother, Marguerita whose fiancé was in prison, and all the serving women were in the dark woods on the hill far behind us. Pedro, the white-coated perfect waiter, was among us and went up and down the stairs on soft-soled shoes to bring us cognac from the hidden store. And the familiar tree tops stood by empty houses, the town half-empty, and all of us were slowly acquiring the new importance of the sky. Our people, men and women of the town but now not in it, had always felt significance of sea, the small and tiny monsters with gills and fins and gleaming spots and stripes of Sheba's Queen, calm nights in dories, nights of terror in the storm. The hills they had known, the valley of the shadow of life —and now the sky. I was thinking of El Greco and of Father Clapés, the seraph-faced young priest, to whom Heaven in all its glory had been peopled with endless possibilities.

An orange shattered arc of falling star.

"*Olé*," said Pedro at the head of the stairs, and tilted, then recovered, his tray of glasses of reflected starlight.

Across the street in front of the Casa Rosita we saw an orange tomcat glide silently to the eucalyptus tree, and approaching from the direction of Can Xumeu his brother, the panther-like Simon. And they sat with tails switching, keeping tomcat distance (glint of amber eyes) as the Formentera light flashed dash-dot-dot. White buildings half empty and the shadows of trees. The fugitives in the hills like Joshua's thin host, afraid to invade until their own white walls should miraculously fall to the ground. In other words, the dawn.

Just after daylight a number of the townspeople straggled back uncertainly, in the hope that they could reach their houses before they were missed by the Guardia Civil, but the Guardias had remained out of sight through the night, did not molest us sitting on the roof so near the *Cuartel* or take official notice of the exodus. Before bus time I met Sergeant Gomez, and he tried to smile as he greeted me and held back so much he was longing to explain that I was on the point of risking everything on an impulse and offering to testify, in case he found himself in difficulties later, that he had acted under duress and with conscious humanity. For that sin of omission I have asked pardon many times.

The sergeant's errand that morning concerned Colonel Fairchilds and family. A British destroyer was expected (I have neglected to mention that the Colonel was refused transportation by the French), and the sergeant believed the British would take Americans, since they spoke the same language.

"Did I wish to go?"

"No, thank you," I said. "Ibiza is *un poc mi pajes*" (a little my own country).

"I knew that," he said wistfully. "The people were very glad when you arrived."

I told the colonel about the British destroyer and sent someone to inform Mrs. Gramkow, and not long afterward there was an excited powwow, hasty packing of valises, and Alice Frankfurter set out in search of gasoline, which she found and purchased, in spite of the fact that there had been none for several days. Mrs. Gramkow had spent the night in the hills, having persuaded the honest José and Catalina at Can Josepi that they should take the same precaution, and Edmundo, who had been employed by her at odd times as motorboat chauffeur, had gone with them. Francisco Guasch particularly disliked Edmundo and that night had taken upon himself a duty which the Guardias preferred to leave undone, namely, to slink through the woods with his rifle and find out who had disobeyed the Commandant's orders. He came upon Edmundo and, with rifle in hand, said he had been authorized to draft able-bodied men into Mestres' service in order to defend the island against the government, if necessary.

"Come with me," Francisco said.

There is no language like the Spanish for invective, and Edmundo (black shirt, fists clenched) explored all its possibilities. He raved and cursed and damned Francisco Guasch until he was out of breath, turned his back to him as Joselito would have turned from a bull he had fixed with the cape, and walked away. Edmundo's tirade had carried with it so much force of language and defiance that it took the armed Guasch several second to recover his wits. Then he began shooting at Edmundo's dim and unhurried back. Four times he fired, into darkness that contained his neighbors' wives and children. Edmundo began to *ook*. The Ibicenco *ook* is an ancient traditional battle cry which is more derisive and not less terrifying than the warwhoop of the American Indians, and on all the hillsides, back and forth, the young men and old men took up the cry until roosters all over the island began crowing to add to the unearthly din. What Guasch did is not certain, except that he was not seen in the woods again that night. Edmundo was in town at daylight, roaring and looking for him, not with gun he had never used but with a hand-carved Ibicenco dagger. Young Andres, socialist and painter, obstructed his way and drew him inside his father's small café. He implored Edmundo to wait just another day. If the government forces were coming, they would need the help of loyal men in town, perhaps. Why throw one's life away, even for the rare privilege of killing Francisco Guasch, when before the week was over the tables might be turned?

"I don't want someone else to kill him. I want to do it myself," Edmundo roared. Then Magdalena, tearful and distracted mother, became suddenly calm. She went to Edmundo, took his knife in her beautiful hands, and said:

"Let me keep this, Edmundo. You shall have it at the proper time. I give you my word, you shall have it back if ever we are free again, or whenever we are sure that we are lost."

Grumbling, Edmundo acquiesced.

As the morning wore on and no planes appeared, nearly everyone returned home and the town lost much of its emptiness. Around the Royalty there was much bustling preparation—the Fairchilds and Miss

Frankfurter packing, Pedro lugging suitcases back
and forth, Mrs. Gramkow scattering broad a's and
indecision like six-inch-wide confetti, José and his
mule cart from Can Josepi loaded and in readiness to
transport as much of the baggage as the auto would
not contain.

Early that evening we all said good-bye to the departing Americans and saw them go chugging toward
the port. José of Can Josepi having preceded them
with a cartload of their baggage. Juanito, proprietor
of the Royalty, set out for the Arabie road at once to
recover a lot of groceries and supplies he had sold
Mrs. Gramkow and which she had not used. All of us
by that time had exhausted our supply of Spanish
money. No banks were open to cash our checks, and
the merchants of Santa Eulalia, hard up for *pesetas* as
they were, and not knowing when they could replenish
their diminishing stock of goods, had without exception assured us and made us deeply feel that anything they had was ours for the asking. We could pay
a month later, or a year or any other time that suited
our convenience.

That evening Mrs. Gramkow and her sons came
rattling back to Santa Eulalia, making null and void
no end of elaborate farewells. Her dancing with naval
officers as a débutante in Baltimore and Boston had
not prepared her for the sight and odor of a crowded
destroyer, its meagre deck space packed with refugees
and chaotically unassorted baggage.

August 4. The morning as now you know it to be,
the bus and the heat of noon, the *Diario* in the
Royalty (but empty again), the hearty lunch with

wine, the *siesta* and with the afternoon breeze, *olé*, a
plane, over Ibiza and then straight for us, our way.
It skirted the shore and was shot at by Harpo (concealed in a cave on the *Vei Isglesi* cliff) circled and
passed high over the slope behind the town, near
Rigoberto's house, and there let slip wind-blown
parabolas of messages. Away, toward San Miguel.
No, turning. Back to us again. I was on Cosmi's roof
with others, including Marc Colomar, and as Francisco Guasch and another fascist fired at our visitor,
Marc from the other side of the broad chimney
waved his broad white apron back and forth. Did
the aviator see it? Ah, yes. Perhaps not. Surely yes.
Back over our roof (swish swish of white flag) and
all of us felt better. Not only a visitation but an
acknowledgment. The town had made its double
reply, futile bullets, white denials. Not many minutes
later Eulalia had the message. Her sick brother had
found the first one, and it had been taken away by
the sergeant, but the boy gave it up so reluctantly
that Gomez did not search him, and the final score
was Noguera 7, Gomez 1.

"TO THE SOLDIERS OF THE GARRISON OF IBIZA

"Your legal government expects your loyalty and
hereby orders and authorizes you to shoot your officers
and any fascist officials who persist in claiming authority."

I did not mention that in the previous messages
the population was urged to refrain from revenge
upon fascists, but to rest assured that the enemies of
the Republic would be dealt with justly and punished "according to the degree of their responsibility
for and participation in the *Movimiento*."

This message and its negative result cheered Commandant Mestres no end. He was convinced, and so were all the officers, high priests and civilian collaborators, that the government had no ammunition. It was difficult for them to believe that their enemies could be patient and try to impress with forbearance and humanity a population that had been for centuries accustomed to coercion. Of course, the soldiers of the garrison had been carefully guarded from contacts with the population and had seen or heard nothing to convince them that the cause the great majority of them favored had a chance. To shoot an officer openly would be suicide, and the officers took good care not to give the men an opportunity to pop them off on the sly.

In truth, I myself was beginning to be doubtful. The thankful elation I had felt when the first of the planes arrived was giving place to an anxiety I would admit only to myself. I was less in fear of arrest than my Ibicenco friends and therefore could speak more freely, and for this reason I felt it my duty to repeat in houses and cafés my testimonials of faith in the people of Spain and their government. This I did, but on August 4th I did it with some misgivings. How could the government spare armed forces and warships for small and distant Ibiza? I asked myself. Would it not be good strategy to bluff a little in districts that could not at first be protected? But would a government directed by men of high ideals advise helpless soldiers to shoot their officers if it was intended to leave them flat? You know how it is, when you want so badly to have something happen. You are afraid to let yourself go, to believe too thoroughly,

for fear you cannot bear the disappointment. You
have moments of thinking you were not born for too
much luck, that somehow you are destined to pick
the losing side, that you are an awful sucker to say
that right will prevail. That was August 4th. Call it
yellow if you like, but when I was stopped by
Angeles' great aunt—if I could reproduce for you
somehow the tones of her voice as she said, her hands
clasped rather prayerfully:

"What do *you* think, Señor Paul?"

And I knowing where her heart was, in a starving
hut in Palma. And reflecting that if I loved Angeles so
much, how much more that old woman was feeling . . .

I told her I believed Ibiza would be saved, and
shortly afterward Mallorca, that soon she would be
able to communicate with her grand-niece and that
Angeles would come through proudly, and never rat,
survive a diet of roots and herbs if that was all she
had, and that Spain should be proud of such daughters and that such young girls were Spain—but in the
back of my mind was a gnawing. Am I, knowing all
this woman has to suffer, tossing on the heap of stones
that bruise her body my pebbles of insincerity?

When a few moments later Mousson's blind woman
spoke to me, calling me by name for the first time,
and saying, "What do *you* think, Señor Paul?" I
broke down, and gave her the works, not my hesita-
tions, mind you. Then and there I decided that a man
who could not believe in the right was a damned poor
stick and a worm. Never mind the circumstantial
evidence. To hell with history! Those messages from
heaven were my gospel, and in the excitement attend-
ant upon being born again and all that, I talked too

much once more. I was standing in the doorway of the Royalty when I heard the fascist owner of the building whispering with Dr. Torres and Mallorqua Pete (now fascist radio expert) and the bad-smelling schoolmaster.

"The only thing that will save Spain is a firm hand. The army has power . . ."

"The only thing that will save Spain is to exterminate the fascists—exterminate them," I said loudly, and again I saw that Rigoberto (who had been worried enough about my safety before) was in hearing-distance.

"Elliot," he said, the moment we were alone, "for the love of God, control yourself. . . ."

"My eye!" I shouted, this time exultantly, for I was facing Tagomago, and Tagomago was just then handing out a caravan of gifts that made all the tribute received in a lifetime by Genghis Khan look tawdry and second-rate. The cliff I had seen so often and whose contours I had admired so much, the lighthouse that had welcomed me (straight searching unwinking orange blaze to the bridge of the Barcelona boat) had just produced, was in the act of producing (remember the steady ocean motion)

> One grey destroyer
> Another
> One light cruiser
> One submarine
> Another
> Another
> And another.

I shall not enumerate the hearts that were thankful

and those others who were deathly afraid, those whose faith had been rewarded and the purveyors of print whose lies turned belly-up like shot fish. Only shall I mention Cosmi, who had seen that sea procession from his hiding place near Estañol and whose joy was so great that he could express it only in action. He jumped into a rowboat alone and started rowing after the loyal fleet, on the magnificent thousand-to-one shot that those lean grey vessels would somewhere stop and wait for him and permit him to serve his country.

18. The Man Hunt

THERE were so many happenings the day of August 5th that the mood of tense and fearful waiting was lost and could with difficulty be remembered. It has been said truthfully that the immediate past is most remote from us. When the grey warships and kitetail of submarines filed past the town, Tagomago to Cala Llonga, Santa Eulalia looked like the finale of a first act in a widespread opera. Familiar figures stood gaping on the main street, in groups that seemed to have been pre-arranged, and from the doorways of white houses on the slopes (boys on rooftops) women in attitudes of interrupted housework watched and trembled. Pep Torres, Ferrer, Vicente Cruz, Costa the mason, deaf Antonio Cosmi, the eloquent-eyed Catalan who played the triangle and castanets, old patched Vicent, the young painter, Andres, and the Royalty's headwaiter were about the only ones left of the republican men, and their joy was too complete for demonstrations. Eulalia Noguera, Catalina's irrepressible aunt, Señora Ferrer, Magdalena (the painter's mother), the cool white-hot Maria on the farm near Can Josepi, the statuesque Eulalia who carried water jars—those women young and old, to whom freedom was a fresh clean garment they had never soiled and in which they had sewn careful

stitches, reacted as did the men. Our turn is coming.
No excesses.

The trees were green and the shadows grey on the
old *Cuartel*, but not greener or greyer than the faces
of Francisco Guasch and Harpo who stood in the
archways with rifles in their hands. The bug-eyed
portero, who since the day the first plane appeared
had found himself a uniform coat, went muttering
terza rima along the way, not afraid but disgusted
with the turn events had taken. He had been led to
believe that people's government had ceased to exist
and his prominent eyes saw long strings of warships
which, according to him, should not be there. Muttering Homerically. Sergeant Gomez was on his balcony,
leaning against the rail indifferently, wishing it all
were over. To die like a Spaniard, of course, but the
ache to explain, to understand, to place his heart one
hundred meters distant and wearily take the gun
from those who were missing it and skillfully pop and
flop. Farewell, Madrid.

"The sergeant's a good fellow," men had said who
now were hunted in the woods, and did they know
how carefully he had not found them?

The women, except the small handful I have enu-
merated, were silent, sighing with apprehension. No
shooting. Resumption of mail and household supplies. I even heard Anna Cosmi say quite truthfully
that she didn't care whether she became English or
Italian. What was the difference? I didn't attempt to
explain.

Guillermo the blacksmith, whose mind worked so
quickly in reading a guitar part, remembering the
spots on dominoes, sketching patterns for iron gates,

and whose deeper thoughts rose slowly and infrequently mudfish and tilted flatly to descend again, had reached a conclusion. The fascist volunteers, Nicolau and Francisco Guasch, had been too eager to take up arms and hunt their neighbors, he said. Like old man Serra, who had hanged himself, they had been guilty of exaggeration. That was as far as he would go, except that he refused flatly to leave his house and take his family of wife, seven splendid boys and grouchy reactionary father-in-law to the woods because of possible bombs from the air. *Cacahouettes* (peanuts) he called them. The reason for his firm stand in that matter was that his father-in-law rebuked him constantly for keeping his family in danger. Guillermo, little as he cared for politics, would have supported any government that might bomb his father-in-law.

We all waited expectantly, after the fleet had rounded Cala Llonga, hoping to hear the boom of cannon. Silence. Disappointment. Act One over for the day. The town, except for Sindik working feverishly, talked fearfully and gleefully. So many important characters had been absent from rehearsal, and not a fascist in sight except the two supernumeraries who held rifles and controlled their bowels perilously in front of the *Cuartel*. The Royalty absolutely clean. No. I am mistaken. Here for the first time, tanned and beaming from his farm across the river, is Ignacio Riquer, richest man on the countryside, owner of well inexhaustible and two dozen prize Holstein cows.

"*Bon dia*, Don Ignacio."

"Good morning" (in English).

An involuntary glance at where the battleships no longer are.

A smile and a shrug of the shoulders. "*Venga que venga,*" this time in Spanish because *Venga que venga* means at least sixteen times more than "Come what may."

From store striding most cordially, Toni Ferrer. "*Bon dia,* Don Ignacio." Impact of blacksmith's hand. "Glad to see you" (meaning that if anyone tries to lay hands on you, they'll have me to fight, and all the other men around here, too). Don Ignacio, understanding, broadly smiles. Syphilis was *nada,* Madrid much fun. Land not neglected. Town full of friends. If he died for being cousin of Mestres, *nada.* Still he was mildly amused by the conspicuous absence of Don Rafael Sainz. Better to be drinking, and much better plump wife banging piano than Sainz's tight-lipped Secora constantly praying, and pregnant every year.

I do not think Don Ignacio was at all ashamed of his cousin Mestres. He thought the commandant was doing what was natural for a commandant to do.

"Spanish people much fool," was the way he summed it up.

After noon over the city of Ibiza four planes came wheeling in that casual and non-military fashion that marked them as Spanish. No V, no hollow square, no four abreast or two and two, simply four planes that took care not to bump one another, then two of them headed for Santa Eulalia and two for San Antonio. This time, when Harpo raggedly fired there were outspoken protests everywhere. The planes soared over the main street, turned, and when they were over the slopes behind the town let drop a stream of messages, but a difference was seen at once in the way the papers came down. They zigzagged erratically, were awkward and larger.

"Newspapers," someone shouted. And newspapers they were. Newspapers from Valencia, crudely printed, and on the front page large headlines. They bore the date of the day before and announced that "*Hoy tomaremos Ibiza*" (Today we shall take Ibiza). A three-column cut showed a company of cheering sailors and civilians with guns aboard a destroyer, decks crowded. It was announced that an expedition from Valencia and Barcelona, with one transport, two destroyers, four submarines, six hydroplanes, five thousand men, eighteen portable radio sets, a stated number of shells, cartridges and bombs, under the command of Don Alfredo Bayo, captain of aviation, had set out from Valencia amid the cheers of an admiring populace. That the plan was to take Ibiza first, then proceed to Mallorca.

Coincidentally, by means of the mysterious island telegraph, we learned that the planes had dropped over Ibiza a demand that non-combatants be evacuated from the city within two hours.

I took my copy of the newspaper to a quiet corner, read it carefully and tried sanely to estimate its importance. Evidently it was propaganda of the crudest sort, quite as blatant as the stuff that had been passed out by Mestres. Nevertheless, it seemed to contain a germ of truth. I had seen the fleet described in the front-page article. It must have set out from somewhere on the mainland, and I knew Valencia, Alicante and Barcelona, in fact the whole Levantine and Catalonian shore were traditionally republican in sentiment. All my friends were jubilant, and I did nothing to discourage them, but having worked in print factories where similar bilge had been manufactured (with especial reference to the *New York Herald* in Paris), I was discouraged and depressed. I had such high hopes for the distinguished conduct of the people's government of Spain that I had foolishly thought its publicists might have seen the folly of undermining the people's faith by continually misleading them. Also I had grave fears for the success of a military expedition the strategy and resources of which had been published in advance. On the other hand, if the government could afford to pay attention to such an unimportant place as Ibiza its plight could not be so grave as the fascists had claimed. I told myself that I must keep in mind that we knew less than nothing. In fact, I used the old methods of insuring myself against too devastating a disappointment.

For a while it seemed as if my misgivings were well founded. The afternoon came to an end in a superb sunset, the glow of which threw a halo of light around the church on the hill and was reflected in the southeastern sky behind Formentera. Stragglers from Ibiza arrived in carts and on foot (there was no more gasoline for civilians). The warships did not reappear and there was no bombardment. Half the inhabitants of the larger towns were in the woods; hysteria was spreading among those who remained at home. In Santa Eulalia one or two of the fascist bodyguards, chauffeurs, etc., came out of seclusion and laughingly read Mestres' new proclamation, to the effect that the "enemy" had no ammunition and that the so-called expedition was composed of adventurers and communists who had intended to rob the people of the island. When the morning of August 6th passed without incident, the lesser members of the Royalty's clique assembled for beer at noon and the republicans, who the day before had rejoiced, were doubtful and sad. Eulalia Noguera's family were still camping on the hill a half mile west of us, but she reached our house before seven o'clock and did not fail to produce for me a new and beautiful ancient melody each day.

Thursday afternoon I was in the Royalty, playing checkers with Juanito, when the bombardment of Ibiza began. We heard the rumble of the naval guns and the sharper explosion of bombs dropped from the planes.

Juanito and I stood on the corner, gazing toward the Cala Llonga divide and listening to the ominous cannonade. It was not a heavy bombardment, perhaps two dozen shells and half a dozen bombs.

"Murderers," Juanito's mother said. He must have seen the angry look on my face, for he looked at me in a deprecatory way and I remained silent. It was difficult to keep in mind that the women of Spain had been kept in a backward state so many centuries that the remarkable restraint and patience of the government leaders were lost on them. Nearly all of them felt that in opening fire the government had sinned. In half an hour the bombardment was over, and it was not long before we learned that no one had been hurt and little damage done. Primitivo's wife and mother-in-law had continued their sewing on their little balcony, pretending not to hear the sound of guns, knowing their husband and son-in-law was in a cell in the conspicuous fortress and that gunpowder had been heaped around the stone floor. When I told them no one had been wounded, they smiled proudly and thanked me. One of the houses that had been damaged belonged to Guillermo's brother but the family had escaped unhurt. In fact, they had vacated the house less than an hour before it was hit.

Two interpretations were current that evening concerning the lack of casualties and property loss. The fascists ridiculed government marksmanship, the republicans said Captain Bayo did not want to kill innocent people or destroy the city he was soon to occupy. Not more than half a dozen families slept in our town that night—Ferrer, Jaume the carpenter (whose wife could scarcely walk), old Vicent and his sister on the back street, Guillermo (to annoy his father-in-law), and the Pauls. At dusk I noticed that the women and children were being removed from the *Cuartel* of the Guardia Civil, and that many of them were offered refuge in republican homes.

Late that evening Pep Torres, Juanito of the Royalty, Pedro the headwaiter and the taxi-driver Durban were in our house. Pep had his violin, I had my accordion. Both Pep and Juanito had good voices and knew plenty of songs. We were unrestrained in making noise because the Rosa family from upstairs had gone to Paja's father's house in Cala Llonga. Mateo Rosa had found it prudent to join the fugitives in the San Carlos woods. Edmundo spent his nights prowling through the woods in the hope of meeting Francisco Guasch, who had distinguished himself the day before by standing in the midst of women and children refugees on the hill and firing at the airplanes.

At one o'clock in the morning we heard a tap on the door. I opened it and saw a strange man standing there. Pep Torres recognized him at once and when he beckoned followed him to the dark street. Juanito turned pale. In a few minutes, Pep returned, also pale and distraught. We waited until he had time to compose himself. There was trouble in San Carlos, he said, at last. The people there were on the point of rising against Mestres. In fact, large numbers of men (including all our friends and led by Guarapiñada who had disappeared from his store) were already in open rebellion, armed with knives and (hear the echo, Americans) pitchforks from the farms. The priest and his father, who was known as the island's most pronounced fanatic, were in the church with rifles. Also the Guardia Bravo had said that the next day the fascists were going to draft all the young men of Santa Eulalia into their service, forcibly if necessary.

The night messenger I was soon to know and admire. He was the hitherto inconspicuous friend of Pep Salvador who was one of the very few communists with *bona-fide* party standing.

The next morning, having in mind what we had heard the night before, I suggested to Pep Torres that I had better take Peanut for his daily swim and that Pep, Juanito, Durban and their friends of military age and republican sentiments would do well to organize a picnic without advertising where it would be held. Pep could not consent to this without a struggle. It was hard for him to hide when he was right.

"Just an hour or two," I urged. "Something surely will happen today."

Returning from the swim near the river's mouth I

met Marc Colomar, the Barberet's assistant, Antonio the young barber and the strong young son of Antonia of the fisherman's bar. They were hurrying southward along the shore, but Marc stopped long enough to explain that Francisco Guasch and a lieutenant from Ibiza had tried to round them up for the fascist army. They had no food, no blankets, no fixed destination.

"Can I help?" I asked.

Marc smiled. "We'll be all right," he said.

The small boy beside me watched with large greyblue eyes the grown young men go hurriedly away, knowing they were being driven from their homes. There is nothing children understand more keenly than injustice, be it applied to them, to old men or women, to a dog or mule or cow.

"Does someone want to kill Marc?" Peanut asked.

"Someone wants Marc to kill someone else," I said. "He doesn't want to do it, so he's going away."

"Do they want him to kill some good people?"

"Yes. His friends," I said.

"Oh."

The child's "oh" carried slowly along the familiar roadway made by wheels of mulecart filled with seaweed. Between rows of vines, right angle of stone wall, sweet potato field in which Sindik, blue shirt drenched with sweat, was concentrating fiercely, foot on spade to drive it down. Loam rich and dark. Plants green. Now very high seemed Santa Eulalia's hill, cliff rising upward and us at the foot. In his carpenter shop honest Sindik could no longer escape the facts he tried to keep out of his mind. Things happened in blankness on blank street before the windows. The

town around him, deserted, caused his broad forehead
to tighten from pressure inside and he had gone to
work harder alone in the field. I did not call to him
as we passed, for his back, bent over spade, was not
to be called to, lightly. Had I known what his solitude
was costing him I should have shouted, raved. For on
deserted dusty street, between Guillermo's cold forge
and the Barberet's closed shop Juan Sindik, the carpenter's older son and principal helper, had been accosted by a fascist lieutenant and offered what he
dearly loved, a gun. A gun to shoot with and a day
or two away from the grind of the shop. To Juan's
simple mind, the proposal was alluring. He had never
shot at men, had never seen communists or robbers,
but he longed for the slopes where the smell of bay
and thyme was sharper than sawdust. He was a simple young man who liked to do what was asked of him.
Without knowing what a fascist or communist was,
he became a member of the fascist army, and in a
thousand cities sound-film bands rejoiced. There were
street parades, tanks tumbling, gas-masked figures
scurried, planes swooped down. Boyishly smiling,
goose stepping, broad Sindik face, *heil* Hitler. Upturned face of carpenter's son who instead of being
old when young was young at twenty-three, smiling
Juan under balcony of dog-faced Mussolini. Trium-
phant message to Quiepe de Llano at Seville. . . .
Father, bonesetter, carpenter, saviour of so many
lives on the countryside, unknowingly bending over
spade.

I enter the main road, dusty in the heat of noon,
refreshed by swim, awed by exodus of youth, hushed
by honest man's back, inwardly sick with waiting.

Where were those planes and ships and guns? Where
were those volunteers, shells, radio sets? Did none of
those men at sea know that on land were men who
were desperately waiting? I walked through the
empty town. Loriano Barrau, Barcelona *prix de Rome*
1881, was painting a lyrical Ibiza scene. Villa, assorted flowers and potted geraniums—blank. Ditto,
a few feet back. Small villa, Derek Rogers and blond-
Irish wife. Blank houses, the blank mansion of Ignacio
Riquer, blank house of Francisco Guasch, the blank
hot fountain in the plaza in front of womanless *Cuartel*. Royalty devoid. In Can Andres pasteboard sign
regretfully slanted over cockeyed mirror behind eight-
foot zinc bar, *Café 15 centimos*. Coffee had always
been 10 *centimos*, but coffee was scarce, sugar was
scarce and coffee without sugar impossible. Local
cognac only mildly impossible. Young Andres sick,
as I was. Not asking "*Que piensa?*" because he knew
what I thought and did not want to make me say it
painfully. Sensitive boy, sick from fever of public
ownership of natural resources and mother weeping
because he would not run. Cosmi's empty, except for
Antonio, impressively and quite grandly deaf in
kitchen, forbidden dagger in belt. Lunch well under
way for handful of possibly unfleeing workmen. Women
chattering in woods and moaning. In Mousson's doorway, blind aunt. "Oh, Señor Paul . . ." The question.
The troubled and worthy old woman's question.
What was dropping just now from the grinder of my
brain?

Should I have said, "Old sightless woman, I suspect we are all washed up (*foutu*). Dust and gravel
for your belly. Drain water to sluice it down. Those

warships you did not see yesterday, I do not see to-day."

Can Xumeu. There was really a desolate place. Wife in dull black unweeping in kitchen door, sallow daughter fungus, Xumeu in patio-Gethsemane. The reading for the day had to do with the man of many talents, the man with only a few, and the man with one, and if Xumeu was inattentive it was because he had a graver question to decide. Should he have been dead already, and public telephone in other hands?

My own house, *Can Pedro es Mallorqui'*. There coolness and woman's patience. Not a word about absence of cannon, nor even about Pep Torres who had not gone to the woods but had sat all morning grimly, taking off his aching head, bouncing it on the wall, catching it mechanically, replacing it, bouncing it again.

Lunch. *Siesta* which I for one did not enjoy. No sleep was in me, and much heat pressed down. In the late afternoon, a truck filled with soldiers from Ibiza and containing ex-Captain Nicolau, red face, loud voice, rifle in hand. In the plaza he descended and spoke for a few minutes with black-mantilla wife whose eyes gleamed with satisfaction. The truck went toward San Carlos and the manhunt was on. Those men, the best of Santa Eulalia and San Carlos, whose spirit had prevented them from condoning treason, were about to be sacrificed. No use to say this sort of thing has happened many times before. No avail to pretend that because I was a guest in that country its tragedies concerned me less than disaster might at home. I was saved by Eulalia Noguera who approached the standing truck and looked at the soldiers from left to right, sadly shaking her head and saying softly, "Well, I had known there were cowards and *ladrones* in Ibiza, but not such a contemptible cartload as this." Then she laughed aloud, threw her head back and laughed sweetly, like an Ibicenco song, and slapped her thigh in merriment until the truckload of soldiers and volunteers began to move nervously like hens in a crate. Suddenly she had seen how frightened they were, how their knees were knocking, how the machine-gun mounted on the front of the truck, the rifles, commanders, sharp-shooters and absence of government fleet were not enough. Could she picture her cousin Cosmi thus? Pep Salvador? Edmundo? Uncle Edmundo? She laughed until someone led her away, and meanwhile, her growing in my heart and that of Pep Torres, my mind turned a flip-flop and I was sure that relief was coming. I was breathless. We must have music that night, loud music, long after ten-thirty. I must go at once and comfort the blind woman and Vicent's old sister.

Toward the north, where the Arabie road branched off, I saw Maria-Moll Pitcher, farm girl with slender beauty hidden beneath cumbersome clothes. She was walking rapidly toward Cosmi's famous well, from which point pink petticoat gleamed like evening star for eyes of Maria-Belle Livingstone, daughter of Pep Salvador, and I knew that before that truck got started, plastered with Eulalia's laughter, our friends in the woods would know of it and take what steps they could.

Food. Darkness. Star patterns. Tenor song about the young man from Granada whose father told him regretfully that the girl he wanted to marry was his half sister, and who mourned until the last verse when his mother cleared it all up for him by admitting he was not his father's son. Good song. Pep alive again. Juanito and Pedro shaking their heads at first and saying, "It's true that Americans are crazy. The Señora buys tomatoes and carries them down empty street. They go right ahead with music, no matter what."

Soon all of them gay in a thoroughly deserted town.

19. The Bombardment

ON THE morning of August 8th we saw the fleet again. The two destroyers cleared Cala Llonga first, followed by the transport and the four submarines. There were few men on the street to watch them. Ferrer spat disgustedly and turned away, Vicente Cruz tried unsuccessfully to look hopeful, Pep Torres went wordlessly back to our house. The warships were following the course they would take if they were headed for Mallorca, standing out about a mile from the shore as they passed Santa Eulalia. They disappeared in due time behind Tagomago and left me struggling with a bitterness I could not control. No ammunition, haphazard leadership, foolish boastful publicists. What would happen now to Cosmi and that brave company in the San Carlos woods?

The answer was not long in coming. Within an hour another truckload of fascists passed through the town, shouting feebly and raggedly (at a prompting sign from their noncommissioned officers) "*Viva España.*" The outlook was so hopeless that all I could wish was that our friends would stone and pitchfork as many truckloads as possible before dying in their turn. Whether Ferrer's ingenious grenades would explode or not, I did not know. Neither did Ferrer. It had been his first job of ammunition manufacturing.

Dead silence in the street. Heat, miraculous and beneficent sun on white plaster walls. Dust settling.

Filed past us very sadly Sergeant Gomez, rifle slung. All my desperate wishes swarmed like bees above his head. Be a man, *Madrileño! Hombre!* A while ago you were as good as dead. Please, for my sake, do as you are longing to do. Take a pot shot at a truckload of fascists, release those two good men who walk behind you, the Guardias Ferrer and Jimenez. Freckled-faced Ferrer with flushed face, downcast eyes, almost tears. To be or not to be Jimenez. Your question is a simple one, now, and you are giving the wrong answer. Their footsteps down the street. Concrete sidewalk by the Royalty, silent dust passing Can Andres, the butcher Mousson's closed shop, the post office (where green-eyed Maria sat in doorway), long step over drainage ditch, heels on concrete again. For the first time Sindik's carpenter shop has no sound of hammers or whine of the lathe.

They go. They are carrying the prescribed field equipment and in the holsters at their belts a parcel of my faith in mankind. Hell! I am not the one who has to die. What am I, anyway? The truth is hard and shameful. In setting out to tell the truth, yesterday I funked the fence, for I did not mention that in my dusty progression through the street I picked up a copy of the *Diario* and found that the United States, the good old freedom-loving *Estados Unidos*, was preserving "an attitude of strict impartiality." My beloved country! I cannot, one faintly articulate observer on an anguished isle, set you right, but let no one say that I did not try. . . . Are filing down the street. . . . With rifles. The priest and his father in the church tower, San Carlos, with rifles. Our Father Who art in Heaven, give us this day our daily round of ammunition, and blunt pitchforks to our enemies.

Eulalia Noguera again. Especially we pray God to bless our sister Eulalia. She is not weeping, but grim. She is taut, like a mare before the race.

"I think they have disembarked," she whispered.

"They've gone to Palma," I said. No more hope.

"*Tio* Mateo (Uncle Mateo Rosa) went out last night in Edmundo's boat. There's something afoot," she said.

"They've gone," I repeated.

Another truckload of fascists. Cheers feebler. Dark coals of murder in Eulalia's eyes.

"Bravo, the Guardia, has deserted," Eulalia said when the dust had died down. "He's alone, without a gun, on the hill." She pointed back to the western ridge, near which, in groves, the townspeople who had no relatives near by in the country were camping. Old Frog Bravo, scars of burns from Cosmi's lamp still on his neck. The slow one, never completely neat like his comrades. The mind unbrilliant and plodding but solving the equation by placing his life on the scales. Mrs. Bravo ashes. Hillside ashes and rusted cans. Trees no more, nor smell of shrubs. *Venga que venga.*

The emptiness of Cosmi's café was a refinement of the emptiness of the town. Shutters were drawn, doors closed, and in the dimness sat Antonio, dark eyes glowing. He had let the charcoal fire go out, had removed whatever food he had on hand. Merely on the chance that some fascists that noon would demand to be fed. He had arranged the disposition of his forces methodically. All the women were in the hills, forming a rear guard. His forces armed with dagger he had placed in a chair in the darkest corner. His strategy was simple, he would tell the fascists there was nothing to eat in the house and that he didn't know where food could be obtained, and in case they found some supplies, he would assure them he had forgotten how to cook.

We endured a long afternoon (another truckload), and even Eulalia did not know what was happening. Her sources of news were all elsewhere, and her brother, only recently recovered from pneumonia, had caught cold in the night air. That obscured other issues. The love she had for that frail boy was one of the most catastrophic emotions I have seen a young woman possessed of. About four o'clock there was a tapping on my door and Toniet Pardal, who was acting as caretaker of Don Carlos Roman's house on the fisherman's point, held up smilingly an octopus in several shades of greenish-grey and brown. He knew I had no money and was thinking happily that some time when he was an old man I would send him a postcard from America, or any distant port he longed to see. I was glad to have something to occupy my time, and octopus in Catalan style is a delicious dish, in wartime or out. I fashioned myself a stout paddle, took the creature to a flat rock by the seaside and proceeded to pound the tentacles as one in California pummels abalone to insure tenderness. And I pounded to a good American army song which runs:

I'd rather be a stinkweed in a nigger's back yard
Than a brigadier general in the National Guard.

And between taps of the paddle on non-resisting dinner-to-be I tried to translate that excellent figure of speech into Ibicenco and make it rhyme with *fascista*. A little later when I cut up the octopus preparatory to cooking it, I saw that the brute was so big it would make three dinners for the hearty eaters of my family, and I was wondering who was left in town to receive a portion of it. No candidate then presented himself, so I heated the large skillet, put in two tablespoonfuls of olive oil, and when the pan was smoking I dumped in the *poulpe*. When the pieces were well browned, I put a little bacon into the hot center, let the grease fry out, then added a cupful of *Marques de Argentera* (*tinto*) and let simmer slowly. Slowly bubbling, with especial care, for I wanted so badly to pay strict attention and watch slow bubbling, smelling tones of bacon and the sea and the wine from sunny slopes and thinking after all that it was a simple dish to make since worthy pig the sea had been working on the octopus for at least a dozen years and the sun had conjured vines from the earth and grapes that gave wine of an inimitable flavor. . . .

Jumping of heart. In the air. A droning. My wife. Eulalia. Pep Torres. All in the doorway. A plane. A plane coming straight, our way. Purposeful. Flying very low. Disregardful of guns. Turning abruptly. Dropping papers. It was seven o'clock.

There being no one young to retrieve the papers, the *Cuartel* being guarded only by young Guardia whose sweetheart (the daughter of Butcher Jaume) had become ugly again because of impossibility of marrying enemy, Eulalia did not find out what the message contained. I saw the bug-eyed *portero* mutteringly carry one into the telephone office at Can Xumeu next door (across the lot), and at seven-fifteen I entered and asked what was the news.

Portero silent, sullen. Not wishing to be impolite but obviously not telling me. "What is the message?" I asked Xumeu. He groaned. I lost my temper.

"Give me that paper," I said, and took the message from his hand. A truckload of fascists drove up at exactly that moment and Xumeu's son (the lame Francisco) hopped awkwardly down from the tail-board. They had given him a lift from Ibiza. Quickly I read:

If the civil authorities of Santa Eulalia and the Guardias did not present themselves before seven-thirty to the commander of the gunboat that would enter the cove for the purpose of receiving them, and if said authorities did not bring with the them available supply of gasoline and firearms in the town, the town would be bombarded at seven-thirty o'clock. . . .

Glancing seaward I saw, with mixed feelings, but quickly exultantly, with gladness, the nose of a gunboat coming out from behind the *Vei Isglesi*. Continuing with my reading, I saw that all noncombatants were directed to leave the town at once.

Pep Torres was by my side. I glanced at the truck-load of volunteers, recognized several acquaintances who very palely and formally saluted me and one little man like the son of the man who used to be the cartoon of the common people, with a tin helmet too large for him, baggy coat, tight trousers and what in sterner hands would seem to be a gun. To this day I am puzzled about that little man, for when I looked at him and his eyes met mine he turned green and mauve, dropped his rifle and his teeth chattered so loudly I could hear them as I read. I had never seen him before, nor have I seen him since, but I shall always be curious as to why or how I frightened him so badly. We all were standing on the sidewalk, Xumeu, the *portero*, Pep, Francisco. Jaume approached for the octopus I had promised him. I told him we had about five minutes to get out of town, and pointed to the gunboat.

"Where shall I go? My wife cannot walk," he said.

I was already at my doorway. "Come," I said. "We've got to go. We'll be shelled at seven-thirty. It's now seven-twenty-five."

"We'll go to Paja's house," (near Cala Llonga) said Pep Torres.

My wife had placed in a straw basket her jewel case, a loaf of bread, an extra sweater for Peanut and a roll of toilet paper. . . . "What else?"

"That's enough. Let's go," I said. If government troops were about to land, I did not want to be mistaken for a fascist, and after the warning for noncombatants to leave I would certainly risk that humiliation. Also we were situated next door to the telephone office, which might well be a target, and bystanders have notoriously bad luck in Spain. Because the door latch would not hold of its own accord, I locked the door behind us and we set out in the direction of the Roman bridge. By the time we had reached the post office I remembered that the octopus was still cooking on our stove.

In front of the Royalty I met Guillermo and his wife, seven boys and father-in-law, Guillermo grinning sheepishly.

"We were the last two to go," he said, both of us having sworn we would stay no matter what happened. But to be mistaken for a fascist, or hit by accident by a bullet or fragment of shrapnel from the troops I wanted so desperately to win . . . Oh, no. Rapid retreat is indicated.

The *portero* and Xumeu had not informed anyone that the town was to be shelled, probably afraid to act without orders from someone higher or more thoroughly uniformed. Consequently we told a few, as we passed. Derek Rogers, Irish wife . . . Señora Barrau, wife of eighty-year-old Catalan painter.

"*On s'en va,*" she said, with matchless French logic.

"*Conforme,*" I said. Uncomfortably reflecting that the gunners would probably train their gun or guns on the hill, thinking it was vital to the town and that to reach the Roman bridge and the clear slopes beyond the river, we must skirt the foot of the hill. We reached it, Pep carrying Peanut on his shoulders, stepped across the river on moss-covered stones, and found sitting on the opposite bank a very nice Englishwoman and her gimp-legged husband. Their dog, a Sealyham, chose that moment to fly at Moritz, who patiently slapped him with huge paw, then got mad and started to destroy him. Forcibly and not gently I lifted Moritz from his feet.

"They're going to bomb the town at seven-thirty," I said.

"It's about seven-thirty now?" asked the Englishwoman, with pleasing inflection, remaining where she was.

Her lame husband pulled out his watch. "I don't know if I'm right on the dot," he said, looking doubtfully at the watch which said seven-thirty-two. "But perhaps we'd better move on a bit," he added.

"Let's," she said, and in the dimness of the evening a golden glow burst forth, a great light as if the skies were rent, and wavering experimentally the strong searchlight of the gunboat rested on Santa Eulalia's hill, up to the church and into reams of space beyond, down to cliff and road too low, jerked up to middle again. We continued walking, and before we were two hundred yards along the Cala Llonga road, Durban overtook us in a strange chugging roadster, by his side the two Catalan pharmacy girls.

"Jump in," he said.

Flash like lightning. Stifled scream of shell on mild trajectory. Unmistakably explosion. Very brightly the younger of the pharmacists smiled, blond hair, dark lashes, light-brown eyes. Pep Torres clapped his hands with glee.

"They have ammunition, all right," he said.

Most worshipful whine, up and up. O Proooooooo miss muhhhh! Another. I looking back from rumble seat. Pep and Peanut happily. Old homefire search-light still is trained on hill. Our invalid friends a small handful in town below. Old Vicent, old hard-working mason, pipe in lips and hands at side. Pep, Peanut and Vicent. Atta boy! A bump and swish. Ruts and corner, and the scene changed. There were quiet age-old hills, dull glimmer of white farmhouse and the smell of wheatstraw in the fields, of summer shrubs and early *frigola* and somewhere tuning up for night a *chibolee*, the crazy stony curlew. *Chiboleeeee*. The small roadster, springs groaning, strong fishtug ceased.

"Here's where we get out," Pep said. Then a walk over narrow rocky roads, road becoming pathway, veering, fork. Pep stood, "Which one?" Peanut sat on rock, munching piece of bread. Dull flashes in the sky toward San Antonio.

"Perhaps they're attacking San Antonio, too. They had another gunboat," I said.

"*Pod se*," remarked Pep, still deciding on road. We chose the lower one, walked in very velvet dark a while and paused before a gateway.

"I'll enquire," Pep said, ashamed to be lost in his own country. Returning with Pep an Ibicenco young man just out of jail the night before because at the port he had *ooked* and startled fascist guard at midnight. He walked with us, talking happily with Pep about underwear (the same being worn just then by certain of their Matutes acquaintances in town). "Here's the turning," he finally said, and hurried home to give news to newsless menfolks.

A mile, up hill around and down but rising and extremely rocky under foot. "Here we are," said Pep, and turned into a narrow lane between high plaster walls. With faint chirp of "*Dios Mio*" small black bundle of woman collapsing in clothes came falling to be caught and held by Pep.

"Paja, *calma*!" he said, but it was no use. She could not stand on buckling legs, chest frightened bird. It was Paja Rosa, wife of tall handsome Mateo, our second-story neighbor. No use to try to reassure her or comfort her. Pep carried her to the wooden gate and we stepped into the quietest courtyard in the world —her girlhood. There, with peasant grace, her wizened father and another. Oh, yes. I remember you,

Xumeu. (He had the name the townspeople had given me, and I had seen him last singing *Caramelos* in the church on the day of the Mass of the Angels.) Depositing the shuddering Paja in low cane-seated chair by open doorway, farm women fluttering, repeatedly accepting welcome for my Señora, then gathered around wooden gate once more the men. The father, the son, another adolescent boy I had seen very rapidly on bicycle, Pep Torres and I. Unreal. Beneath such copious farness and resplendence of sky, surrounded by dark lines of hills. White courtyard stone-paved from the time of the Moors. Terrace, ghost of almond trees, fiend fig, stone walls and terrace down into terrace again. By doorway women welcoming and weeping. By gateway patriarch and sons and travellers footsore from afar. Pep told them what was beginning to have happened as we by accident warned, and in chugs retreating had craned our necks and ears to observe, and that Xumeu (the writer) understood Ibicenco. . . .

"*No pod se.*"
"*Verda.*"

Wizened patriarch looking searchingly. Namesake son Xumeu nodding. Pep understanding and assuring them they could speak quite freely. It seemed that for the news we brought they had news to give in return most fearfully, in whispers. Stepping over our dog who was standing, worried forehead at the gate, we placed more quiet distance between us and the women's doorway, and in hoarse whisper and unreal isolation the old man told us that the priest and his father had been killed in San Carlos, and enormity of sadness sifted down from the star-curdled dark and

fell lava flakes from volcano of eternal woe. Pep,
awed not for life of priest but all it meant, said:

"Now it never will be over."

Old man sighed.

Just how that information had flown from hill to
hill, avoiding Santa Eulalia between, I could never
ascertain, but each dark hill I saw in middle-distance
or background had that knowledge to tinge its night
and ancient hillness, and it was as if an island (wine-
dark sea) that had seen so many conquests, galleys
and quinquereme and frigates and destroyers—le-
gions, elephants, spearmen, slingers, dash of Arab
cavalry, conquistadores and the sight of sights reserved for the morrow—men stoned and crucified,
women and babies put to the sword—it was as if that
island, rising from the silent fragrant depths of sea to
form a center for centuries of impressive strife, at last
had seen men go too far in killing off a symbol in
temple of symbol-symbol and unleashing all the
hordes of symbols in pent-up *Nada* with tools.

"Now it would never end. . . ." The world with
seven-day hash beginning, blood steam belching middle, and no end. In silence of hills, no end. In silence
of men, no end. In chattering of women, caught,
plugged, ripening, yielding, withering—no end. Then
symbol of eternal life burst upon us, beauteous young
girl *en fleur*. Maria, handsome pearl-flesh daughter
of black clothes heap and handsome mariner, coming
from well, so glad to see us, smiling. Not knowing the
end of all things had been broken off and thrown
away. Oh, beautiful Maria Rosa, daughter of God,
protect us, send young mercy streaming over us! We,
who are all washed up, salute you, and take water

from your hand. And Moritz—*pobrecito*—he is thirsty, too. Dish of water for the dog. Lap, lap.

Indoors the women were making hospitable preparations. Crowded already by the Rosas, they were receiving new and foreign guests with exactly the right amount of ceremoniousness. Food, such as they had and would have eaten on holidays. Old mother directing, such a one to fetch water, another to bring wood for the fire. Of course we had had no dinner. . . . I remembered the octopus, simmering in Marquesan majesty on stove in incense-empty house. Had Toniet known, he would have left him in the sea.

"We never know." (Old lady.)

I had eaten in many Ibicenco houses, and as long as I live shall eat my heart in memories of them again, and sometimes when I dream of food it is not caviar or terrapin or any of the dishes with French names. Quite frequently it is chickpeas, as we ate them in that quiet farmhouse that night. The entire family and all the guests sat around the long table, and for us plates were set and glasses for the wine. Our hosts ate from the common dish and drank from the wine pitcher, catching the stream at a distance of four or five inches from the spout. We had boiled chickpeas seasoned with pork, a potato omelette, dark home-made bread in huge slices, almonds and dried black figs for dessert. The women were unbelievably shy until we got well started, then thawed and liquid laughter when we spoke Ibicenco (not one of them understood Spanish). We assured them that bombs were *nada* (blessed word), and that everything would be "regulated" without delay. They believed, not our words, but the plaster walls and the ceiling beams from which hung peppers and *sobresada*, the sound of their mules in the stable, the night stillness of their nest of hills. They believed in old clothes for workdays and new clothes (now not used because in mourning) in carved chests. They believed in growth and yield of fig trees and in work, not prodded but in Ibicenco tempo, with natural rising from bed and after span of hours the grateful sinking into sleep. Things old and dependably familiar are received in the bosom of *nada*, than which no greater peace occurs for objects, plants or bones.

Girl's laughter and exclamation. "Moritz! Supper for Moritz!" And hearing his name, the dog squealed hopefully. Young Maria put chickpeas on a plate. Titter of young aunts. A plate for a dog. Strange ways of *foresteros*. But not to be outdone, young Xumeu's wife rose daintily and offered also a spoon. I explained that Moritz did not use a spoon. More laughter, but she would not have been impolitely surprised if he had used a knife and fork.

After dinner we sat in the courtyard beneath the harvest moon, and there was no singing because the house was in mourning, and the talk was not of what some of us had on our minds. The tiny wife Paja sat wrapped in black kerchief and shawl, hoping by her henlike stillness to shelter her hunted handsome husband in the San Carlos woods. I think that small woman may be more tranquil now, having lost her Mateo (although not knowing by what means and not feeling perhaps that he is living), for an actual bereavement cannot but give relief to a lifetime of apprehension and prophetic nervous fears.

If hard work has many virtues, one of the most

considerable is that it induces sleep. Our hosts were really musically polite but noticeably exhausted, and Peanut's bedtime had long passed. The Ibicenco children have no bedtime, when the older people are astir. Before midnight my wife and I were shown to the best bedroom, wide carved and posted bed and clean hand-woven sheets, and a cot had been brought in for Peanut. No use to protest. Of no avail to speculate how many of the family were sleeping on the floor. I consulted Pep Torres. I begged him to tell them I could sleep magnificently under a fig tree. He made it clear that I must accept, and we agreed that at the first crack of dawn he and I would go on the hotfoot to Santa Eulalia and see what was happening. And soundly in peaceful room and linen sheets I slept until something in sleep became diluted with receding light of stars, and a streak of window roused me and quietly I slipped away and closed the door behind me. Pep was washing in the courtyard, dripping silently.

Bon dia.

20. *Victory*

PEP and I had not walked a mile from the farmhouse, white courtyard which at night was of the stars and in early morning very much a part of the high terraced countryside, before we saw a man approaching on foot and alone. There was something familiar in his carriage, the high-crowned black felt hat, broad shoulders. He looked as if he were walking (arms not swinging) because he thought he could cover more distance that way.

"It looks. . . ." I said, then relapsed into silence.

That morning we had no use for guessing. The possibilities were so many and so divergent that by common unspoken consent we had walked side by side, as rapidly as the man who was coming toward us, saying nothing. Aware of cool air, subdued grey-green and brown of dry land, drabness of rocks, grace of undernourished trees.

Pep, at last, "It's Francisco Guasch."

Guasch it was. Tall. Well-knit frame. Perfidious face, loud voice and sharp and shifty eyes.

"Good morning," I said.

He paused a moment in his easy stride. "Good morning," he said. Nothing more. Pep did not speak. Just waited. Pep and Guasch and I on lonely countryside. It occurred to me that he was not armed; at least he carried no long rifle.

"How is it in town?" I asked.

"*Mol tranquil*," he said, succeeding even to smile. Then he hurried on, we staring at his nervous back. A little faster, or was I imagining? No imagining that cool morning. Firm. But we knew that our firmness had been broken.

"That's strange," Pep said.

"What's he doing here?" I asked.

"He's got relatives all over the hills," Pep said.

"He didn't have a gun."

"That's strange."

On we went, and then for a stretch particularly silent, for a half mile ahead at the turning of the road we should ascend a steady grade and soon would be seen the church and Santa Eulalia's high hill, or would it? What should we see, that last night, craning necks from rumble seat, had been brilliant in spotlight of gunboat (the whine and explosion of shells). We walked steadily, side by side, against the undertow of impatience and anxiety. We reached the turning, mounted the grade.

"There it is," Pep said. We stopped and strained our eyes. The church was there, the priest's house. A smaller dab of white was the churchside café and the nearby hut of Platé the Admiral. I remarked the windblown dwarf pines dark against the white of the cemetery wall. All there. On higher range behind, high shrine. The landscape told us nothing.

A little farther and we should overlook the valley and the Roman bridge, the junction with the stage road, the steep cliff and the mill. We hurried on, and just before the picture was about to change a shot

rang out, and echoed in the hills. No question what
it was. A rifle shot. Another.

Stopped again. Pep ruefully smiling. He had learned
about war and the eating of corn on the cob from the
very patched and jerky old American films. To me,
a veteran, he looked (rueful smile) for cue. What to
do when shot is heard. Very willing, but expecting
me to take the lead.

"We may as well go on," I said.

The point of vantage gained, the valley spread below, but the sun was rising and was square in our
eyes. The same instant we saw a figure (gun and uniform) by the bridge at the approach to the town, and
blinded by the sun we both made the same mistake,
and instantly were drenched with weariness and disappointment.

"A Guardia," Pep said.

I said nothing. Apparently nothing had happened
for the best. Guardias still in town. No landing after
bluff bombardment. Sick and tired. The sentry moved
his arm and beckoned us to come on. We walked toward him and suddenly were bees wild drunk with
wine of transformation.

"Guardia, hell!" I said. "It's a Spanish sailor."

"*Olá*, comrade," shouted Pep.

"Comrades," pleased and hearty from the transformed sentry.

"It's a Formenterenc," Pep said, as he hurried
with outstretched hands. The best handclasp of my
life. "*Hombre!*" Not only a sailor and a Formentera
man but one I had known for several years, a steward
on one of the Palma boats. So purposeful. He was
only five feet tall but he had a businesslike way about

him. He handled his gun as if he knew what would
happen when he pulled the trigger. He walked his
post in a patriotic manner, with no military tosh, no
self-consciousness. "Boy, I'm glad to see you," I said.
Then Pep noticed an empty bicycle by the side of the
road, and furthermore the bicycle of the boy from the
farm we had just left. The sentry explained. A young
man had come riding down the hill about a mile a
minute, and when asked to halt had tumbled off and
run. Our Formenterenc had fired twice to scare him
(he could hit a corncob at one hundred meters) but
the young man kept right on going. He could run as
fast as he rode a bicycle, the sailor said.

"He's all right," said Pep. "We just spent the
night at his father's farm . . . Xumeu has a house in
town," nodding toward me.

"You'd better take care of his bicycle," the sailor
said. "The militia'll be here before long and . . ."
Gesture of evaporating wheel.

How marvellous of this war to take on a familiar
tone just now, I thought. We promised to take care
of the bicycle and apologize in behalf of the sentry to
the young man when we found him.

"The Captain's over there," said the sailor, pointing to the low roof of a small white house by the river
bank not far from the mill. "Would you like to see
him?"

"Sure," I said. I wanted to see everybody. I was
feeling intense love for the human race and destiny.
I was sorry I had been pessimistic all my life and at
times had felt that nothing ever would go right. My
long shot had won. By all means, see the Captain.

"Come on," I said, and the sailor walked with Pep and me to the end of his post and there yelled:

"Captain Bayo!"

A powerfully built man of medium height, in white collarless shirt and military trousers, binoculars in hand, motioned us to come to him. Eagerly I jumped the small ditch and clambered to the roof beside him. He greeted me in Spanish. Then Pep mentioned that I was an American. Captain Bayo genuinely smiled.

"You are a republican then," he said.

With a lump in my throat I stammered, "Naturally . . ." Much light had left the morning. "Yes, of course . . ." American-Republican.

"This is a quarrel between Spanish people . . ." he began, in very good English. What a break! He spoke American. Learned to fly in Ohio and Michigan . . . Republican.

"I know," I said. "I've been here, off and on, five years."

"Then you understand the situation."

"Very well."

Perplexed and admiringly stood a small group on the roof beside us, pleased that there was eager conversation, understanding only it was friendly.

My enthusiasm and surprise had made me forget many things which at that point began to nudge me insistently. The last I had seen of the town around the corner, there were fascists and Guardias with loaded guns. Our group on the white roof top was within easy range and completely exposed.

"Er . . ." I began, wondering how I could suggest in a dignified way that we get the hell away from there as quickly as possible. He began to ask me many things he wished to know.

"But, Captain," I said, "are you not in danger here?" I pointed to the town, out of sight.

"I don't think so," he said, glancing across the river through his binoculars. There I saw a detachment of marines, perhaps fifty men on the vacant slope. "How many guns were there in town last night?" he asked.

"In Santa Eulalia, about a hundred," I replied. "More in San Carlos to the north. . . . They were not Santa Eulalia men, most of them were from Ibiza."

"I think they've gone," the Captain said.

"Do you know the town?" I asked.

"Not at all."

"Have you a map?"

"It doesn't show much."

"Here, I'll make a drawing," I said. I took a stub of pencil and drew a rough sketch of the town in his notebook, marking the *Cuartel*, the telephone, etc., and the roads leading in and out. As I was drawing, the Captain told me he had landed four thousand men on the northern coast (beyond San Carlos).

"Militia," he said. "I had to take what I could get. If they steal or misbehave I'll shoot them." He said it dispassionately but with exactness. Much he would have preferred to be flying, for that he knew, but officers were scarce, trained soldiers needed elsewhere. Here he was with whomever he could get.

A fisherman and a mason's helper had been picked up by sentries on the road, about to enter the town. Captain Bayo looked at me, enquiringly.

"They're all right," I said. "A mason and a fisherman. There are no fascist fishermen."

He smiled. "How many fascists are there here?"

"Not many in Santa Eulalia or San Carlos," I said. "Not more than a dozen . . . And the Guardias . . ."

"*Carabineros?*" the Captain asked, anxiously.

"I haven't seen a single *Carabinero* in arms," I said.

"Good," he said, with relief. He had hoped there would be loyal *Carabineros*.

A few more of the townspeople straggled along, escorted by sentries. I passed upon them happily. "Ah, Xumeu," they said to me. God, I was glad about the gladness in their voices, seeing that I could explain for them and that they knew it and had ceased to worry.

"I am entirely at your service, Captain," I said. "Most of the people here will be glad to see you. They have been helpless, unarmed."

"How many will be glad?" asked Captain Bayo.

"More than half," I answered.

He looked toward the road. "The militia will be here soon," he said.

"What have you got those men over there for?" I asked, pointing across the river. "There are no guns there, nothing at all for miles."

He raised his arm and shouted. From far riverside voice and arm responded.

"Come over here," Bayo shouted, and the marines got up from the rocks and the grass they were lounged upon and approached us so eagerly that they forgot to use the stepping stones. Captain Bayo pointed toward the church on the hill. "That commands the town?" he asked. I nodded. "Take the church," he shouted, meaning his command for the top sergeant of marines. Our blithe young Formenterenc at the roadside heard and took it all upon himself. Alone and with incredible speed he scrambled up the cliff, disappeared over the top, appeared in a moment again.

"All right. I've got it," he shouted.

"Let me see our flag there," Bayo said, and the flag sergeant and all the marines streamed up the hill. But they could not climb as fast as the Formentera sailor and while they were mounting the steep cliff those of us below were treated to a spectacle the like of which it is not given to many to behold, for the Formentera sailor had come upon the only man who had spent that night on the barren height, namely old Platé. The old man looked wilder than ever, beard and uncut hair streaming in the morning breeze, trousers rolled to knees of pipestem legs.

And there against the sky the wild old man and the five-foot sailor danced the most exquisite and dainty *jota* that ever flew out of Aragon, and, dancing, they felt on church, on highest belfry, the sun morning ripple of the Spanish republican flag, for which men died one hundred years ago, were buried and after a certain number of days were resurrected from the tomb by an accomplished Spanish peasant named Goya, for which men were dying all over Spain at the moment of that burst of flag on Santa Eulalia, for which quite surely each boy then on our hill since has died or soon will perish.

I began to believe we were safe on the rooftop, but

Ibiza and its well-armed garrison began to trickle uncomfortably into my mind.

"There are several hundred soldiers in Ibiza," I
said.

"We'll take Ibiza today," said Bayo. "I've men
enough."

It did not occur to us then that after Mestres had
committed the island and all its helpless population
to a treasonable adventure he would surrender without a fight.

And on the hill, by sun illumined with back drop
of flat sky behind, Platé's historic *jota*, danced by
two, to be seen by all. Salomé with head on platter
was overstrained, in fact, a trifle vulgar. Isadora in
red in Red Square theatrical. Best of dances was that
of old man stripped of everything but spirit and young
man who when freedom rang came right up with the
tray. Our Formentera man was, I learned later that
morning, the brother of an inventor. He and his
brother had fought in the streets of Barcelona on that
first bloody morning, and the brother had discovered
a way to stop machine-guns firing that was not to be
found in the manual of arms. By pressing his body
against the muzzle, hot lead streaming, he buckled
the troublesome machine and got sudden red oyster
cocktail, and for a moment sailor face without belly
held expression of fullback waiting for a punt.

"Now, the *Cuartel*," Captain Bayo said.

When he started to move I saw he was limping
badly. He had been wounded in the foot, three weeks
before. I stepped down from the rooftop, which was
near enough the ground on the uphill side of the
house, and offered my shoulder to bear his weight.

Ah, yes, Don Alfredo! I remember not only your simplicity and bravery and the justice of your cause but
the drag of the earth to your good two hundred
pounds. Solid honest weight. A man, please God.

The Formenterenc clambered down the cliff and
resumed his post by the bridge. Captain Bayo, Pep
and I walked three abreast past the mill, the Buena
Vista on the left, the row of villas around which the
riotous flower gardens complained of emptiness within, and I saw in front of the town residence of Ignacio
Riquer a broken heap of furniture, paintings and wall
decorations, household goods of all sorts. The wide
front doors and French windows were open, exposing
wreckage within. Next door, in front of the residence
of Francisco Guasch, a smaller and more thoroughly
broken heap. A detachment of marines were just in
the act of cleaning out Nicolau's house across the
street.

"Here comes the Captain," I heard one of them
say, a tall and villainous-looking type with a bandaged
eye. The men stopped breaking furniture and eagerly
got into line.

"Attention!"

Eyes front, hands to sides.

"As you were," the Captain said.

At a glance I could see that he needed no folderol
to stimulate the loyalty of those men. They did not
resume their demolishing of Nicolau's goods at once
but maintained a loose formation, listening hopefully
for whatever news their leader could give them. No
mumbo-jumbo of theirs not to reason why. They
would smother machine-guns with their bellies, but
were human and enjoyed the news. Bayo assumed a

military posture himself. The marines followed suit quickly. Bayo's left arm was raised, determined fist clenched tightly. With snap left arms, fists arose.

"*Viva la Republica!*"

With boyish glee came running Ferrer from Las Delicias. Joyously I stepped to meet him, slapped the palm of his hand, his back. "*Arra va be!*" (Now things go well.) Appeared in our midst with noiselessness and glowing eyes Antonio Cosmi, dagger still in belt. Down the street sunlit flash of yellow, red and purple. The boy who worked on Cosmi's farm came happily toward us with the huge flag that had been hidden in Cosmi's attic.

"Put it on the *Cuartel*," the Captain said.

"*Si, mi capitan*," proudly said the boy.

The flag was on the *Cuartel*. Incredible. No Guardias. Hats and uniforms of Guardias strewn in front, where the town boys practised football. At the door of the mayor's office, stains of blood. Little else was left, I learned, of the bug-eyed *portero*. He had stood his ground when all others had run away and had been dispatched with bayonets and bullets by the advance guard from the gunboat. Old Vicent, pipe in gums, stood in his doorway just a few yards away, eyes flashing satisfaction from beneath his saturnine eyebrows. Husky voice with happiness. "Now we'll see. . . ."

I give you my word that up to that moment I had forgotten I had a house. Pep gently reminded me. I took leave of the Captain, after assuring him again that I would consider it an honor to do anything I could for him. We had an extra room in our house, I said. I had a typewriter.

324   *Victory*

"Is there a typewriter in the *Cuartel*?" he asked a corporal.

"Here it is," the corporal said, and brought it in his hands.

"I should like to post a decree," the Captain said.

I took the machine to the Secretario's empty desk and said, "Fire away."

His message to the townspeople was to the effect that the false state of war declared by Mestres was at an end, that each man was urged to continue his work and his activities as usual, that complaints as to property loss or misconduct on the part of the troops were to be reported instantly, and that the people's government had no object other than to insure the inhabitants of Ibiza a peaceful and pleasant existence and protect them from marauders with traitorous intent.

"Already I have established strict order on Formentera," he said.

"Ah, that's what detained you," I replied.

"I had hoped Mestres would have sense enough to surrender," he said, resentfully. "The fool makes *me* shed blood."

How can I tell you of the joy there was in that nearly empty town? I had not progressed five yards before I saw Andres the painter, with his quiet sensitive smile, and he had on the usual blue shirt and faded dungarees, but with his instinct for effective touch of color he had sewed on one scarlet beltstrap at his left hip and the other young men who had fled as the fascists tried to press them into service, upon returning, took up the fashion. How can I tell you that the Spanish are a people with remarkable restraint? Others would have plastered red all over the place. Andres and Marc and their friends found one small bright red beltstrap more eloquent. It was.

It is because the Spanish people have been so patient for centuries, have suffered such an untold accumulation of wrongs, that the excess of shameful submission is impossible. Italians have become sheep, Germans automatons. The Spanish are men, please God. And as much as I love them, I prefer to see every decent Spanish man die, my best friends, their great artist Quintanilla whom I love more than a brother, Cosmi, Pep Torres. I could see each and every one of them riddled with bullets and hold my head up proudly. But to see them grovel, gradually and eel-like to modify their ideas and remarks and friendships, to taste boot-polish, ah, no! God will spare us all that. If the fate of my friends is now wormwood, if they have lost all the fruits of their life's labors, their mouths will be filled with red soil of Aragon and yellow dust of old Castile, but never say you heard them chirruping "*Heil*, Franco."

I was greeting young Andres, when, stumbling down the street, slanting like two catboats unskill-fully racing, came the idiots Anfita, Pepe in the lead, the forty-two-year-old Chicu (as always) trailing. Smile on face of Philip IV (chin gone wrong), smile and squeal from Chicu. It was true that their green-eyed sister Maria was desperate about her fiancé but the boys had caught the holiday spirit in the air outside, and for weeks they had missed it sorely. I saw Pepe fumbling grinning with a Guardia's hat in hand.

"The house," again admonished Pep Torres.

We passed Can Cosmi, where at the bar, Antonio

now presiding, a small group were whooping it up. Not a roar like Liverpool on Saturday night or a barroom in East Boston, but a pleasant sound like running stream and contentment somewhat *mezzo-forte*. Then a short split second of sadness, a faint and ineffective piercing of my mood. Can Xumeu was a wreck. The café and its contents had been destroyed, except for the walls. The house and *telefonica* were empty. Broken window-panes, shutters wrenched from their fastenings. My own house, next door, was intact. I fumbled for the key, opened the door, and was greeted by an angry smell of octopus in more than Catalan style. The odor drew me through the living room to the kitchen and I saw that the charcoal fire had burned itself out before doing damage to the pan or even to its contents. We had a meal all prepared for a very busy day. Not a minute later Eulalia Noguera came breathlessly in and we clasped hands and made strange motions and noises, collectively symptomatic of thanksgiving and exuberance. She had saved our house, when the first marines demanded that all doors be opened, by telling them that it belonged to a member of her family and that she had lost the key. From the hill to the west she had seen the Guardias and fascists in flight toward the interior, and as we talked hum of airplane drew us to the door, and we saw the plane following the shore all around our side of the island. The search for fugitives had begun.

"They can't escape in boats," Eulalia said, and slapped her thigh with glee.

"What about Don Rafael Sainz?" Pep asked. He

had worked on Don Rafael's house and rather liked
him, as he detested his wife Secora.

"He's hiding. They've taken his house. He has no
more house than a *chibolee*." (Nestless night bird.)

"And Secora?"

"They won't hurt women, worse luck," said
Eulalia.

The pulley of the pump creaked outside our doorway.

"Who's upstairs?" I asked.

"It must be Uncle Mateo," Eulalia said.

Eulalia is too young and has too much vitality to
be mourned just yet. Her life had not been an easy
one, and from now on will probably consist of dreary
weeks and months, but for a few days she was happy,
she felt gladness coursing in her veins. In short, she
had a taste of freedom, her town and country's freedom, and no doubt that brief glimpse of a promised
land will keep the Nogueras hopeful another century
if necessary.

The tall handsome fisherman Mateo was all smiles.
I told him I was hurrying back to his father-in-law's
place near Cala Llonga to bring back my Señora to
the house. Mateo's face showed mild alarm.

"Please tell *my* wife to stay there until I send for
her," he said. He wanted no black bundle of tears,
or handsome young daughter, where soldiers were,
and on day of celebration.

Pep and I started out hurriedly for Cala Llonga,
so hurriedly that somewhere along the rough stony
road I developed a severe Charley-horse, and those
who have had one may judge how pleased I was with
events, for I kept on my feet busily and constantly

that day and the days that followed, almost grateful
for the twinges of pain that seemed to remind me all
was well. The black-shawled Paja was a little calmer
than she had been the night before. I left Pep to tell
her we had seen her husband safe, and rushed into
the bedroom to arouse my wife and Peanut.

"Come on," I said hilariously. "The government
troops are in town. Guardias gone. Everything's wonderful."

"Jaume?"

"Jaume's all right. So's his wife. And Vicent. Nobody was hurt," I said, quite honestly forgetting the
portero.

Ibicenco farewells are not easy, no matter where a
war is raging. We had to drink coffee, eat *sobresada*.
Figs and other forbidden foods were forced upon Peanut and regretfully refused. I had brought back a bar
of chocolate for the children. At last we got away and
walked rapidly toward town, I limping ludicrously,
gesticulating and talking disjointedly. Pep was afraid
of my enthusiasm. He had not seen four thousand
men. Ibiza had not surrendered. No news from the
heroes of San Carlos. His dark presentiments were increased when we reached the summit from which the
church could be seen.

No republican flag. No flag at all. Bare belfry.

Since I had promised Flora a sight of the flag on
the church, she and I were wordlessly disappointed.
On we went (it was not yet eight o'clock in the morning). No five-foot sentry at the bridge. In fact, no
sentry at all. In the bay off the river's mouth was a
gunboat, and approaching it in calm water a launch.
On every house, in morning air, white flags adding

white to white plaster walls. The countryside a
clothes yard. Then, just after we had crossed the
bridge and were right at the foot of the cliff, a company of scarecrows marched around the bend in our
direction. Men without shoes or shirts, in overalls,
shorts, streaked with dust and sweat, guns at haphazard angles. The leader stopped us and we in turn
halted raggedly the column. Pep explained we were
Americans.

"You ought to wear American colors," the leader
said. "We are told to be very careful of foreigners.
But how are we to know?"

"*Hombre*," I said. "Do you think I carry flags
around in my pocket?"

Everyone laughed.

"Where are you going?" I asked.

"Ibiza. How far is it, comrade?"

"Ibiza," I repeated with concern. "There are
hundreds of fascist soldiers in Ibiza."

"They've just surrendered," he said, with a wave
of his arm toward the launch at the gunboat's side.
"They came to surrender just now."

We shouted with joy. Flora, Pep and even Peanut.
Too glad to do anything except laugh and shout.
Surrendered, the *ladrones!* The column got in motion,
and now we saw not their insufficient clothes and the
dust they had collected, but wholesome boys' faces,
smiling and touched by my wife's simple demonstration of glee. They raised their arms, and I saluted.
Then one of them stepped from the absence of ranks.
"Not like that, this way," he said, and for the second
time I saw the spirited left fist raised salute of the
Frente Popular.

"That's right. *Viva la Republica*," they said, and off, two and two, across the bridge.

"How far?" one shouted. I could not be inconsiderate.

"Just a few kilometers. About five," I said (it was fourteen). That was all I could do for them, although God knows I should have been willing to do more. That was our first view of the *milicianos*, the volunteer militia. Another large detachment was just around the corner, appearing even more like pirates, and a group had halted in front of the neat-vined house of the old Catalan painter, Loriano Barrau. The Barraus, of course, were in the hills.

"Is that a fascist's house?" a militiaman demanded. "It's locked. Why is it locked?" A few of the men started to scramble through the gateway.

"Stop," I said, and Pep with me. "That's an artist's house. A Catalan artist. He was a patriot before you were born."

"Come on . . . An artist. A good Catalan," a sergeant shouted, and the detachment moved on.

We made our way through the street, now crowded, receiving loud greetings from young Andres, Ferrer, Marc Colomar, and in front of Primitivo's balcony we paused to salute his wife and mother-in-law, industriously sewing.

"*Viva la Republica*," shouted Primitivo's four-year-old son.

"Ibiza has surrendered," I said. They nodded. None of us dared to speak of Primitivo and the prisoners. What had become of them?

We stepped over the débris in front of Can Xumeu and entered our house, but not a moment later

Eulalia came in, kissed Flora, and while they were embracing let fly the word that the church was burning. I hurried to the back door. Sure enough. Black stream of smoke from the rear. No wonder the flag has been lowered. The harmonium! We must get the harmonium out.

Pep and I rushed out the door, through the crowded street and up the spiral pathway of the hill. Smoke pouring restrainedly from rear. At the priest's house an angry group of militiamen. We passed, saluting, and to the men by the churchside bar made hasty and excited plea.

"*Hombres!* Put out the fire a moment. There is *musica* inside, a harmonium."

"*Musica?*" delightedly.

"Yes. An organ in the church. It's right there. Let me show you," I said.

A sergeant shouting, "Boys! Put out the fire!" And at the risk of burning hands and what was left of their clothes, they snatched at smouldering saints and paraphernalia. I entered the side door, choked with smoke. Some of us lifted the small harmonium from its place at the left of the stripped altar. Fresh air again. Drinks at the bar.

"Let her burn!" the sergeant said.

And, the harmonium safe, we started down the hill with a sense of duty well accomplished. This time, at the priest's house, the militiamen stopped us to show the stack of arms and ammunition they had found hidden in the tunnel. The priests had all disappeared the night before.

"Don't burn that house," I said. "It's the best one on the island, the best architecture."

The militiamen surveyed the lovely Arab walls with new respect, and seemed to be impressed with the exquisite proportions.

"You don't say," said a corporal. "Well, in that case, let it stand."

"There are plenty of ugly ones to burn," I said.

"*Conforme,*" he agreed.

And on the Sunday morning air sound of the church bell spread out suddenly through the smoke to the slopes and the fluttering white flags.

21. *The Internationale*

MY NEXT recollection persists in form of a painting, as if I had seen it on the walls of the Prado or like the St. Moritz in a chamber of the Escorial, a Spanish painting with the movement of a Greco and the warm colors of Zurburan and especially the tones of white (Beruguette to Morales to Zurburan), for the central figure was in clean white shirt and so cleanly shaved, and the mirror was a sky (arched with shelves of angels) and standing, smiling, serving his friends, as he spoke, rubbing glasses with towel, was Cosmi. There he was, unharmed, returned. The café, where by day there had been shade from reactionary sun and by night a wavering candle of liberty most carefully tended, was filled with our friends we had not seen for many days—Pep Salvador with cartridge belt and rifle, the republican mayor looking extremely unpolitical, Edmundo, black shirt and peering eyes through spectacles. I winced when I saw Edmundo, knowing that Pep and I that morning had let Francisco get away, but where, after all, could Guasch go? The vigilant airmen were patrolling the coast, squads of militiamen were searching all the houses in the interior.

In came Ramón, full face perplexed. "Mestres has hanged himself," he said.

I felt a slight disappointment, as much as I could feel on such a day, but the others shrugged their shoulders. As long as he was hanged, why quibble about who did it?

"There will be a *matanza* (pig-killing) in Ibiza today," said Edmundo happily.

"Now wait a minute," sternly said grave brother Mateo. "A regime that begins with blood will end that way. There must be trials . . ."

"And Matutes? I suppose you want to give him time to buy himself off," said Edmundo, but not angrily.

"Don Abel is very sick," said Cosmi with his inscrutable smile. "He's in the hospital."

"Bah!" Edmundo said.

My joy in seeing Cosmi and the numerous reunions with friends at the bar had deterred me from going into the backyard and kitchen. On my way from the church (now leisurely smoking) I had passed the Royalty (all shutters down) and had felt the sharpest concern for Juanito. What would happen to him, boy who had worked so hard and was fundamentally so decent but whose place had been the hangout for all that was vilest from the republican point of view? Could strangers, hurried militiamen and harassed leaders, be discerning? In Cosmi's back doorway my doubts and fears were resolved, for there with a hen in one hand and a knife in the other, working with feverish skill over bloody basin, was Juanito. Cosmi, who could have destroyed his competitor so easily, had sought him out in hiding and had suggested that since there were so many to feed that day Juanito had better bring himself and his force to Cosmi's larger hotel

and share the work in that way. In other words, the
safest place in all Ibiza, under Cosmi's watchful eye
and within the range of his powerful influence.

"*Olá*, Xumeu," said Juanito happily. Happy not
only to be alive and the object of such decency, but
happy also that he was free from an atmosphere he
had secretly detested. "*Estic foutut*" (I am ruined),
he said to me later that day, "but I would rather be
foutut with things as they are than to have my café
as it was." Beside him was Vicente Cruz, working like
a tiger. And all the workmen Cosmi had fed through
the lean weeks just past. Antonio at the bench was
proceeding with his Olympian calm, and for once had
the chance to demonstrate how effective were his
simple motions. He fed thirteen hundred at lunch
and eleven hundred at dinner, in a place where one
hundred guests had seemed to be a crowd.

Blue-eyed Catalina's eyes were wide. She was
grateful that Vicente was safe, but the smoke from
the church filled her with childish horror.

"*Mol malamen*, Señor Paul," she said. (Very bad.)
Her mason-fiancé grinned and nodded. "It's better
toasted," he said.

The public square was an amazing sight. Sentries
paced in front of the *Cuartel*, groups of peasants (such
ones as dared come in from the hills) stood looking
through the windows and archways as if the familiar
building bereft of Guardias and filled with strange
half-clad young men were a sideshow in some widespread and incredible *fiesta*. The town fountain was
two feet deep with suds and around it the militiamen
were washing themselves down to the waist, scrub-
bing, borrowing and begging soap and towels, and

to a group of them walked that wonderful Eulalia, tall girl who carried water jars with inimitable grace. And over her arm she had some shirts, laundered by her mother and belonging no doubt to someone who had good reason not to be in Santa Eulalia that day. Eulalia, girl who walks as a cup defender sails, who never had spoken to a strange man before or left the house at night without her mother, in the midst of shirtless men seven days aboard ship (day and night battle), long march in hot sun. No self-consciousness. No ribald words.

"Take them, comrades," she said. "I wish I had more."

"Thanks, comrade," the reply.

Could I believe my eyes and ears? Militia in the *Cuartel*, troops filling the broad *paseo* from the square to the sea. Mixed with my friends all along the street, strange figures, and not the least arresting a tall gypsy woman in Spanish colors who had volunteered as a cook. Other young women, purposeful, with armbands denoting their branch of service.

Then an auto, a large open touring car, raised dust trail from the mill to where we were standing, and as it came to a stop a cry arose, faint at first because the strangers did not understand, and I saw the pale face of Primitivo, of Fernando the communist schoolmaster, of Carlos, thinly smiling. The prisoners! Roar from crowd and troops. Eulalia, butcher's daughter, Catalina of the fishermen's café weeping and shouting with joy. And almost forgotten when the others had stepped out, a plump embarrassed girl. Catalina Pedarcx. The girl who had stabbed young Nicolau. I found myself with my arm across Primitivo's shoulders, shaking hands with Fernando. . . . An occurrence in black! A sweep through the crowd, and Marguerita sobbing, Marguerita in black. Fernando, one arm comforting, sustaining, face still responding to friends.

I grabbed Pep Torres, no explanation needed, and we ran (I limping) to the house, snatched up trumpet and accordion and started down the street playing the republican national hymn in spirited march time. Files formed behind us. Primitivo's balcony. Four-year-old son in arms. Left-fisted salute. Wife and mother-in-law now quietly smiling. Still with dignity. We played the hymn again and the crowd around us sang, and Pep and I, accustomed to the voices of Santa Eulalia, were thrilled with strange tenors and resonant bass.

"The *Marseillaise!*" "Yes." "Please."

You remember how it goes, or do you? *Allons, enfants de la patrie.* Our crowd beneath Primitivo's balcony had grown. Perhaps fifteen hundred voices and faces. This time they let loose. No such sound had ever been heard in Santa Eulalia before. I felt as if I was at the throttle of some huge engine in a dream.

Move on, to the Royalty for Fernando. Fernando and Marguerita, standing together. He had suffered more than the others, it seemed. His face was gaunt, unshaven, but smiling pale blue eyes. Twice he had been told he had been sentenced to be shot. Twice fake reprieve. No food but bread. About the time the town had surrendered, Fernando had spoken to the guards, explained how much worse it would be for them if the prisoners were harmed, then led a break for the door. A few straggling shots behind them, but all were free. Mestres had not hanged himself, Fernando insisted. Another officer of the group had done so, but not Mestres. Mestres was in hiding.

On a bench on the *paseo*, near the sacrificial tree of the butcher-shop owl, Pep and I installed ourselves, and around us two thousand volunteers of many nationalities. Four-fifths of them were Spanish, laborers, students, soldiers who had refused to follow their traitorous officers. By my side stood a *Madrileño* sergeant who knew all my friends in Madrid, Quintanilla, Araquistain, Negrin. Near by were several Frenchmen who had crossed from French Catalonia to help their kinsmen in Barcelona.

"Play the *Internationale*," someone shouted. Pep looked uneasy, for he had never learned the tune, but a soldier standing near him sensed the trouble, and after polite asking of permission took the trumpet from Pep's hands. The town resounded to that unfamiliar stirring song, and the volunteers from Valencia, Barcelona and other lands sang until they were hoarse. They never had enough of singing.

"The *Marseillaise!*"

"No. That's a bourgeois song."

"Not yet," explained the first man, and an exact and technical argument arose as to whether or not the *Marseillaise* had passed its usefulness. The consensus was in its favor, so we played, and everyone, including the tenor who had led the opposition, sang it lustily.

Ah, Rigoberto! Now we'll have music. Rigoberto Soler, pale, happy and still obviously worried.

"Rigoberto, sing a song."

He held up his hand and began a Valencian march

he had taught Pep and me not many days before. It had not then become known throughout the town, but within a week it was the local favorite.

"*No te vayas, no te vayas
Niña a Alcoy. . . .*"

A sailor's song with sailor's farewell and ending with the comforting phrase "*Paloma mia, t'escriberé*" (My dove, I'll write you).

The Valencia contingent knew the words and the melody and we had verse (Rigoberto's baritone most poignant solo) and chorus with all Valencians *fortissimo*. A pause at the end. Old man's cry. Platé. Old Platé again, and from near me a young man springing. It was Platé's son, who had left a good job in France to help save his country, and fearing his eccentric father might be dead, he had been timid about asking for him. It is healthful, after martial music, to see years roll off in cascades of tears and smiles from old man's wild black hair and beard.

I was treated to another such spectacle in the Royalty a few minutes later. The owner of the cliff called the *Vei Isglesi* was an aristocratic and handsome man with white flowing beard, very rich and a cousin or nephew or uncle of everyone who had mattered, and with the best of intentions I think the worst painter in the world. I had always assumed that Puget (yclept Narcisse) was like the rest of his relatives. For that injustice I publicly apologize. He was sitting near one of the sturdiest of the soldiers, one who had been a first sergeant in the army, and who wore a communist band around his arm. Puget's only son had come home to show his white-haired father that the precepts the old man had obstinately taught had taken root.

Rigoberto at my side. Anxiously tugging. "Elliot, for the love of God. . . ." I followed him to the go-down in the backyard. "Elliot," Rigoberto said. "You know Captain Bayo? You have been with him today?"

"Yes. Fine man," I said.

"Take me to him, please. . . . I can't wait. . . ."

We went out the back gate and across to the *Cuartel* My Madrid sergeant fortunately was at hand. "We must see Captain Bayo. It's important."

In a moment the sergeant beckoned. We entered the mayor's office, I introduced Rigoberto, then withdrew. . . . The conference had to do with Don Rafael Sainz, who had taken shelter in Rigoberto's house, Secora and the various children having gone to a nearby American's house. Cosmi had been shaving when the first squad of militiamen had started up the slope to hunt fugitives, and, seeing them headed for Rigoberto's, had run across lots to head them off. They had reached Rigoberto's house ahead of him and had seen protruding from behind a pile of paintings that unforgettable bottom of Don Rafael and had dragged him out in a state resembling jelly. While the *milicianos* were tossing a coin to determine who should shoot the millionaire, Cosmi interfered. And I have not yet disclosed that Cosmi had been with the Bayo expedition several days and had commanded a column in the battle of San Carlos. The militiamen at once took his word that the fat man should be spared. Don Rafael was simply spending the summer on the island, and had taken no part whatever in the *Movimiento*, Cosmi assured them. Nevertheless, there were other squads roaming the slopes, and Rigoberto was in terror on Don Rafael's account. He wanted Captain Bayo to give orders, some kind of credentials, that would protect his guest. Captain Bayo sent for Cosmi and issued at Cosmi's request safe conduct papers for Don Rafael, Don Ignacio Riquer and Don Carlos Roman. Without hesitation. Cosmi knew the town. Bayo did not. Many thanks. You're welcome. If all the lives Cosmi saved that day were placed end to end, they might reach that year in the future when Spain will rise from this year's ashes.

And now to my house again. My wife had sent word to the women volunteers that they could consider our place their own, if they wanted to rest or refresh themselves after their harrowing voyage. The gypsy woman had thanked her, but said they were comfortably installed in the schoolroom at the *Cuartel* and would not trouble her. As Pep and I approached the house, Eulalia Noguera came to meet us. Could I spare a shirt for a boy who was too bashful to ask? Flora had given shirts to others of his group, it seemed, but he had none.

"Of course," I said, and stepping in, asked the two boys near the doorway to enter. Smell of octopus, lustily. I quickly produced my last shirt, and one of the boys, Ramon Casas of Barcelona, went into Peanut's room to wash and change. Antonio Roca, his companion, was reluctant to ask for anything, already having received a shirt, but at last let it be known that he wanted most of all a pen, some ink and a sheet of paper. His family would be worried about him, he said. We brought out writing materials and cognac. Both young men were "real soldiers," that is, they had been performing their compulsory military service when the rebellion broke out and had remained loyal when some of their officers deserted.

Casas stepped from Peanut's bedroom a clean pleasant-mannered young man and was so pleased at the sight of ink and paper that we urged him not to stand on ceremony but to write whatever letters he wished to write. Like Roca, Casas had a family concerned for his safety and welfare. Their fiancées were with them, serving in the commissary. We invited them to have lunch with us and bring the girls, but they refused politely, being non-commissioned officers and having certain responsibilities at mess time. Had I not seen the rice that Cosmi was preparing, I might have pressed our invitation, but I knew that a magnificent meal was in store for them at the hotel and told them so. Before leaving us they promised to return with their fiancées before setting out for Ibiza in the afternoon. The Barcelona contingent, they said, had been ordered to Ibiza, and Santa Eulalia was to be left in charge of a detachment of Valencians. There was some rivalry between the militiamen of those two cities because of slightly different views on communist doctrine. Casas had left his dirty shirt in Peanut's room, and Eulalia Noguera offered to wash it for him and have it ready before he departed for Ibiza. He shuddered.

"I don't think I could ever look at that shirt again," he said.

In the doorway he paused and took a cartridge from his belt, and handed it to Peanut.

"Keep this, in memory of a Spanish soldier," he said.

Oh, shirt! I wonder where you are mouldering. Are you fluttering empty from some bare branch or barbed-wire fence? Or have you the honor to be buried in the ground? Casas and Roca were such courageous young men, it is impossible to expect that today they are alive. Their families in Barcelona get no letters, their girls who called on us that afternoon have but to add to that ashheap of girlhood, potential mothers of the free, their own crushed ideals and femininity. Impartially one watches an anguished democracy die.

Let us leave for a moment the crowded street of Santa Eulalia in the heat of that Sunday noon, the thousands singing, the prisoners return, and even on the back street the family Pedarcx (Catalina home from jail). She had served a year without trial, and really they had little to say except that the mother and the fisherboy smiled and the old man thought of being shaved. But the Barberet's shop had been ransacked because it was part of Can Xumeu, and talking incessantly and spirally, the damage was mounting in the Barberet's mind until the whole town was inches deep in straps, mugs and razors. Let us forget for a while in burning sun the meal being prepared and nearly ready in Cosmi's back yard, the mountain of hens, mosaic of chopped goat, rice yellow with saffron, glowing coals of outdoor fireplace, the huge *paellas*, workmen toiling merrily as K.P.'s. Forget the church, now scarcely smoking, its structure intact and much as the Arabs had left it. Silhouette of church on hill. Inside, no trappings.

On the verdant slopes northwest of town a squad of soldiers are returning for lunch. They meet a young man, bewildered, rifle in hand.

"Who are you?"

"Juan Sindik."

"Are you a fascist?"

Puzzled. "Yes."

The carpenter's son, who had been given a gun two days before, had fled to the hills when the men near him had run away but, not grasping the seriousness of the situation, had got tired of hiding and decided to come home. The gun had been given him by a strange lieutenant and he hardly dared throw it away. He could not have explained what a fascist was, except that he seemed to have become one.

He was led to a nearby haystack, not far from the large residence of Don Rafael Sainz. His hands were bound behind his back and, dimly and fearfully aware that he or someone had made a terrible mistake, Juan was shot. Not many of the townspeople knew about it until the next day.

One must think also about a house on the *paseo*, and of Guillermo the blacksmith, who was tied with me for last place in leaving the town the night before. In every crowd that had gathered on Santa Eulalia's main street since the day he had escaped from the stern apprenticeship in his father's shop, Guillermo and his blue-striped shirt had been conspicuous. This Sunday of jubilation and woe he was to be seen, but with less jauntiness of shoulders, not quite up to standard with the cape. Decidedly gauche with the *muleta*. Guillermo, it must be remembered, occupied the ground floor of a house occupied by the gay Madrid priest, Father Margall. In his hasty departure for the woods Guillermo had left open the communicating door to the stairway, and the marines, strange to the town and with no one to guide them, had thought the house was all priestly and had taken some of Guillermo's clothes, and about thirty *pesetas* in money. Government, to Guillermo, was a strictly personal affair. He had been dealt with unjustly and was sulking. It is true he could smile when he saw the old files of nudist magazines the gay priest had collected. Nevertheless, he was definitely chilled and offended. Ramon, his noontime pal, was also far from exuberant. Old Julian, monkey-faced owner of the bus, had been taken to the fortress as a fascist and Ramon thought his job had been destroyed. Julian's son, who worked in Matutes' bank, had fled from Ibiza at the approach of the republican forces and had reached Santa Eulalia just as his father was being arrested. Sadly he prowled through the back street of the town and I felt sorry for him, he having always been most accommodating in the bank. I did not believe anyone would shoot old Julian, although he might have been put in a cage and provoked to chatter, still a father is a father and he had got his only begotten son a good job with excellent prospects, and now the whole structure on which prospects rested and buses rumble was collapsing.

Teresa, the fat solid Catalan wife of the fascist Bonéd, stood in the doorway of her new house, eyes dry and very hard. She could not join the dancing in the public square because her husband had been arrested and the hidden arms and ammunition removed from his cement shed. He had not told her of his full complicity with the fascists, knowing how she felt about Catalan independence. Juana, in whose eyes those tragedies had lurked, remained as ever, aloof, resentful, passionately hostile. Shame dangerous, love dangerous. Father to be killed, mother to receive no pension nor any more *pesetas* henceforth and forever.

On the fishermen's point was Toniet Pardal, and it had been due to his eloquence, to his blazing eyes insistence that no shots had been fired at airplanes from the roof of the house of Don Carlos Roman that the property of that convivial monarchist had been spared. There was a story circulated by those who wished to discredit the republican troops to the effect that failing to catch Roman they had shot his pet monkey. Not so. The fisherman, who in protest had burned Don Carlos' shack and motorboat, made amends by saving Don Carlos his house, and Cosmi, unsolicited, had secured an order of safe conduct for Don Carlos. His only obligation was to keep out of sight until things blew over a bit.

Don Ignacio Riquer had decided to give himself up when Cosmi came back on the scene. Instead he was a guest in Cosmi's apartment.

Noon of sun, hot dust and the shrunken patches of shade. Of chicken saffron rice in hotel dining rooms (din of forks and voices), of plates under trees on the *paseo*. And Spain and now old habit, historic *siesta*. Tired boys stretched on the ground, on floors, under stairways, also men and women of the town, fragments of strange sights fluttering and flashing under eyelids, humming and numbness of brain. All stretched for that blissful after-rice experience, and let the war pass on for an hour or so. Enough when on awakening to take up colored threads. Enough to start slowly, like boat leaving dock, inches widening barely. At four o'clock would come the sea wind and the skyline of the island would be there. Other hordes had swarmed and fought, had imposed their burden on island towns, delivered captives, taken hostages, but also had not Hannibal and Caesar and old sea-wise Phoenicians and women from all the Mediterranean shores as pilgrims to the shrine of Astarte at San Vicente—had they not slept when noontide sun so neatly had murmured "Rest my children"? Astarte, Mary, Zeus, Allah, Jehovah. All had had *siestas*. If a sparrow falls, *siestas*. If a town gives birth to an army and an epoch, *siestas*. Family saved and deep freedom, to sleep. And to sleep if father is in jail, and father in fortress sleeping also. If shot by haystack, sleep. If gypsy, sleep. The night has peace, awake beneath the stars, so give us sleep when most 'tis needed, in the afternoon. And after sleep, a bugle!

There was a townwide upward movement, erratic but not startled, as men got up, yawned, extended arms, brushed off dust beneath the trees and indoor sleepers came to doorways. In the swarm of unfamiliar faces were now to be seen at intervals the familiar faces of those who had returned to their homes from the woods. Another bugle call, and the center of the main street thinly cleared as the Barcelona *columna* began forming there, company front, two ranks. Hurriedly to our doorway came Casas

and Roca and the two girls with commissary armbands.

"They have provoked this civil war," said Casas.
"We're going to finish it. Good-bye."

"Many thanks," said Roca. He gave us their ad-
dresses in Barcelona and a small snapshot of himself,
and we promised to send them some postals when the
war was over.

"Some of the women here look at us as if we were
circus ladies," said one of the girls. "You" (to Flora)
"are American. You understand that women too
must fight."

"Good-bye."

I passed along the ranks the full length of the
street, receiving greetings, wishing everyone luck,
especially the singers I best remembered. Andres in
the doorway of his café, white-coated Pedro on the
Royalty's sidewalk next door. Women fearfully on
sidewalks in groups, men grouped around their favorite cafés. Within the memory of no one living, nor any
living person's great-great-grandfather, had troops
formed in that street, and still there was an echo of
history that kept the sight from being strange. To
Ibiza, for weeks in complete isolation, seeming remote, on the edge of the world, had been brought an
awareness of its centricity, of hovering civilizations
on all points of the compass and of time.

Before lunch I had said good-bye to Captain Bayo
who had pressed on to Ibiza to take charge of the
city with a handful of marines. He was much relieved that he had not been obliged to sacrifice more
lives.

"I shall try to make soldiers of these men," he

said. "They are loyal and willing, and filled with large ideas."

"I have never seen troops behave as well," I said.

"They haven't seen much bloodshed yet," he said sadly.

Oh, yes, Don Alfredo! I caught the drift of much you could not say. I know how you felt your frightful responsibility. To young men who should have been in shops and school, you must teach relentlessness. Youth unfamiliar with butchery, you must inoculate with that incurable plague. You, a flyer, must remain on the ground. You must be misunderstood by extremists because of your moderate judgment and cursed by the dupes of those who gag when the word liberty is pronounced. In distant lands it will be advertised that you have burned a church, and not a word about those instruments of death secreted by the ministers of Christ.

Just before leaving, Bayo introduced me to Captain Pastor, leader of the Valencian column that was to remain in Santa Eulalia. Pastor had none of Bayo's force, but a very level head. It was he who persuaded Andres, Marc Colomar, Antonia's son and many other young men not to join the expedition at once but to wait for the formation of a local militia. I thought this strange until he explained to me, after many Masonic high signs (to which I was unable to respond) that men all over Spain were ready to volunteer, but it was difficult just yet to equip and arm them properly.

Again the bugle. And Spanish bugle, unmistakably. The British bugle with a cockney stutter; no two French buglers can keep together or would if they could; American bugle is sturdy and square but a trifle hard-boiled. A Spaniard can keep time, he can be tough and insistent, but he cannot play even a bugle call without that subtle *rubato* that is the heat, blood and dust of Spain. I have heard the Madrid Symphony play Haydn, but lurking somewhere in those conventional patterns was the same suspension of rocket flight and more effective arc of arrival that Segovia finds in Bach and Teresa Careño found in the *Appassionata*. Die, Spain, when your music dies. Die, liberty, when your sponsors become neutrals. Die, Greco and Morales and Goya. Die, Christ and your brotherhood of man. Die, *enfants de la patrie*, oppressed of earth. Die in mud and in memory, in honor and obscurity. Die. Just die.

The afternoon milk was delivered by José of Can Josepi while the Barcelona column was standing there, waiting for the order to right face and forward march. There was a happy smile on his eager face, and also the desire to ask questions.

"What did it mean? Would things be better now?"

I assured him that they would, that the men and women of Ibiza now were owners of their own island and could show what good men and women they were by conducting their affairs justly.

"Then we won't have to work so hard for nothing?"

"No," I said.

"And the Guardia?" He mentioned the owner of the farm he worked on shares, who was sergeant of the Guardias of Formentera.

"I'll inquire about him. Meanwhile, go on as before."

"Will it be like your country?" José asked. "I've heard it's much better there for a man who works."

"We've had a republic for one hundred and fifty years," I said.

"Ah, *fotre!*" said José in awe.

The long ranks stirred, from Gork's all the way to the plaza.

"Attention!" Shifting of feet, eyes right, that's better. Then I heard a cheer, for Cosmi in white shirt, so cleanly shaved, had appeared in front of his café and was saying good-bye to the men he had led to their victory in the mines of San Carlos.

"*Viva* Cosmi!"

I have never seen a man blush so thoroughly.

"Attention. Right face. Forward, march!"

Two and two, right hand swinging high and across the chest in Spanish fashion, the Barcelona troops moved on, through the plaza, past the wreckage of the furniture of Nicolau, Francisco Guasch, Ignacio Riquer, the row of villas with gardens, turned right at the mill and disappeared two by two, tail now at the plaza, by the villas, the mill, out of sight behind the cliff. Dust. Thinner. Then the Sunday afternoon crowd, minus farm girls with holiday costumes, began milling lazily up and down, discussing, wondering.

My friend, the Madrid sergeant and socialist sought me out. Would we be so kind as to have music that night? Of course. Any time they wanted music, Pep and I were ready. There was a cool evening hour and much settling down. Valencianos in the *Cuartel*, and a few camped on the *paseo*. Non-coms at the Royalty, non-coms at Cosmi's, officers (so few) in

the *Cuartel*. Peasants after sleepless nights in the
woods went to bed before sundown. Happy on the
back street was Catalina's aunt, and even smile on
face of invalid mother with white hair as Vicente
Cruz sat close to Catalina on the doorstep and said
now they could be married without a priest, for there
was not a priest in town. Not quite. But as a matter
of fact a squad had found old Father Coll in the house
with three very old women who were frightened. Such
a harmless-looking old man in black and old women
with fingers rough from sewing. The four militiamen
performed a feat of Spanish duty, that is, they wordlessly agreed as a matter of course to consider they
had not seen the old cassock at all.

There are some men, priest or not, whose faces and
manners indicate congenital incapability to join in
plots and store fire arms. Such a one was old Father
Coll and for that he was denied martyrdom. And
made no complaint.

Dominus vobiscum.

Just die.

22. *Dios Foutut*

EARLY Monday morning, August the tenth, the
town awoke, stunned and refreshed, streaked with
joy and mourning, white flags fluttering and everyone
knew it could never be again as it was before. A
leaven of modernity stirred those who were receptive
to it. Old people knew that their day and age and the
build-up of island life since the time of the Moors
would pass away with them. Around the *Cuartel* a
large crowd of men from the outlying countryside and
all the regulars from the streets of the town stood
waiting in slowly resolving groups. The three hitching spaces for mules were filled with two-wheeled
carts and animals that switched and shuddered
casually to stir the flies, along the lane beyond Gork's,
in the vacant lot on the back street between Eulalia
Noguera's house and the new baker's shop, behind
the transformed *Cuartel*. Scrawled on walls around
the plaza were huge initials and insignia, the hammer
and sickle, C. N. T., F. A. I., and more frequently
the U. H. P. (*Union Hermanos Proletarios*, or Union
of Proletarian Brothers). "No truce" was painted in
letters two feet high on Nicolau's empty house.
Printed catechisms and stories of the saints, torn and
untorn, littered the space around the fountain. Beneath the archways of the *Cuartel* were rocking-

chairs from the residence of Francisco Guasch and Ignacio Riquer. In the street, from Can Cosmi to Can Gork, two detachments of recruits were doing squads right and left with varying success and much good nature.

"Is that discipline?" would ask my Madrid friend, the sergeant, when a boy would pause and break ranks to say good morning to the statuesque Eulalia or the voluptuous Mexican servant girl whose voice was like Libby Holman's.

"Excuse me, Sergeant. I have sinned." (In Latin.)

Brisk crackle of volleyed raspberries along the line.

"Enough," from the sergeant. Another go at squads right and left.

Damn me, if I wasn't homesick for the A. E. F.

I watched a while the soldiers of the people in the making, and seeing old Miguel Tur, head shaking furiously and with long important paper in his shaking hand, making for the *Cuartel*, I followed impelled by curiosity. Turning the corner by the Royalty, I was startled and genuinely alarmed. Guillermo, my dear friend right or wrong, was standing by the guardroom door, gawking crowd of peasants all around. He was gesticulating, speaking passionately.

"For the love of God, no! No, Sergeant," he was saying.

I hurried to his side. In the center of an open space half the size of a prize ring was a sergeant holding by the scruff of the neck an unpromising boy, seventeen, perhaps eighteen, with eyes slightly crossed, vacant chin and forehead, dangling hands. Relieved, I saw that Guillermo was pleading not for himself but for this lad who looked like all the photographs of young public enemies.

"I have my orders," the sergeant said.

The boy was cross-eyedly crying, and tears were in Guillermo's eyes

"I gave them to him," said Guillermo. "You can't shoot a man on account of a pair of pants. Look at them. Full of holes. Not worth two *reals* . . ."

"It is such as you," said the sergeant to the boy, "who spoil the reputation of the rest of us. We come here to be honorable, to save these people, and you steal their clothes."

"He's welcome to them," pleaded Guillermo.

It seemed that Guillermo had seen on the boy a pair of the pants that had been taken from his house the day before. The boy insisted he had found them. It is possible he had.

"Give me that gun," the sergeant said, disarming the lad. "You are a prisoner. Take him inside."

"You won't shoot him?" Guillermo asked. The sergeant, softened by the horror of the crowd, winked reassuringly, but Guillermo was trembling and drenched with sweat. I think it was the worst experience of his life. All that day he shook his black curly head and muttered to himself, thinking of an old pair of trousers on one side of the scales and the blood of a fellow-being spilled over the other. His old clothes the cause of a life snuffed out, a cross-eyed pitiful boy. That such things were contained in the grab-bag of what days had become, that seven sons might violently become six! The touch of the trousers Guillermo was wearing became hateful to him. Had he escaped narrowly from death by a bomb he would not have been as profoundly impressed, and from that time on his avoidance of contact with anything or anyone in an official capacity was high art.

Captain Pastor, soft-voiced and with much elaborate politeness, had formed what was known as a Local Committee, which was from that day forth to administer the affairs of the town.

"You must organize and take care of yourselves," he said. "We must hurry on. We have other work to do. While we are here we will keep order, but you, the citizens of Santa Eulalia, are supreme."

"Ah, *fotre*," groaned assembled peasants. Order to them had meant Guardias and *Carabineros*. It was no concern of theirs. Their farm work left no time for order. What they wanted to know was why they had been told to come to the *Cuartel* and register.

The Local Committee consisted of a chairman and four committee men, namely, Carlos, the San Carlos schoolteacher who had broken out of the fascist prison the day before; Miguel Tur, old-time republican, storekeeper, lover of legal phrases and exile under Primo de Rivera; the republican mayor who loved hunting; the anonymous workman who had knocked at my door a few nights before to tell us of the uprising in San Carlos; and that irrepressible patriot and buffoon, Pep Salvador. I was astonished and so were Pep Torres and Vicente Cruz, that Cosmi was not the chairman or even a member of the committee, but later in the day I learned that Captain Bayo had asked him not to take any local office. Knowing the needs of the island so well and the way in which Ibiza's commerce had been monopolized by Matutes, Cosmi had been selected to represent the island at Valencia, keep supplies moving, arrange for the sale or exchange of produce. I was saddened at the thought of the town without Cosmi's presence, but saw at once the wisdom of Bayo's choice.

The Secretario became secretary of the committee as a matter of course. No one thought of questioning his loyalty to whoever might occupy the *Cuartel*. One of his sons was a fascist but guilty of no overt acts, another a vehement republican, his wife was a bit of a shrew, his mother-in-law a real *tremenda*. Smiling he took up his duties, but (finger lacking) he was inexpert with the typewriter, so I told Carlos and Miguel Tur to call on me when they needed quick results. I typed merrily all the rest of the morning. First they posted notices on the doors of Nicolau's house, the Hotel Buenavista, the residences of Riquer and Francisco Guasch, Can Xumeu, the mansion of Don Rafael Sainz and Teresa Bonéd's new house to the effect that those premises had become public property and that no one might enter them without permission of the committee. Each citizen within the limits of Santa Eulalia must obtain a passport from the committee, in order that fascist stragglers and fugitives might easily be identified. I was voted full citizenship in the town and given the first passport to be issued, of which I am proud.

Mateo had been delegated to issue permits to the fishermen, who were ordered (like all other men in town) to resume their usual trades and occupations. A motorboat patrol had been established to watch for fascists trying to escape in boats, and any man in a sailboat or dory was liable to arrest if he did not carry a permit.

One of the most uplifting moments occurred just before noon. Ramon had been given government gasoline and had been told to drive the bus one trip a day. He returned at mailtime with the *Diarios*, but such *Diarios* as had never been seen before. Across the front page was a banner headline announcing that the newspaper had become the organ of the Popular Front, and the leading article was a proclamation signed by Captain Bayo.

"The enemies of the republic," he began, "have held forth, to discredit the legally constituted government of Spain, the spectre of communism. The expedition under my command has no object except to restore to the people of Ibiza their inalienable rights. Among these, the right to hold property will be scrupulously respected. . . .

"Those who have taken up arms against the government or have given material aid to this detestable *Movimiento* will be punished according to the degree of their participation in the same. . . .

"The state of war falsely proclaimed by ex-Commandant Mestres is hereby declared at an end. . . . Continue to do your daily work. Come and go as you please, provided you have registered with the local authorities. . . ."

In the news columns we read that affairs were proceeding in a normal way in Madrid and Barcelona, that train and trucking service between Valencia and Madrid were running on schedule, that the post-office employees were making superhuman efforts to keep mail in circulation, that President Azaña had remarked to the foreign press: "A military coup which does not succeed in the first days never succeeds."

We read that Franco was attempting to bring Moors into Spain on the promise of unlimited spoils and freedom of action with Spanish women. In short, we read and read and drank to the *Frente Popular* and the men and women of Catalonia who were fighting side by side, and to the destruction of traitors and tyrants everywhere.

The air hummed with rumors and with stray bits of fact, and many of these wounded me. Sergeant Gomez, who had been shot in the foot near San Carlos, had dragged himself as far as San Lorenzo, where the militiamen found him and gave him the permanent relief of death. There died a man I might have saved, had I only followed my impulse and persuaded him to obey his conscience and not his orders. The Guardia Jimenez hanged himself in Ibiza, to escape being tried for doing what he knew was wrong. Bravo, who had refused to fight against the government, and Ferrer who had always been a republican and had saved Cosmi and the others from arrest, seemed to have vanished completely. Not a word could I learn about their fate, but their wives and families, wandering homeless on the countryside, their former friends half afraid to offer them food or shelter, mourned them as dead. One could not be glad that the best men had been rescued without feeling deeply sorry for the strays. It would have been easier not to notice had it not been for the dogs. What change had come over that company of animals who had known and enjoyed that pleasurable existence and dog order in which they had their place!

A large red-brown hound, part solidly mastiff, was running distractedly from place to place in very straight lines, sniffing, bristling, raising his patient eyes. Even if the government did not love old Bonéd, and his homeless wife and coal-eyed daughter were only half loyal and mostly resentful, the red dog searched for him endlessly and was set upon by other dogs who sensed that he had become an outcast. One may say, "It is good enough for Nicolau, the first to be willing to shoot his neighbors," and still notice regretfully that his three pure white Ibicenco hounds (a breed unchanged since the days of Tut-ank-Amen) were demoralized and stained, that they did not find their daily food and were unaccustomed to rustling for themselves, and saddest of all that the other dogs were unkind to them. And in crushed nasturtium bed in deserted garden lay the tomcat Simon, and none might enter those confiscated premises, and no rockfish were cleaned on slab of concrete walk, and no women busy or talking by the well. Xumeu was ill in the house of his brother José the diving champion, in a state of complete collapse. Roaming over slopes and through the back streets were his dignified wife and his pallid listless daughter, limp with anguish. Francisco, Xumeu's lame son, had been arrested. Their property was gone, had been confiscated, and it would go particularly hard with that family because when the marines had entered the telephone office they had found there a large stack of messages to and from anxious men and women and their relatives which Xumeu, acting under Mestres' orders, had failed to send or to deliver.

I had lived next door to Xumeu Ribas and had seen his son Francisco hourly during all the trouble. The lame boy had accepted a lift from the fascist volunteers and had been seen on their truck. That was all. He was fascist by education and temperament, an unlovely product of the Catholic seminary in Ibiza, but he had not borne arms. I found his mother and sister on a back lot with some tethered goats and promised to testify in Francisco's behalf. He would soon be released, I assured them. Their gratitude was more than I could bear. I sought out Teresa and her daughter Juana and advised them to go to Barcelona as soon as they could. Teresa shook her head. I think, from the hardness in her eyes, that she could have strangled her scheming husband with her sturdy hands, but she could not leave the island while he was in prison. Juana, hating everybody, shrinking from the touch of her mother's hand.

There had been screaming in the woods the night before. The wife of Francisco Guasch somehow had got the idea that one of her sons had been shot and had raved like a madwoman until Eulalia Noguera, who detested her, had brought the boy and pushed him before her and upbraided her until she grew quiet again. Not a word about her husband. I heard that he had been caught, that he had escaped to Mallorca, that he was in hiding near Cala Llonga—a dozen conflicting reports. Señora Guasch was calm about her husband and hysterical over her sons.

At sundown that day I saw Harpo being marched into the *Cuartel* and could not care, so help me, whether he was shot or let go.

But the darkest cloud was the shooting of Juan Sindik. The poor hard-working young man, not too bright but very willing. Shot to death in the shadow of the millionaire's mansion, and Don Rafael excused

from death. Was it to be the same old story, the rich
unscathed, the poor more mercilessly scourged?
Sindik's grief was too deep for description. He walked
beneath tons of suffering, completely numb, hands
twitching and bereft of labor, avoiding everyone he
knew, and his friends pretending they had not seen
him. Next to Juan's own father, Cosmi was the chief
mourner. If only he had known, if he had been able
to be everywhere that first Sunday morning. He had
saved nearly everyone, and missed his honest and
hard-working neighbor's son.

I have not told what Cosmi had been doing, after
his quixotic pursuit of the battle fleet in a borrowed
rowboat. He had been correct in assuming that the
gunboats would anchor just south of Formentera, for
that long lean island offered perfect protection against
shell fire from the batteries in the Ibiza fortress and
was near enough to place the guns of the destroyers
within easy range of the city. It was a long hard row
but the last few miles of it were easier because he
could see his objective, the flagship, and knew that
soon he would be on board. Eventually he came alongside, exchanged a few joyous words and a line was
hove to him. Captain Bayo had recognized him instantly as a valuable aide. Cosmi told him that the
people of Formentera were almost unanimously loyal
to the government and that the force of soldiers and
Guardias there was negligible. The next morning
Cosmi and a small detachment of marines made a
landing unopposed and received the surrender of the
lieutenant in charge. This officer was the only rebel
officer of the Ibiza garrison who was spared.

Captain Bayo had expected that Mestres would

surrender when he saw he was outnumbered. It would have been possible for Bayo to take the city of Ibiza by direct assault, but that would have meant waste of life and destruction of the property of innocent men. The plan finally adopted was suggested by Cosmi, who knew every inch of the island and every quirk in the character of its fascist leaders. The slowest of the submarines could make twelve miles an hour on the surface, and the distance by sea from Ibiza harbor to Estañol, a convenient landing place on the northeastern shore, was half the distance by road. If Bayo's fleet steamed out of Ibiza early in the morning they could get to Estañol hours before the Ibiza garrison could get there to oppose a landing. In case the garrison was drawn out of the fortress, the fleet could hurry back and take the city before its defenders could get back.

The night of August seventh, Cosmi was taken in a launch to Escanat, a beach near San Carlos, landed, and within a half hour was in touch with Pep Salvador and Captain Juan the fisherman. He learned of the San Carlos uprising and the necessity for haste. The morning of August eighth, Bayo landed four thousand militiamen at Estañol and Cosmi explained to him how by sending a column with a machine-gun by way of an unmapped pathway along the shore he could get behind the fascist volunteers and cut them off from escape through Santa Eulalia to Ibiza. Cosmi was placed in command of a column and told to go ahead. So it was that when the fascists found they had armed militiamen to fight, and not unarmed countrymen, they tried to retreat through the region of the abandoned mines and found Cosmi's force there waiting for them. Those who were not killed then and there were forced to take refuge in the interior of the island and were tracked down within a few days. It was in that engagement that the fascist mayor of Santa Eulalia was killed, and his body was thrown into a Phoenician mineshaft. So many of the fascists caught in Cosmi's trap had relatives who might prove sulky or troublesome that he set a story in circulation to the effect that the mayor and several of his friends had escaped in a sailboat before the patrol was organized.

Paler and most listlessly, with death in her posture and only life in her suffering eyes, Odila Nicolau sat in a corner in the pharmacy and shared the bed of one of the Catalan girls. Her father, the loud-voiced ex-captain, was a prisoner and one of the guiltiest of a very guilty company. Francisco Guasch was caught on the second day and was locked up with Bonéd, Harpo and one or two others in the Santa Eulalia guardroom of the *Cuartel*. The meals of the officers and prisoners were prepared at the Royalty and carried across the square by the white-coated Pedro, who stepped as lively and whistled as gaily as if he had been serving a favorite client on the terrace. Francisco Ribas, the lame student, was in the fortress of Ibiza and with him his friend the Santa Eulalia schoolmaster who never took a bath.

In the living room adjoining the Casa Rosita sat Vicenta, wife of the proprietor's son, sad but tearless, very dignified. Her brother, a lieutenant in Mestres' command, was one of the first to face a firing squad. Mestres was found hiding in the house of two old women, distant relatives, and was shot within an hour. Matutes, the banker, was ill in the hospital. The nature of his illness was not announced.

According to Bayo's instructions, he was to seal the doors of the banks (all three of them controlled by enemies of the government) and guard the funds and the account books until officials of the Bank of Spain could take charge of them. For goods bought or commandeered for the maintenance of his troops, he had been instructed to issue signed receipts which later were to be redeemed by the government. This caused much anxiety and dissatisfaction. The small storekeepers and farmers wanted cash, and began hiding away their wares and produce.

The churches in Ibiza and in the other towns were burned, if arms and ammunition were found in the premises or in the houses of their priests, but exceptions were made in the case of the church at Jesus, which contained valuable fifteenth-century Catalan frescoes, the church at San Miguel (whose priest had taught music to the children free of charge) and the architectural gem at San Jorge near the salt mines. Captain Bayo, extremely modest about his ability as a critic of art, took the advice of Rigoberto Soler and nothing of artistic value was lost.

Father Margall, who occupied the second floor above Guillermo, renounced the priesthood and joined the republican forces. Father Torres, one of the ringleaders of the conspiracy in Santa Eulalia, was held as a prisoner.

I heard an old man ask Guarapiñada, who was present when the priest at San Carlos opened fire on the crowd from the belfry of his church and in return was promptly shot: "How does a *cura* look when he is shot?"

"Oh, he just sits down" (hands over belly) "like anybody else," said Guarapiñada.

Eulalia Noguera's father, the lanky master mason who had lost so many contracts because of his republican loyalty, was beset with appeals from the members of fascist families to help them and to intercede for certain of the prisoners.

"This is not a matter for civilians to decide," he said. "The decisions must be made by the military authorities."

Eulalia, whose influence with the troops carried surprising weight, went to Captain Pastor, as did Cosmi, to ask for the release of young Francisco Ribas. For years she had been drawing water from Xumeu's well, which was one of the best in town. Each morning she had chatted with Xumeu's wife and daughter at the kitchen door. The sight of those women wandering homeless on the outskirts of the town touched her heart and she was determined to save their son. Miguel Tur persuaded the local committee to lend its influence. As a result Francisco and the young schoolmaster were provisionally released, but instructed to report to the *Cuartel* once each day.

Francisco, with ill-advised bravado, paraded up and down the main street until Cosmi took him aside and told him to go to his uncle's house in the country and not to be seen again, except for his daily appearance at the *Cuartel*. The boy was not wise enough to comply with this suggestion, and his friend the schoolmaster went into hiding and tried to escape in a boat.

Within two days, Francisco found himself in prison again, this time in the *Cuartel* of Santa Eulalia, and his parents and his sister were more terrified than ever.

Primitivo, never much addicted to work, was too excited to settle down to his nightly grind at the electric-light plant. Instead he joined the new militia, as recruiting sergeant, and Derek Rogers, the English painter, volunteered to tend the dynamo. But the lights were not always extinguished at midnight. If for any reason anyone wanted light at a later hour, the lights were glowing. Halbique, the French owner of the plant, flew a French flag over his house, a flag so big that all strangers mistook the building for a Consulate.

Tuesday morning before bus time I met Ignacio Riquer on his way to the bus, accompanied by Anna Cosmi and her dogs. He was cool and smiling, rather hurt because his furniture had been destroyed and thrown in a heap with that of Francisco Guasch and Nicolau, but quite prepared for any turn events might take. The greetings he received all along the street more than compensated for the loss of a few rocking-chairs. Every republican made it a point to be seen at his side. As he progressed from Gork's to the plaza he accumulated as an escort the republican roll-call. That Mestres had been his cousin and had been shot as a traitor the day before made no difference to Don Ignacio's friends. If the people had become sovereign, he knew he had nothing to fear. A man in Spain can be a man, rich or poor.

The *Diario* on Tuesday announced that Ibiza was to become a part of the new Catalan Free State, and in view of this it seemed fitting that Barcelona troops should replace the Valencians in the various *Cuartels*. Late that afternoon the Valencian company formed in the dusty street, farewells were exchanged, presents of fruit and *sobresada* passed out and acknowledged, toasts were offered in all the cafés. The sight was no longer novel and astonishing. The town had adapted itself once more.

It was then I had a most embarrassing experience which later was repeated several times. As a sort of joke, I had claimed a slight knowledge of palm reading. Some of the soldiers heard of this and crowded around me, extending their palms. It was their life-line that interested them, and I was horrified. No use to pretend I knew nothing of the art. They had heard of my reputation and insisted that I tell them the worst, but their faces were so anxious for the best that my eyes were blurred and my heart pounded fiercely. I spent a harrowing fifteen minutes, and finally told one of them (a man I believed could take a joke) that he would be shot, but by some woman's husband.

Just before the order to march was given, along the line came Don Pedro, the Dutch poet who preferred to be mad.

" '*Dios, 'dios,*" he shouted.

Catcalls, raspberries. "*Dios esta foutut*" (God is all washed up), the soldiers shouted. "Say *Salud*."

" '*Dios, 'dios.*" Don Pedro, feigning fury.

"*Salud*," roared the Valencianos. Men and women in doorways weeping with laughter.

"Attention."

" '*Dios.*"

"*Salud.*"

"Attention. Right face. Forward march."

Pursued by the explosive Dutchman, amid sharp cry of '*Dios* and resounding *Salud*, the Valencian volunteers began to march in dust and laughter, and as the column (head disappearing around the cliff) began to shorten and recede Don Pedro remained in possession of the field, yelling '*Dios* to the horde of small boys who jumped up and down with joy and cried, "*Dios foutut.*"

Now why, in the midst of the tumult and shouting, do memories persist of utter quiet, of hours so still (silver and indigo of moonlight) and shadows so familiar, of reality idealized and purified until it grows unreal? I am thinking of that evening. No need of lights of electric lamps or candles, with the bright moon streaming across the sea and spilling over the plaza. We lounged, the nocturnal handful of Catalan guards, Don Pedro, Juanito of the Royalty, and I, sprawled in confiscated easy-chairs beneath the archway of the old *Cuartel* and with very soft needle from the phonograph (formerly of a Guardia) endless *Cantos Flamencos*. It is said by some that these songs, so near the stratosphere of music, had their origin in the songs of Spanish cowboys to calm the cattle grazing on the plains at night. Others have it that the Spanish troops in the Flemish wars brought back the germ of these haunting melodies that are nearest to the Spanish heart, the result of infiltration and blending with songs of the North. Still others build upon the resemblance of the *Cantos Flamencos* to the songs of the Moors, their Oriental persistence and non-intrusion. Minor flight of the ribbons of tone, guitar response, rise of melody, and hanging perilously in air and in convolutions descending. Guitar. *Olé*, softly. Two o'clock, three o'clock. Smoking, saying almost nothing. Apotheosis of repose.

23. *La Lutte Finale*

IT IS a soul-shaking experience to see a fellow-creature demoralized with fear. Death is not nearly as impressive. One sees death all around, the rule that admits no exception. Everyone dies, but few of us are obliged to beg for our lives. This supreme misfortune overtook young Dr. Gonzalez, whose very timidity (reared a Catholic and a royalist) had made him cling to the hopes of the fascist movement. I have told you how he went from house to house, warning women about the ferocity and unscrupulousness of the leaders Spain had elected, of the menace of irreligion and socialist doctrine. Now the reckoning had come. He had not enlisted with the fascist forces when the fighting began, but had gone into hiding, and in hiding he was found by the Catalan militiamen.

Perhaps I should mention that his young wife had gone to Albacete for her first confinement just a week before communication with the mainland had been cut off. The doctor had been unable to follow her as he had planned and had received no word as to her condition.

At any rate, the progress of his days had brought him to the situation in which I saw him, half led and half supported by contemptuous militiamen, moaning, "Please don't kill me," and clasping and unclasping his hands, not daring to pray. This time it was not Eulalia Noguera who came to the rescue but her calm and resolute mother. For the day Dr. Gonzalez had come to town, Maria, the lovely older daughter of Señora Noguera was suffering from child-bed fever (which a large percentage of old Dr. Torres' obstetrical cases developed) and the young doctor, knowing Maria was as good as lost, had sadly and patiently cared for her, aided fiercely and efficiently by her mother, and the miracle had come off. Maria got well. It was Señora Noguera's turn.

"What! Kill a good doctor," she said. "How many good doctors have you?"

"None," said the Catalan sergeant ruefully.

"I'll work. I'll work. Just give me a chance," begged Dr. Gonzalez. "I can give you references. Professor Negrin . . . He's a socialist. . . ."

"Negrin," the sergeant said sharply.

"Yes, Professor Negrin in Madrid."

"What do you know about Doctor Negrin?"

"He was my teacher. Ask him . . ."

"This doctor saved my Maria," Señora Noguera said, not interested in Madrid.

The name of Negrin had a powerful effect, for all alert young Spaniards knew that not only was he one of the best teachers of medicine in Europe, but that in the dark days of Alfonso he had kept alive the revolutionary organization in the capital city and had escaped death only because of the regard in which he was held throughout the medical world outside of Spain. I wish I could make you understand how grateful the Spanish workmen are to their scientists, artists and intellectuals who have stood by them.

That wholesome relationship between workers and men of culture does not exist, in the same degree, in any other land. Scarcely a dozen Spaniards of high achievement in the professional world were in good standing with Alfonso's backward crew.

Dr. Gonalez was given his chance, and the work he did on the hospital ship more than repaid the militiamen for their merciful decision. It is too much to expect that Gonzalez revised his political ideas. But he watched his step, and the last I heard was serving faithfully as he had agreed. He was too good a doctor to be left in Santa Eulalia, of course, so the town was left with only the slothful and untidy Dr. Torres, who somehow escaped imprisonment.

Late that same afternoon I had a most embarrassing few moments. I had seen Pep des Horts and his wife go into the Royalty, and suggested to Flora that we join them there. The big Dane, who was more afraid of communism than old Father Coll was, had stayed close to his Arabie house and his amazing garden since the government troops had landed, but this afternoon by chance he came in for supplies. On the terrace of the Royalty I was accosted by one of the slimiest of the Palma fascists who had wormed his way into the good graces of the bishop and the young aristocrats there by his willingness to do anything they asked him. To see him alive, perfumed and nattily dressed in the midst of the Catalan soldiers surprised me so that I could scarcely understand his bad English.

"Do you want to go?" he asked, as if he were offering me an inestimable favor.

"Go?" I repeated. "What for?"

"You'd better see the Commander," he said.

"What Commander?"

"The American Commander," he said, I turned in the direction he indicated with a gesture and saw a naval officer in white uniform with epaulettes and braid, and beside the stranger an American who had organized certain public utilities in Mallorca and who had cheated the people so badly that he was known and despised all over the Balearic Islands. He was the Commander's interpreter, encyclopedia of Spain and European politics, and apparently his bosom friend.

"Good afternoon," I said, politely to the Commander and coldly to the other unwelcome type.

"Are you an American?" the naval officer asked.

"Yes," I said.

"Do you want to get away?"

"Why, no. I like it here better than ever," I replied.

He took out a notebook and wrote "Mr. and Mrs. Elliot Paul, No."

"Thank you for coming," I said. He was the only commander of a rescue ship of any nation who had penetrated as far as Santa Eulalia in looking for refugees, and I was pleased by his thoroughness if not his choice of company. That was not his fault, probably. One Spick looked just like another to him. The public utility gent he had picked up wore stylish clothes and spoke with disdain of the Reds. The officer knew not a word of Spanish, had no grasp of the history of Spain or of the situation into which his duty had projected him. He was a middle-aged babe in the wood with a destroyer, several high-powered cannon and a crew of hearty gobs under his command.

An old Englishwoman hurried up to ask him for passage.

"You think it is necessary to go?"

"Madam, I'm supposed to be neutral, but I've seen plenty." He lowered his voice and spoke in a horrified whisper. "I never thought that I'd have to ride behind a red flag, but in Valencia that was the only way I could get by. The communists are the *conservative* party there."

"Do you think we should go?" Derek Rogers whispered at my side.

"When he says the situation is bad, he means it is good from our point of view. He wants the rebels to win," I said.

Just to my right, the well-dressed business man was saying with apparent satisfaction, "The insurgents have two-thirds of Spain under their control. In a month, they'll have Madrid and Barcelona."

Pep des Horts came up. "What about it, Commander?" he asked.

"My advice is to go," the officer said. "Look at these kids with guns." (He pointed to the Catalan militiamen.) "It'll be the same old story. Their leaders will run away, get out of the country and leave them holding the bag."

With difficulty I restrained myself. Remember he's only a dumbbell, I repeated to myself. But I could not help thinking of Largo Caballero, with whom I had talked in Madrid and whose son I had known before and after he was in prison for his part in the 1934 uprising against Gil Robles. Big-hearted and courageous Caballero leaving his followers in the lurch, indeed! And Julio del Vayo, my friend and one of the best newspapermen on earth. And Araquistain and Negrin and Prieto. Picture them, after a lifetime of heroic service (of which this well-meaning fellow in white ducks had never heard), showing a yellow streak and deserting their comrades.

Guillermo approached. "Are you going?" he asked.

"Of course not," I replied. The Catalan sergeant smiled.

"Xumeu is one of us," he said.

And, surely, I am nearer that Catalan sergeant than to the envoys my country so thoughtfully sent to that island town. At least, I aspire to be.

I was not even angry, but only a little sad. Those ragged boys with guns had learned what kind of faces reactionaries have and knew on sight that the visitors were sympathizers of their enemies. They would have given a right arm apiece to get that mangy Mallorquin interpreter alone for five minutes. But they did not hold the incident against me. I saw no flaw in their comradeship, no suspicion or distrust.

Often, by day and by night, I think of that naval officer. He bothers me. He was essentially a decent sort, nothing sly about him, a man to be trusted. His manners were pleasing, his intentions of the best. With another set of tenets in his head, like peas in a pod, he would have viewed the situation differently.

Well, he impressed Pep des Horts, and to Mrs. Lange's horror her impulsive Danish husband decided to abandon their home and garden within the hour and sail for parts unknown. Probably it was the lack of medicine for his treatments that drove Lange away. We were sorry to see him go, but Derek and Eileen Rogers stayed, and that night we ate chicken and sweet potatoes with them and tried to get back into a proper island mood. Mrs. Gramkow, who had changed her mind at the gangplank when the British destroyer had called, could not resist the invitation to sail on an American destroyer. With the usual confusion and explosion of Junior League brogue she contrived on that occasion to get off with her two protesting boys and eventually to reach Baltimore, where, by all means, let us leave her.

In connection with Dr. Gonzalez' removal to the hospital ship, I forgot to mention its effect on the Halbiques. With that tendency toward a rough sort of balance that Providence seems to show, Halbique, much worried Frenchman, just as he was about to lose his light plant and his savings (or at least he thought he was) had to face the fact that his wife was to give birth to a baby. Madame Halbique had been troubled, in fact almost hysterical, on account of the bombings and battles and troop movements, and when she learned that the only doctor who might help her was old Torres, who scattered puerperal fever among the young women of Ibiza as Don Carlos Roman bestowed peanuts on small boys, she collapsed. She wept, and simply refused to be comforted.

Building was at a standstill. There was no cement or other materials and supplies, no one had money with which to pay the contractors and of course the contractors could not pay their men. The amiable hours of trading in the stores had dwindled and their tone had sharpened. At the Casa Rosita old Juan the Cowboy and his fat complaining wife sat on the sidewalk or in their living room, where Vicenta mourned her brother, abusing the new regime as loudly as they dared. Ferrer's automobile had been idle in the shed for some time, there being no gasoline except for military purposes. The country people who were unwilling to part with money but had produce to exchange came to Las Delicias and Ferrer did the best he could for them. Guarapiñada found it more amusing to stay in San Carlos on his small farm, so Tot Barat was closed. At the Casa Miguel, the dropsical old woman pottered here and there and kept the few customers waiting an interminable time. Her husband, Miguel Tur, was busy all day at the *Cuartel*.

The question of payment for the supplies needed for the soldiers was a difficult one. The storekeepers and bakers were obliged to accept the *vales* or promises to pay from the military authorities, but there their circulation stopped abruptly. No one else would accept them from the storekeepers. Cosmi gave out everything he had, and accepted the *vales* without murmur, but at the Royalty Juanito's mother was sullen and indignant and did not even try to be polite to the men who had spared her son and his enterprise. The bakers were hard hit, because in order to buy flour they had to pay cash (at a very high price), and the bulk of their output went to the soldiers and was paid for in what was (temporarily at least) completely worthless paper. The dynamo of Halbique's light plant turned merrily each night, but he knew it was useless to try to collect his monthly bills. The fishermen were not anxious to fish, since the army was the only large purchaser and *vales* could not be exchanged for drinks over the bar. There were not more than two dozen men in Santa Eulalia who had the slightest conception of the problems confronting the government, and the fears and suspicions of all the others were raised because of the cessation of the flow of money. Guillermo, Ramon, the Barberet went around with long faces and a dejected air.

Captain Bayo knew that his four thousand militiamen were a burden on the island and announced that he would go on to Mallorca within a few days. The transport had been sent back to Valencia and Barcelona for more men. Even before the Bayo expedition departed, two men had begun to stand out prominently among their colleagues of the Local Committee in Santa Eulalia. They were Carlos, the young schoolmaster with light curly hair and blue eyes and always a warm smile, and Pep Salvador. The latter showed promptly that he knew the exact point at which joking should cease, and he addressed his attention to the principal malcontents and frightened them into line. Because the old folks at the Casa Rosita were complaining, Pep, rifle slung on shoulder, took the mess sergeant there oftener when goods were needed, and favored Ferrer at Las Delicias, who would have given the soldiers his entire stock without regret. All day Pep roamed the countryside with his silent communist friend, giving warnings to recalcitrant peasants. Ramon's sour face annoyed him, so he found repair work to be done and had the bus driver spend his afternoons patching together broken-down machines.

It is strange that because Joachim Guasch, Maria Anfita's fiancé, had been so bold and reckless in the days before the *coup*, Pep Salvador seemed to like him better than the other fascists. And so it came about that when Pep found the young man's hiding place in a farm house on the outskirts of San Miguel, he sent word there by a relative of young Guasch, advising the latter to give himself up. The next morning, the young brawler and arch-enemy of Pep Torres presented himself at the *Cuartel* and was locked up in an upper room, where he paced the floor restlessly, smoked cigarettes constantly and thought about getting away.

It was in the course of those first few days after Bayo's arrival that I began to appreciate how much damage the fascist *coup* had done to the island life. Families, hitherto friendly and to whom political differences were of sixth- or seventh-rate importance, were now aligned in bitter feuds.

"It will be two hundred years before people here will be friendly again," said Pedro at the Royalty, sadly.

The farmers kept on working, but without zest. They knew there would be only a local sale for their crops, and that no money was available to pay for them. Carpenters, blacksmiths and other tradesmen made no pretense of working and felt that vague uneasiness that idleness produces in habitually busy men. The women, having nothing to fear in the way of death or imprisonment, moaned and protested incessantly. But those among them who had expected that a government by a local committee would be no government at all were rudely disabused by Pep Salvador. It hurt me because so many honest and likable people had no political perspective, no ability to fix the blame, no awareness that they were members of a nation and the human race. Too many years they had been fed upon the priest-ridden *Diario* and *Voz*.

Too many centuries the march of world events had passed them by. They were capable of suffering but not of understanding, except for those few who had always understood. On them fell the burden of the island's inertia.

The old blind woman at Mousson's and Vicent's old sister still were pathetically eager to talk with me, and to have me reassure them. I could not tell them that there were lean and terrible years ahead, that Spain, even if she could save herself destruction or the ultimate degradation, would be crippled, that the flowering of all her hopes would be deferred, that the excess of perfidy and unscrupulousness would breed a frightful reaction and revenge. The people of Ibiza, except for a half dozen arch-conspirators, had not brought the disaster upon themselves. They had been forced to be traitors; now they were obliged to pay dearly for their rescue. Young Carlos, a teacher, saw the problem in terms of education. All the people, young and old, must be educated, he said. Those who had little education of the sort the church had dominated had the least to unlearn. There were many whose minds could never be opened, and Carlos knew that somehow they must be prevented from doing harm. Men could be shot, if necessary, but what to do with the women just one step removed from Oriental seclusion? His views he explained to me in long hours of conversation. The old people, he thought, should be allowed to go on as they had always done, even to go to church if they wanted to. The young must either work for freedom and self-government or be weeded out. There was to be no more special privilege. Each attempt to get back into the old grooves of Matutes' monopoly must be stamped out at its inception.

Old Miguel Tur was busy with his legal papers. Each prisoner had a hearing before the committee, the minutes of which were meticulously transcribed by Miguel, and he wrote the decision of the committee in such perfect language that no lawyer in Madrid could have found a flaw.

What beat upon my brain, making itself felt in spite of my thankfulness and enthusiasm, was that life in Santa Eulalia, which had been so pleasant, well-rounded and naturally abundant, overnight had become grim. Where there had been harmony and no struggle, relentless purposes arose, distant and thorny objectives. The blue waters of the Mediterranean no longer isolated the island from the peninsula. What unscrupulous men had torn down must be built up, not on old designs but with a modern structure. Ibiza, which had nearly always been abreast of history and social evolution, had rested calmly in a sheltered backwater since the expulsion of the Moors seven hundred years ago. August eighth and ninth of 1936 had landed it in the swiftest current of modernity.

Knowing the hopes and prospects of the individuals who made up our pleasant community, I had to face the fact that they had been swept away. Toni Ferrer could not continue his progress as a merchant. Arabie would not blossom in Cosmi's lifetime, according to his cherished plan. Odila would die, not become a pharmacist; Angeles was starving; Maria Anfita would not escape the halfwits in her home. Her fiancé was a prisoner and soon would be a corpse. Men and young women now must be content to work for others in a visionary future, and what was there in the world situation of 1936 to convince them that humanity was forging ahead? Education? What comfort could be found in history for these lost generations? It was a bad moment to preach the gospel of faith in mankind. Our town, in all its essentials, had been destroyed.

The stamina of the people, however, had not been destroyed and their courage and adaptability at once began to assert itself. During a few days depression and despair were given full rein, then I heard remarks like these:

"Don't bother to pay me, Señor Paul. You can't pay me, I can't pay anyone else, so it's all the same."

And in the bars, instead of the traditional "*Salud y pesetas*" as men raised their glasses, smilingly said Ferrer and soon afterward the others, "*Salud y vales.*" Who can resist such people, or think of them as dead until they are under ground?

The people of Santa Eulalia, unaccustomed to quick changes, trained to think in terms of donkey carts and sailing boats, could not in one day catch the rhythm of airplanes and torpedo-boat destroyers. Their food supply was low, their means of selling their grain and vegetables and fish and hogs cut off. No money was in circulation. Four thousand strangers were there, to be fed. No wonder their first reaction was one of dismay, but it was dispelled by Bayo's prompt and business-like departure. Thursday morning, August 13, they saw a transport filled with new troops from the mainland steam past the harbor, bound for Ibiza. Four hundred Barcelona volunteers were drilling in the main street. The non-coms had spread the word that they all were to embark for Mallorca that afternoon. I received confirmation of the rumor from Captain Pastor and Carlos, chairman of the local committee. Young Carlos, intelligent and willing, was to be left in charge, with only four days of preparation.

At three o'clock a transport and one destroyer weighed anchor just inside the *Vei Isglesi*. A few moments later four hydroplanes circled low above the town and swooped gracefully to rest in the quiet waters of the cove. The Barcelona troops, with packs and bundles slung over their shoulders, formed loosely along the street, from Gork's to the plaza. All the people of the town were gathered on the sidewalks, the fishermen in front of Antonia's café, Ferrer, the young barber, the blacksmith's helpers near Las Delicias, across the street the staff and customers of Cosmi's hotel. At Gork's Vicente Cruz and the mason's helpers. Juanito and Pedro at the Royalty. Can Xumeu's emptiness and broken windows. The dogs of the town went up and down the line, sniffing, barking, enjoying the excitement.

We watched from Cosmi's roof. The cove, with the huge grey transport, the lean destroyer, the swaying hydroplanes to augment the fishing boats which belonged to the scene. The double rank of volunteers was thinned and fed by men dashing in and out of cafés, farewells were exchanged, good-natured banter. An hour or more the troops stood waiting, not at all impatiently. Then Captain Pastor appeared, the ragged ranks straightened and a detachment was counted off from Gork's end.

"Right face!"

The first detachment faced north. "Forward, march." They started marching, turning right at the lane which led to the shore and were halted on the low flat rocks two hundred yards away. Four whaleboats put out from the transport and the first men clambered in. Slowly they were rowed alongside, and scrambled up the gangplank. Another load.

The ranks now occupied the stretch between Can Xumeu and the plaza. Another detachment was counted off, faced right, and followed the same course to the shore. The whaleboats gathered them in. They swelled the distant throng on the deck of the transport, shouting and waving. Now the ranks on shore extended from Can Cosmi to the plaza.

"Right face!" Cosmi appeared and a shout arose.

"*Viva* Cosmi!" Ah, yes. *Viva* Cosmi. *Viva* the banquets he had served them as meals. *Viva* the flanking movement he had executed, *Viva* the *vales* he had cheerfully accepted, knowing it might be for years and it might be forever. *Viva* good men, everywhere, who will not knuckle down and grimace and eat crow and play with the big boys, and to hell with the rest.

"Come on. Why not come with us?" Captain Pastor held up his hand. Cries from non-coms. Silence!

"Comrade Cosmi has work to do, important work. Our leader, Captain Bayo, has asked him to stay where he is for a while," the officer said.

"*Viva la Republica!*"

"*Viva!*" rang out above the chorus the hearty voice of Ferrer.

The detachment came to attention, faced right and marched to the shore. Then I saw Guillermo cover his face with both hands and turn away, as if he were overwhelmed with grief. For several paces to the rear, with an armed guard in front and another behind him, staggered the cross-eyed boy in an old pair of pants, bearing on his shoulders a live sheep he could barely sustain. We all were aware of the detachment marching two and two, ahead, turning into the lane, falling out by the shore, but pitying women and awestruck men could not seem to take their eyes from that struggling figure, the boy with the sheep, stumbling, no doubt weeping from eyes badly crossed. Would he fall? Caught breath. No, he'll make it. And fainter the bleats of the sheep, down the lane and lost in the crowd on the rocks.

There was only one detachment left, from the post office to the plaza and on the steps of the post office sat the green-eyed Maria whose devil-may-care young man was pacing a room of the *Cuartel*. For a moment she seemed the focus of attention, embarrassed attention on the part of the troops and the townsmen. Everyone knew the story. She sat among the members of her defective family, forehead so perfect and cool, shawl so precisely wrapped around her shapely shoulders, a jewel of cool womanhood and misfortune on a dusty velvet cloth. Heredity, environment, circumstance all against her. I had never seen her weep or cheer, but I had felt, and the strange throng now felt her emanations. I am sure she is the Lady of Elche. Does no one want to place her in a niche? Will no one make that journey to reclaim an unmistakable work of art, and wrap it and ship it and let it stand in some distant hall, away from the foaming old man who passes for her father and the idiot brothers she has taught to be clean?

"Right face!" This time Captain Pastor takes his place at the head of the column. A voice begins the *Internationale.* They sing. Ferrer, all the men of the town who have just learned the tune, Pep Torres standing at my side. All sing. They pass Can Cosmi, the broken Can Xumeu, the old baker's shop, Tot Barat, Can Gork. Wildly singing and head thrown back, among his fellow-masons, is the Catalan who plays the drums and castanets.

"*C'est la lutte finale!*"

Would to God that it were! If those were the last of the boys to be served up to foreign machine-guns, to be betrayed in all the capitals of the world, to be scorned by well-dressed American Commanders, to wind my bowels on a drum. Oh, no, *enfants de la patrie!* Nix, oppressed of earth! Not yet. Not half. Go get yourselves killed. Go, fire those pathetic old-fashioned rifles, what few you have. So long!

They are gone. The last boatload is rowed to the transport. Then a young boy comes running up Cosmi's stairs to our roof.

"Pep," he says. "They've taken your bicycle."

"Ah, *fotre*," said Pep.

Pep hurried down to see Cosmi and a moment later I saw Cosmi hurrying down the lane. He got into a rowboat and a little later came rowing back from the transport with a bicycle, which he rode back to where Pep was standing.

"It's a good bicycle, but it's not mine," Pep said.

Cosmi smiled. "Who said it isn't?" he asked, and went back to his work behind the bar.

Extraordinary emptiness of town. The men in groups, with large contingents missing. The same trees, that seem farther apart. Echoes of white walls, stray bird flying high to Cala Llonga. On the bluffs of Formentera a streak of light from the setting sun. The wine-dark sea, and violet warships. The stirring, rising and receding of hydroplanes. The *lutte finale*. The just a song at twilight. The kingdom and the power and the glory. The cat's nuts.

And sitting in an armchair, in front of the deserted *Cuartel*, is the Secretario, rocking, waiting unhurriedly for other masters to enter and be served.

24. Maño

FROM beneath the arches of the *Cuartel*, long after the ships had gone to sea and the Secretario had gone home to supper, there arose that evening a warm geyser of sound, a voice springing from earth's darkness and reaching toward the starlight. The first poignant phrase of a *jota* of Aragon. Red earth, sturdy people and their own mode of song. To be explicit, Maño. He was not tall, but he was very broad and strong. Swarthy face, eyes black and perpetually gay, nose a bit impudent. He came to Santa Eulalia when the town was on the verge of gloom and filled it with song and laughter. Five minutes after his arrival he was singing a *jota* in the night, and from that moment until the bitter end of this story, the occasion of his leaving, he sustained the morale of that bewildered community. No one there will ever forget him, or what his presence meant. He became a part of the town, and without him the town will never be the same.

Maño was a private in the volunteer militia, a workman who had never been to school. Of all the young men I saw marching to an almost certain death, Maño is the one I feel certain as I write today must be still alive. I cannot believe he could fall, that his strong young heart could cease to beat, that his songs could be silenced without some corresponding pang of death in me. Maño is still fighting. I state that as a fact, without a word of confirmation. *Viva Maño!* I think in less than four weeks Maño taught me more about how a man should behave than I have learned from anyone else in a lifetime.

The period following the departure of the Bayo expedition was unique in the history of Santa Eulalia. A dozen members of the newly formed local militia occupied the *Cuartel* and policed the town. The civil administration was in the hands of the Local Committee. The first sacks of mail were brought from the mainland by government planes; the two-masted schooner *Isabel Matutes* brought a cargo of flour, coffee and sugar from Barcelona under the government flag. Carlos had transformed Can Xumeu into a schoolroom and had started his program of education for the young. The teacher was Fernando, who had been in the fascist prison, and for the first time boys and girls studied together. The country roads were patrolled by Pep Salvador and the republican mayor.

In command at the *Cuartel* was a gentle-mannered corporal who although born in Ibiza had spent his life in Cuba. Because of that he was known as El Cubano. His men were Maño the Aragonese, Pedro, an Ibiza fisherman, two brothers, Jaume and Luis, both students and a laborer from Murcia. If there was any doubt in the minds of the inhabitants as to whether the *milicianos* could preserve order, as the Guardias had done, it was quickly dispelled. Maño and Pedro, always side by side, kept order all by themselves.

The first mail brought news to many anxious people, and, generally speaking, it was good news because the relatives of the inhabitants of Santa Eulalia, if they were on the mainland, were likely to be near Barcelona or Valencia. In both cities an order approximating normality had been preserved and the casualties had been light.

Reassuring news came each noon in the *Diario*. Bayo had landed his forces without the loss of a man. Several Mallorquin towns had received him with joy and thanksgiving. His plan was to close in on Palma, slowly, cutting it off from the rest of the island, blockading it by sea. The hum of the schoolroom on the main street was comforting, suggestive of continuity. El Cubano was not disposed to make his authority felt in any unpleasant way. Maño and Pedro had so much force and determination that no one expected the town to get out of hand. Sindik, stricken man, went with bowed head back to his carpenter shop and hour after hour he worked with plane, saw, hammer and lathe. The death of his son had broken his spirit, but its effect was more far-reaching and disastrous than that. Because Juan had been shot, the committee was embarrassed in each merciful decision. Don Rafael Sainz was technically innocent. There was no fair reason for taking away his house, and still, although the committeemen were unanimous in their desire to be just to the fat millionaire, they hesitated to do so because of Juan Sindik. Carlos was especially anxious that clemency should be shown the prisoners, that only those who had forced others to be guilty should be shot. Again arose the spectre of Juan Sindik. How could Harpo be allowed to live when Juan was dead?

Could Francisco Ribas, son of a fascist and a fascist
at heart, be walking the streets when the carpenter's
son was underground? Miguel Tur was at his best in
the midst of all these perplexities.

"We all know it was a mistake to kill Juan Sindik,"
he said, his head shaking from side to side as he peered
over his spectacles. "That tragic event should not
lead us to other follies." He suggested to his colleagues
that the Local Committee had not been specifically
authorized to try cases of treason and that the prisoners should be held until some competent authority
was ready to conduct their trials. Cheerfully the committeemen of Santa Eulalia acceded to this policy,
and the city of Ibiza and the other towns followed the
precedent. The total number of prisoners on the
island, charged with complicity in the fascist plot or
with bearing arms against the legally constituted government, was two hundred and thirty-nine. Most of
the soldiers of the Ibiza garrison had gladly agreed to
serve in the republican army and were on the way to
Mallorca, a few of the non-coms being left to help
organize the new militia.

A thinning and sharpening had taken place in
Santa Eulalia. I could not shake off the illusion that
the trees along the main street were farther apart. It
is true that at dawn the dogs who had been sleeping
in the dust in the middle of the street would stretch
and shake themselves and walk sleepily to Cosmi's
backyard where the deaf Antonio would wordlessly
receive them. Do you think he relaxed and talked or
even smiled as he handed out the refuse and bones?
Not at all. His eyes had that same far-away look, that
smouldering. He said no extra words and made no un-

necessary motions. Old Antonia Masear arrived, bowed and said *"Bon Dia"* so courteously. It was as if, on her way to her daily work, she had passed through many vacuums. Catalina, the Wedgwood drudge, wore a frown of perplexity. Could she and Vicente Cruz get married now the priests were gone? Sadly she shook her head. She knew nothing of marriage outside of the Church.

Ramon, in tuning up his motorcycle, did not seem to have the old-time relish for noise, and the bus creaked for lack of grease, was painted grotesquely with F.A.I. and U.H.P., and passengers were few. Tuesday was no longer market day in Ibiza; there were no processions of mule carts to be passed in the dust. Still, there were many activities persisting, bearing no apparent relation to the necessities. For instance, through all the strange events already recorded the ice plant on the waterfront in Ibiza had made ice and filled siphons every day, and Ramon brought back several cakes of ice on the back of the bus and on the roof.

Crack! Crack! of rifleshots, all morning long. No pattern. No rhythm of silences between. Witless crack! I was annoyed at first, especially because I understood that in other parts of Spain ammunition was scarce. I protested to Carlos and to El Cubano. The town was kept in a state of uneasiness by the continual, senseless din of rifle fire. El Cubano explained that several of his men had never fired a gun. They needed practice. I told him he should organize the practice, not permit haphazard firing, and he did so, after a fashion. Having been in the regular army, he was glad to be rid of the arrogant severity he had been obliged to assume, and a population that has been unfairly disarmed and forbidden firearms likes to hear guns go off. So in the morning hours, and again between *siesta* time and twilight, militiamen and the idle men of the town popped at targets floating on the sea or set up on the shore. In fact, I took part in one or two small competitions myself, the loser to pay for the drinks. The *paseo* had become an amateur shooting gallery, and the *Cuartel* was the merriest place in the town.

Small boys very frequently mounted the spiral pathways on the hill and amused themselves by ringing the church bell. Always to the delight of Ferrer and Guarapiñada. Carlos, however, believed the old people should not be offended or frightened unnecessarily. Apparently the same difficulty had arisen in other towns in Spain, for the *Diario* announced that offensive statues and church bells in Catalonia were to be melted and the metal used for cannon or ammunition. The Local Committee of Santa Eulalia sent a crew of men to the hilltop, dismantled the bell, lowered it from the belfry and stored it with confiscated fascist arms in a building that formerly had been used by a reactionary organization of peasant leaders.

We were finding Can Pedro es Mallorqui' rather noisy and dusty under changed conditions, and also the plumbing had gone wrong, and there was no chance to get spare parts from Barcelona. Juanito of the Royalty had an apartment across the lane from the *Cuartel*, above the home of the Secretario and his family. The Fairchilds had occupied it when we first arrived. So we decided to move. Our moving was a sort of game, as nearly everything had become. Juanito and Pedro of the Royalty, Pep Torres and Eulalia Noguera assisted with the temporary packing, Ferrer contributed his donkey cart (without donkey) and of course Maño, who had a hand in everything, immediately insisted on taking the donkey's place between the shafts. Cartloads of our clothes, pots, pans and furniture were rushed up the street and across the plaza at breakneck speed. Maño unloaded below and threw things to the balcony, where the sailor Pedro caught them with the utmost ease. Cheers rang out from the *Cuartel* across the way. People watched and shouted from doorways as another cartload came along, Maño bucking and braying, and, yes, quite audibly farting. Peanut's two-decker bed, one of the wonders of the town, became a bishop's canopy, and chanting impeccable Latin, Pep Torres and Pep Salvador accompanied Ferrer, the bishop with a small chamber-pot crown. On each of the four up-turned legs of the bed were partly demolished helmets left behind by the Guardia Civil.

Carlos was a serious-minded young man and had the weight of a new civilization on his shoulders. At first he was disturbed at the tone of levity affairs had taken on. Not so Pep Salvador or El Cubano, and soon I convinced Carlos that he had been wrong.

"The town needs gaiety," I said to him. And gaiety it had. Every evening on Cosmi's terrace the singers gathered. Pep Torres could never memorize a line of instrumental music, although he sang well from memory, so in all the hilarious throngs he could be seen fiddling earnestly with his eyes glued on the notes and around him heads turned skyward, seaward, helter-skelter. I typed several copies of the words of Rigo-berto's songs. He stole away from his house on the hill, in which his German wife remained sadly in se-clusion. She had money galore, but it was not possible for her to take it into Germany or to go there herself. Sadly Rigoberto descended the lane, but before he stepped into the light on Cosmi's sidewalk he placed aside his worries and let himself go. He never had sung as well.

"*No te vayas, no te vayas*"—the sailor's soft but cynical farewell. "*Pescando la sangonisa*"—ribald song about catching eels. "*Dos y tres fon cinq*"—of the properties of numbers. "*No em volen cap que yo stigi borachu*" (I don't want to get drunk).

Accompanied by trumpet and accordion, the crowd would sing, but with ten or twelve strong voices like those of Maño, Rigoberto, Pep Torres, El Cubano, the singing had a new effectiveness. Yes. Maria An-fita, green-eyed goddess. I saw you smile when we sang "I don't want to get drunk." The moonlight touched the Lady of Elche.

Then there always came a moment when everyone shouted "Maño!" Hatless, sturdy arms bare, Maño would throw back his shoulders and nod to me. We then had no guitar, so I played the inevitable tradi-tional and only introduction to the *jota*, and as I re-tarded and paused, up rising went that geyser of sound, a song of Aragon, of a woman, of a bullfighter's sweetheart's handkerchief and another I particularly enjoyed, the words of which (rhyme lost in transla-tion) go something like this:

The executioner turned the screw
My father stuck out his tongue
My mother was deeply affected (*emocionada*).

More singing in chorus, Cosmi with a tray of drinks
and his bashful "*Bona nit, jovens*" (Good evening,
young men), and Rigoberto would be asked for a solo.
Never twice the same, or seldom. Something nostalgic
and romantic. Always of love. And now he sang of
love, and our company listened as if the song were an
elegy, that some precious gift of the ancients had been
known as love, and actually once upon a time men
sang beneath balconies and women peeped through
shutters. Leading the singing of a crowd, Rigoberto
was all smiles. A soloist, he was sad.

Then Pep Torres. Pep always had to sing about the
young man from Granada, but the big moments for
all assembled came when he consented to sing, *Ai,
ai, ai.*

And at midnight, sometimes, Maño and Pedro the
sailor had to stand guard at the electric light plant.
So half of us went with them and there at the fork of
the Arabie and San Carlos roads carried on, to the
amazement and joy of the neighbors, until the hours
of dawn.

We had invented another kind of game for the
mornings, and it spread contagiously through the
town until nearly everyone felt he had some part in it.
Sugar again was scarce, practically nonexistent, coffee
had disappeared, white flour was only for the friends
of someone who had some. Flora and I knew that one
could eat magnificently of the products grown right
there on the island, and began to advertise the fact

to the neighbors whose lifelong habits of cooking certain dishes in certain ways made it hard for them to get along. Each day we had a luncheon party, taking turns in cooking and planning the meals, using nothing imported. The cooks were Flora, Juanito of the Royalty, Pep Torres and I, and each day we had a guest or several. We used the oven at the new baker's. Captain Juan saved the most exotic fishes for us. Pastry was baked at the Royalty. Everyone in town got a glimpse of the dishes as we carried them steaming through the front or back street.

Everyone began to have a good time, and the mood of the town was reflected even in the faces of the prisoners who paced wearily in the *Cuartel*. An ominous note had ceased to sound. They all began to hope they would live and be free some time again and that their jailers were incapable of hate. That the men and women of Santa Eulalia, in spite of centuries of efforts to hold them back, were capable of conducting their own affairs in a civilized and delightful manner was incontestable. We breathed the air of freedom, with all the scents of summer shrubs and flowers. Harvests lay on the fields, the blindfolded mules ran in circles on the old-fashioned threshing platforms. Water in abundance coursed through the white plaster flumes and conduits left by the Moors. Pepper trees on the *paseo*, olives, almond trees, crouching figs, plume-spreading *garobas* silk green on the outlying farms.

Then the knife of tragedy cut sharply through our section of town. The brother of Eulalia Noguera, who had been chilled during his nights in the woods, took to his bed. Only a few months before he had had a severe case of pneumonia and the exposure had under-

mined his feeble resistance. Eulalia was in despair. I
had some medicine given us by an American doctor
to reduce fever, so I went to see the boy and left some
pills for him. The lad did not seem to be dangerously
ill. He lay patiently and quietly, complaining of a
pain in his left side. Dr. Torres was summoned but
did not care to come. Señora Noguera had blamed
him openly for Maria's childbed infection and had
dismissed him from the case the moment the young
Dr. Gonzalez had come upon the scene. The old doctor had been accustomed to run things with a high
hand and did not realize that times had changed. His
failure to visit the Noguera boy came to the ears of
El Cubano.

"Maño!" he shouted. Out of the guardroom like a
clown rolled Maño, adjusting his steel helmet as he
rolled. Pedro the sailor, as always, was with him.
They heard the story from El Cubano and, making
noises like children who had been told of apple pie,
they started out on the double quick. Ten minutes
later the back street saw a spectacle that threw it into
convulsions. Dr. Torres, not completely dressed and
in fact with trousers incompletely buttoned, marched
hastily down the center (rocks and bumps) with
Maño and Pedro behind him on either side. Their
bayonets were fixed and moved in an exploratory way
around the doctor's stern, and from the way he hopped
ahead now and then it was certain that occasionally
he felt cold steel. At the Noguera's doorway, the
husky militiamen dropped their rifles, grasped the
doctor by the shoulders and the seat of his pants and
heaved. Not a quiet way to enter a sickroom, but a
most emphatic one.

"Report each day at the *Cuartel* how the boy is getting on," Maño said to the quailing doctor.

"He's very sick, I tell you," the doctor said.

"He'd better get well," said Maño.

The second night following, the Noguera boy died. It was not the fault of Dr. Torres, much as I should like to blame him. I knew how narrowly the boy had escaped death in his last attack of pneumonia, that his lungs were hopelessly weakened, and in the interests of the people's justice, so dear to the hearts of all of us just then, I sought out Maño and Pedro before the news reached them and explained as best I could. I had only a little knowledge, but Maño had none. He had never been sick a day in his life. He thought it over and promised to take my word, but Dr. Torres had the fright of his life. He ran through the fields to Santa Gertrudis and hid there until word reached him that he would be thrown into jail if he did not come back to his post without delay.

In conformity with the local custom, Flora and I were obliged to enter that stricken household within twenty-four hours and offer our condolences. We were not prepared, no one of our race and temperament ever could be prepared, for the wildness of grief we encountered there. Men and women, wailing and groaning. Heartrending sobs and cries, renewed, frantic outbursts at the sight of us. What can a man say or do? Eulalia, our sister Eulalia, dissolved in tears. Sobbing like a child. All the fruits of liberty swept away, and in the bedroom in plain view through the open door the frail corpse of the boy. The lanky father, face down, grovelling on the floor. The next morning, at the hour set for the funeral, I forced my-

self back into that harrowing area, and when the boy
was lifted into a coffin unbridled howls and tearing of
hair. When the coffin passed through the doorway,
Eulalia completely mad, wailing "*Adios*, Juanito!
Good-bye, brother. For always. *Ai!*" Collapsing. The
father, knees buckling, wailing, struggling as if he
were drowning in a swift current, supported by two
of his friends. The women did not follow the body to
the grave, but the neighbor men, some with black
hats and jackets, others in their shirt sleeves. Cries
and shrieks of women. *Adios!* Women in doorways all
along the street, eyes streaming. Women in Cosmi's
backyard, erect and weeping. I could not see. Tears
were blinding me, and gropingly I felt my way
through Cosmi's gate as the rest of the procession continued to the hill and I sat in the dark dining room
alone until I could control myself. For the first time,
a funeral procession mounted the spiral pathway of
the hill without the tolling of the church bell, no
priest, no altar boys. Just dead.

Poor Anetta, the Barberet's sister-in-law who was
living on his meagre charity, had worked in our
kitchen the summer before and we called on her
again, for Eulalia would spend the next ten days or
more indoors with her sorrowing family. Anetta came,
fluttering at the prospect of a few *pesetas*. On an
island fragrant with wheat and corn, surrounded by
deep blue sea replete with fishes, above the soil in
which coins of Phoenicians and Romans are sown like
sterile seeds, *pesetas*. Death stings, *pesetas* move on
checkerboards and the fewer there are the tenser the
game.

With dismay I learned once again that my courage

was not sterling. I should have called each day, or at
least every other day, at the Noguera home. Could I
do it? No. I cut through alleys and backyards to
avoid it. But daily went Sindik, while the carpenter
shop was silent, and sat beside the lanky father. The
thoughts of Noguera went south to the hill and of
Sindik numbly to a haystack north. Many days.

And as sharply through the plaza cut the sabre of
rejoicing. A wedding. Fernando the schoolmaster and
his Marguerita in black, the plump orphan girl with
hair so black, with finely drawn eyebrows, and skin
as pale as ivory. What she had suffered while Fernando was in the fascists' hands had made her almost
slender. Smilingly waiting, clean shirt, white collar
and black coat, the Secretario. He had pawed through
many books to learn what he could about civil mar-
riages. In a lower room next door to us the bride, the
groom and a few near relatives were gathered. In the
Royalty kitchen, Juanito, Manuelo, the white-coated
Pedro were working feverishly. A long table had been
set in the dining room. Beneath the arbor, Antonia
the Chaste and the small Marietta were working
under the direction of the groom's proud sister, re-
nowned for her pastry. Antonia the Chaste had hoped
in her uninformed way that so many changes in the
town might bring back her husband from America,
but nothing changed for her.

The ceremony took place in the mayor's office and
was soon over. Then Fernando and Marguerita were
borne on a stream of congratulations to the Royalty
dining room, and the feasting began. First wine was
passed around. There were calls for music. Pep Torres
and I began to play, and nearly all the men in town

had some piquant verse of the *Cucaracha* to sing. More wine. Dancing. Then the meal began, and just as the guests were seated, Fernando at the head, Marguerita beside him, men on the west side, women opposite, children grouped at the foot, Vicenta from the Casa Rosita came in and with much dignity took a seat reserved for her. Her brother had been shot, but she had decided to break old customs, lay aside all feuds, and help make Marguerita's wedding day a memorable one. There were elaborate *hors d'œuvres*, a magnificent rice, a course of meat and vegetables, Ibicenco pastry, almonds, figs, cigars and champagne. By midafternoon the whole town was dancing, singing, drinking, unified. It was not until dusk that the bride and groom escaped to San Carlos, where a relative of Fernando's had placed a house at their disposal.

But all during the festivities, it was not one of us who had attended no end of social functions, who had been trained in the use of knives and forks, who had been toastmasters and after-dinner speakers, it was Maño who kept that first feast moving, who seemed to know when the loud pedal or the soft pedal was needed.

"Don't teach the children any lies," he said simply to the schoolmaster. "If you do . . ." Maño reached for a carving knife, and very gaily throat-slitting pantomime.

25. *Shadows of Vultures*

AND no one can forget the night of San Xumeu (St. Bartholomew), that mellowest of August nights, when the moonlight touched all the island from its pathway on the sea and the scent of eucalyptus and pepper trees mingled and the plaza was festooned with lanterns and streams of colored paper along the wires. The town had given me that name, Xumeu, which is used so freely among friends and strangers, and my friends had planned a celebration, the first public dance in the square since the outbreak of the war. After dinner, Maño, in the costume of an Aragonese woman, and the sailor Pedro, in a jersey with fantastic tattooed symbols painted all over his bare arms and shoulders, came to our house early in order to put the finishing touches on their gala dress. I remember Maño sitting in the corner, trembling and perhaps for the only time with fear and dread all over his broad honest countenance, for it had been suggested that he must wear earrings, and he thought we were going to pierce his ears. His relief when Flora explained that she had a pair which could be screwed on, without bloodshed, was eloquent.

The best of the confiscated chairs were ranged side by side beneath one of the electric lights for the orchestra, and that night there was a guitar, brought

from somewhere in Ibiza by El Cubano. Guillermo
was still too cautious for a public appearance, so the
guitarist of course was Maño, and Maño was the chief
ballerina, and to summon the public he was ridden
from place to place in an iron wheelbarrow, at full
speed, singing at the top of his voice. Out of deference
to those who might be disturbed by the use of the
church harmonium we had decided to use the accordion. Pep Torres had his trumpet and violin and had
been granted leave of absence from the municipal
band of Ibiza, which was giving a concert at the port
that evening. The dancers in the plaza were mostly
of republican families, but I noticed with pleasure
that among the crowd on the nearby terrace of the
Royalty were members of the other faction, watching
timidly at first, relaxing as the evening wore on.

Beneath the arches of the *Cuartel* were the prisoners, in easy-chairs, guarded inattentively by the students Jaume and Luis. Can I tell you how I felt when
Maño, before midnight, said to El Cubano: "Let's
bring them over here!" So a row of chairs was set out
for the prisoners, and they were escorted to the
square, all except Francisco Guasch, who did not care
to show himself. The green-eyed Maria came to stand
behind the chair of her fiancé, and young Francisco
Ribas chatted with his friends. The dancing proceeded
more heartily. It seemed as if wounds were healing
and goodness and mercy had descended to Ibiza to
spread from there to the ends of the earth. In token of
this, when Maño was dancing, someone fastened a
newspaper to the back of his sash and set it afire and
he danced round and round pretending not to notice
until Pedro of the Royalty and a squad of young men

snatched up siphons from the bar near by and extinguished the blaze, still dancing.

A few days later, after bus time in the morning, these same prisoners (this time including Guasch) were marched through the square, loaded on a truck, and after much formal counting and checking and perusal of elaborate papers by the spectacled Miguel Tur they were taken to the fortress in Ibiza to await their trial there. It had not yet been decided who was to try them, and it was apparent that the local militiamen did not wish to be their judges or their executioners.

About that time, Ramon one morning came out of the gloom which had surrounded him and smiled. He had a paper in his hand which granted him the bus concession between San Carlos, Santa Eulalia and Ibiza, and what he had done many years for the enrichment of old Julian he was to do for his own benefit, subject to the orders of the committee. There was no question now of meeting boats at proper times, for there were no passenger boats. At infrequent intervals a small sack of mail came in, and we were much amused, upon receiving a letter from a Negress in America who had worked in Flora's family, to see that it had been passed by the Barcelona censors. It was all we could do to decipher its meaning, and El Cubano who read English quite well could not make out four words of it. I should like to know what the Barcelona censor made of it, but his instinct in deciding it was harmless and contained no menace to free government was both praiseworthy and correct.

The *Diario* each day contained items about Bayo's progress in Mallorca, but it was evident to me that something had gone wrong. I felt the same about news from Zaragoza, Bilbao, Oviedo and other points in Spain. The new editors were trying to be reassuring, and they did not go to such lengths as the fascist management had when the newspaper was in their hands, but it was clear to me that the struggle was approaching a sort of stalemate and that victory, if it came at all, would be long deferred.

Primitivo, for reasons he did not disclose, had decided to remove his family to Barcelona and was allowed to do so and to resign from the local militia. On the same boat, a Spanish family named March departed. The husband had been secretary to Madariaga and was in the diplomatic service. How he had contrived to keep out of jail during the fascist occupation I did not understand, nor do I understand it now. The departure of the Marches brought another member to our group. Erica Braussen, a German girl who had joined the German communists when Hitler had begun oppressing them, had been a guest of the Marches. She could receive no funds from her family in Germany, faced detention in one of the lethal concentration camps if she returned to her country, and because of her German passport could not find shelter in any other land. From day to day she did not know what would happen to her, but with fine courage she kept up her spirits and was much beloved in the town.

The first thing that alarmed me definitely was a small item in the Barcelona *Vanguardia* in which it was stated that Indelicio Prieto, an influential member of Caballero's cabinet, did not approve of the Valencian and Catalan expedition to the Balearic

Islands. Available forces, Prieto was quoted as saying, should be concentrated for the defense of Madrid. A few days later, El Cubano told us that nine of his twelve militiamen had been ordered to go to Mallorca, and that Bayo had been sent reinforcements from Barcelona. That did not surprise me. I knew Bayo would not attempt to take Palma by storm if a siege was practicable, and the fact that his columns were being strengthened reassured me. We made preparations for a rousing farewell to Maño, who inevitably would be the first to go to the front, and the whole town was saddened by the prospect of his departure. The town without Maño. . . . No one could hide his dismay. I rode with Ramon on the bus to Ibiza one morning to see how things were going at the port and returned in a horse-drawn cart with Maño, Pedro, El Cubano and the two student boys. As we jogged along the talk touched upon votes for women and the support thrown to the reactionaries when the first Cortes had included full suffrage for women in the Constitution. To my astonishment, it was Pedro the relentless tattooed sailor who defended theoretical justice against expediency.

"The women understand nothing, but that is our fault. We have not taught them," he said.

Knowing that Xumeu Ribas and his family would be immensely cheered to know that Francisco had been allowed to watch the dancing and that I had seen him in good health and spirits I walked to Can Josepi for the early morning milk the day after St. Bartholomew's. The Ribas family had taken refuge in the rooms vacated by Mrs. Gramkow, and all day Xumeu sat near the door, ajar, his face buried in his hands, groaning. His faded clothes flapped loosely on his wasted body. His mind was not sufficiently complicated to go out of gear and thus relieve his suffering. He had been caught in a trap of circumstances, none of which had been in his control, and seeing him so pitiful and helpless I could not hope he would recover, that ever merrily again he would roll the dice on his small zinc bar that now had been replaced by the schoolmaster's desk.

Once I was face to face with Xumeu and his daughter I doubted the wisdom of my errand, for they drank up hope so eagerly I was afraid. I all but promised them that nothing should happen to Francisco. I tried to explain that, not strangers, but their neighbors and townsmen were now in authority, that the spirit of forgiveness was in evidence all around. I had not forgotten the lean and frightful years ahead for stricken Spain, but I was convinced that in Santa Eulalia, composed of my dear friends who I knew to be sound and sane, the hardships would be borne equally in something resembling Christian fellowship. I regained the exalted mood of the evening before. José, hard-working peasant, stood wide-eyed in the doorway. Catalina, a bundle of alfalfa under her arm, watched and listened with shining eyes. I explained how the towns in America had town meetings, chose their leaders, were sovereign in matters concerning only the town. I told them about free education, clinics, co-operative marketing. The essence of American freedom, the privileges of American citizenship were very dear to me at that moment, for it seemed that the evening just past had been a brilliant reflection of America's fondest dream. God forgive me if I was wrong, and hopeful and not omniscient. Meanwhile the morning milk, warm from the gentle black cow (who did not know how the twenty-five hundred *pesetas* she was worth had dwindled on the foreign exchange), was further warmed by the blazing summer sun.

I forgot to mention that while we were seated at dinner on the evening of San Xumeu a knock had sounded on our door and we saw Señora Guasch, almost defiant in her injured dignity. She had a bottle in her trembling hand and addressed herself to Flora.

"I knew I could come here," she said. "My boy is ill." (They had been camping in the henhouses behind the house they rented to the Marches on the slope.) "Could you give me a spoonful of honey for his throat?"

We asked her to come in, but she would not sit down. We tried to make her feel that old friendships could survive political change. In a moment she disappeared into the darkness, bottle in hand.

Thank you for coming, brown-eyed woman. We are grateful for the honor you bestowed on us. It was your boy's bicycle that saved my life not many days later, and I know you are glad about that.

Days passed. No news. On the first Sunday in September I was aroused from my *siesta* by a knocking on our door, and voices. Juanito of the Royalty, Maño (whose departure again had been delayed), Toni Ferrer. Pep Torres was sleeping in the room he shared with Peanut. Quickly we roused ourselves. It seemed that a party was in progress and music was needed. Don Rafael Sainz had asked us to be his guests.

A few days before the Local Committee had considered Don Rafael's case and had given him back his spacious house on the San Carlos road. The fat millionaire, in a burst of enthusiasm and relief following days and weeks of worry, had escaped the vigilance of his pious wife and was celebrating. He had waddled down the main street, his first appearance since the government troops had come, shaking hands with everyone, smiling, red face shining. In the Royalty he had proclaimed open house and was drinking *manzanilla*, cognac and beer in prodigious quantities and without regard to possible results.

"Ah, Señor Paul," he shouted as I entered. "Have a drink. This town has spared my life. From now on, it is my home. I will never desert it. . . ." He raised his mug of beer. "Drink, everyone. To Santa Eulalia. *Viva!*"

"*Viva la Republica*," shouted Ferrer. Juanito looked embarrassed. No one had ever cheered the Republic in Don Rafael's presence before.

Rigoberto was watching his fat friend anxiously. The bodyguard was gasping in a corner, for Don Rafael insisted he drink whenever the drinks were passed. It was not long before the genial millionaire, so glad to be alive, was formulating a declaration of independence. No longer was he going to be cooped up at home. No, indeed. He would be master of his house. The men of the town had saved him. He would drink with them every day.

I thought with some dismay that the supply of liquor on the island would be exhausted within the week if Don Rafael kept his promise. Nevertheless, I did nothing to mar the occasion. We all drank whatever was brought to us. Rigoberto sang. Pep Torres and I played. Now and then the women of the Royalty were asked to retire to the backyard while Don Rafael sang a verse or two of the *Cucaracha*. The Sunday crowd that day included many men and women from the farms. They had got tired of remaining at home and added their presence and their picturesque Sunday clothes to the throng that gathered in the doorways and windows, amazed to see Sainz so drunk and happy, and giggled behind their fingers when they thought of what Secora would say. Before dusk, Don Rafael was carried upstairs to bed by four of the strongest men, but the party went on and the echoes of it were resounding unharmoniously when after midnight the millionaire was helped homeward through the back street, head throbbing and legs unsteady.

Nevertheless, I could not help thinking how fortunate it would be if Don Rafael's gratitude persisted and he diverted a small stream from the river of his *pesetas* for the relief of those who were facing privation in the town that had become his own. I wished, for his own sake, that his manner of greeting men he formerly had ignored was less noticeably different, but in my hopeful state I was ready to believe that the past few weeks had become a part of his education and that his change of heart was spontaneous and genuine.

Then the aspect of everything changed for all of us. Our island was to be sacrificed in the interest of larger and more central areas. A small item on an inside page of the new *Diario* stated simply that the Bayo expedition had been withdrawn from Mallorca, after progressing steadily and successfully, and that,

in spite of previous bombardments by Italian planes
(the first we had heard of that), the embarkation had
been orderly and had been accomplished without loss
of life. Ibiza, which for a few short weeks had been a
part of the brotherhood of free communities, again
was cut off, from the world and from the protection
of the harassed government. It was a few hours' sail
from Franco's base in Africa, even nearer the hotbed
of German and Italian influence in Mallorca. According to the Barcelona papers, Prieto had been instrumental in the move which, although it strengthened
more important fronts, left a large number of helpless
republicans in Mallorca at the mercy of the most
fanatic and unscrupulous fascists and condemned to
sure death all the courageous men of Ibiza who had
been willing to put their shoulders to the wheel and
set in motion a temporary government.

This was not generally understood or admitted, but
Cosmi, Carlos, all of us who were most involved, expected disaster. There would be no more supplies, no
more communication, no more acceptance by the reactionaries of a new and cleaner order. Then two
large passenger ships came steaming into Ibiza with
four hundred volunteers of the F.A.I. (*Federacion
Anarquista Iberica*). This organization was one
which had decided to do without commissioned officers and which at that time had not submitted to
common leadership and effort with the other large
unions and federations. The F.A.I., with only the
slightest deference to the Local Committee in Ibiza,
took command of the town. The anarchists were
orderly, comradely in fact, but the whole population
of the island was uneasy because of the lack of re-

sponsible leaders and the obvious lack of connection between the boatloads of armed civilians and the government of Spain. Considering the fact that each man among the anarchists had equal authority to buy what he wanted and pay for it with a simple scrawled and signed receipt, there was not much abuse of the privilege, but the storekeepers and farmers began hiding everything they had, and the inhabitants who had friends or relatives in the country began to evacuate the port town.

Miguel Tur, Carlos and other members of the Local Committee of Santa Eulalia regretted deeply that they had sent their prisoners to Ibiza. They were as anxious, now, to regain control of their fate as they had been reluctant to judge them previously, for it was evident that the F. A. I. intended to set up a court and pass judgment. The Barcelona men knew that most of the prisoners had borne arms against the government and that many fascist leaders were among them, and they considered the Ibiza committee had been lax in dealing with them. Within a few days, nothing remained of the confidence in people's government and the good will that had marked the Local Committee's administration.

Erika Braussen, the German girl who had been through so many dangerous situations, began to advise us to leave the island.

"I would even risk going on a German boat," she said. Of course, there were no boats at all, and neither were there means of dissolving the ties I had formed with my friends in the town. My disappointment was so great that I could no longer help sustain the morale. Juanito stayed away from our luncheon parties, for now we could no longer protect our friends, but were highly dangerous to anyone who wished to survive the next fascist regime. Pep Torres sank into a state of frightful melancholy. Rigoberto's face was perpetually grey. Only was there a rocket of joy when a wounded boy got back from Mallorca, and, meeting the wives of the Guardias Ferrer and Bravo in black and forlorn by the *Cuartel*, he told them their husbands had been fighting bravely in the Bayo column and that while Ferrer had been shot in the leg, the wound was slight and he was in a hospital in Barcelona. The militiamen, overhearing, brought out the Guardias' old phonograph (their only means of entertainment) and returned it with apologies to the women.

At noon on Sunday, September 13, four planes appeared suddenly over Ibiza and dropped bombs on the crowd of women and children who were promenading on the waterfront and the *paseo*. There was no warning, no attempt to destroy anything of military importance. A small tobacco shop was wrecked, a gasoline pump near the shore, several fishing vessels moored to the wharf, a clubhouse. Of the fifty-five Ibicencos who were killed, forty-two were women or children under ten years old. In the evening, just as the work of caring for the wounded and sorting out the dead was at its height, one of the younger fascist prisoners in the fortress remarked to the anarchist guards:

"Our turn is coming now."

Horrified by the outrage to the women and children and inflamed by the fascist's insolence, the guards seized a submachine-gun and shot down the speaker

and the men around him. The alarm was given and
more anarchists rushed in from the barracks. They
quickly decided to execute all the prisoners that
night, in groups of five. When the prisoners refused
to come out in the yard, machine-guns were turned
on them in the building, and those who were not
killed by bullets were dispatched with bayonets. The
anarchists then marched to the hospital, pulled Abel
Matutes whimpering from his bed, and shot him.
The bodies of some of the prisoners were loaded on
a truck and buried in a common trench, others were
left in the fortress. The anarchists then made ready
for departure the two large passenger boats and
ordered the members of the Ibiza militia to embark
with them. The militiamen in the outlying towns
heard of what was happening and hurried to Ibiza,
insisting that they should not be left behind to be
butchered. They were taken aboard.

Early the next morning, unwilling to believe the
stories that were spreading through Santa Eulalia, I
started to walk to Ibiza. Flora, who had until that
moment been firm in her decision that our duty lay
with our friends on the island and that having joined
our cause with theirs we could not desert them, at
last said that she was ready to go. I decided to send
a telegram to all the consulates in Barcelona, if it
were possible. At that time we did not know what
had happened, but our *Cuartel* was completely deserted. That was alarming enough. We had heard
the bombardment but had had no direct news from
the port. Half the inhabitants of Santa Eulalia had
again taken to the woods.

"There is a white flag over the fortress in Ibiza," the Barberet told me.

"Who put it there? By what authority?" I asked, so angrily that he froze up immediately and said he did not know.

Before I had progressed far toward Ibiza, an automobile overtook me. I had not seen one in motion for weeks. In it was Dr. Torres and he offered to give me a lift as far as the intersection of the San Miguel road. He was on his way to Santa Gertrudis, and the driver kept telling him he had not enough gasoline to get there and return. He decided to drive to Ibiza, get gasoline there if he could, then return to Santa Eulalia via Santa Gertrudis. We chugged along, got near enough the port to see the white flag, and met a survivor of the massacre who had been left for dead. He was in a hysterical condition. He tried to tell what had happened but was unable to control himself. One of the militiamen who had been left behind came along and told the doctor there was not a drop of gasoline in the city.

"Then we'll go straight back," Dr. Torres said to the driver. "I don't want to be seen in town. There'll be too much work to do."

Too disgusted to say good-bye and thank him for the lift, I continued on foot. What I found in that formerly most beautiful and prosperous and hospitable city is too bleak for words to convey. The inner harbor, smashed fishing boats and fish, belly up and stinking. At the corner, the wreck of the tobacco shop and the gasoline pump. Bloodstains on all the walls. On the broad *paseo*, one building still inhabited. There stood old Carmen, wife of Sergeant Ortiz, her

arm around the shoulder of a woman in black, and
very gently lifting the blanket from a donkey cartload of corpses to find one the other woman might
claim. I walked alone through the old Roman gates
to the walled city and through narrow slits of street
and up stairways to the fortress. About a hundred
bodies were still lying on the floor, and the first I
recognized was that of Francisco Ribas, the boy I
had promised to save. Ex-Captain Nicolau's head,
or rather the top of his head, had been blown off.
Francisco Guasch and old Bonéd had fallen side by
side. In one another's arms were the seraph-faced
young priest and the priest who looked like a butcher
boy, and in that muddy lake of blood and corpses he
looked more than ever like a butcher boy of a
slaughter-house of man's most evil dreams.

Alone, I stood in that frightful hall, too numb to
be saddened or horrified, faint from the unspeakable
smell, alone in the ancient town the sight of which
had always raised such thankful emotion in my heart,
alone in blaming or not blaming or what or who, alone
in yesterday's riddled hopes and illusions, unable to
be sick, to vomit, to weep, to tear my hair, unable to
Santa Eulalia or Spain or the workers of the world,
to stay or go away or not do either. Later I snapped
out of it, and numbly and dutifully, as being the only
man alive for miles around who tapped nightmares
on typewriters, I found the fascist boy survivor and
the militia boy remainder, and separately and together I listened and asked and prodded my numb
brain and obtained what facts I have written of
events I did not actually see but only heard and

smelled the morning following, as other mornings and events will be following following ever.

Of the two hundred and thirty-nine in the fortress, perhaps five were innocent, and of the fifty-five dead in the streets *all* were innocent, and the port was innocent, and the island and my town, and honest people everywhere.

I, having mounted the hill of silent terror of the ghosts of Spaniards and Moors, and descended to the death of fishes, communed with corpses, talked with boys—I walked up the empty *paseo* to where the corpse cart stood and the door was marked Red Cross. The woman in black was simply sitting there, perhaps waiting for another cartload. Old Carmen greeted me in her excellent Castillano, and her gruff-voiced husband stood up to shake hands.

"Terrible, terrible, Señor Paul," he said. No more. Only a face for Mantegna.

I told him I wanted to send telegrams, and he regretted that the telegraph office was not in operation. It had died when the city had died. There was nothing to do but to walk back to Santa Eulalia. I left money with the old man, and the text of telegrams to the consulates, and he promised to send the messages whenever, if ever, it was possible again.

I got home after dark, although a San Carlos man, one of whose relatives had been killed by the fascist bombers, overtook me before I had walked many miles. There are many hours of that day I cannot seem to account for or dislodge from the mortar of my memory. I told Flora, Pep Torres, Erica Braussen a few of my facts, and we spent the evening somehow, and listlessly went to bed.

The next morning Santa Eulalia was practically deserted. Not a house in town, now, that did not have its emptiness and death or slaughter and desolation in prospect. Some fascist planes flew over, but dropped no bombs. Eulalia Noguera came to us for the first time since her brother's death and said that Cosmi, her uncle Mateo, Carlos, Pep Salvador and in all seventeen of the best Santa Eulalia men had set sail for some unknown destination before dawn that day in the schooner *Isabel Matutes*. We rejoiced that they had got away. In fact, with so many good men safe I began not to feel completely numb again and to see that much more would be happening and that, if there were no end to injustice and hate and bloodshed and emptying of inhabited buildings, there simply was no end.

At quarter of twelve that day a Belgian resident of Santa Eulalia sought me out and told me there was a destroyer in Ibiza harbor and that a peasant had told him it was German. An Englishwoman in Ibiza had told the Belgian that Sergeant Ortiz had told her that an American and his family wanted to be taken off. I thanked him, and thinking rapidly but with no definiteness I hurried to the house where Erica Braussen was staying. Flora was there with her. Erica turned pale when I said I thought the destroyer was of the German navy. I simply told them what the Belgian had told me. We must do something about it, we all agreed. I suggested that Erica write a note in German to the Commander of the gunboat, letting him know that there were Germans and Americans in distress in Santa Eulalia and asking him to call at our harbor. For pen and ink we hurried down the hill to Cosmi's café, and there, to my surprise, I found Cosmi. He and the other republican leaders had been unable to get away the night before. He was disappointed, but quite resigned to an early death. I told him about our plan.

"I wish I could go," he said simply.

My brain began to function again. I knew Cosmi spoke French fluently, with an Algerian accent.

"Could you go as our cook?" I asked.

"I'll try. I had a French passport once, during the War," he said.

Quickly we consulted Erica and she wrote the note in German. Cosmi said he would go at once to Ibiza, if we could find him a bicycle, deliver the note to the German Commander and ask to be taken aboard. It was a slim chance, but not much slimmer than the one Erica was taking in placing herself within reach of the German authorities.

"Will you tell them I am a governess, that I work for you?" she asked.

"Of course," I said.

Then I went back up the slope to ask Señora Guasch for the loan of her son's bicycle. I have never seen a widow with more thirst for revenge in her eyes, but they softened and she courteously granted my request. Within ten minutes Cosmi, collarless, sockless, with a dirty shirt and torn trousers, was speeding toward Ibiza. To make a favorable impression on the German Commander, we had set forth in the note that Cosmi, Algerian-French cook in my house, had lost his clothes and of course all his papers when communists had raided the town.

Flora, Erica and I thought so little of our chances

that we did not begin packing, but ate a long and leisurely lunch. But as we were finishing dessert, a boy came running to us. An auto was in front of Cosmi's to take us off, would wait ten minutes. Hastily we threw a few things into suitcases, Eulalia, Pep and Juanito helping, and carried them across the plaza, past the Royalty, Andres' café, the post office, to Cosmi's. The driver told us the German destroyer could not come to Santa Eulalia because the Commander had no orders to that effect, but that the German officers, on receiving the note Cosmi had delivered, had taken gasoline from their launch and filled the tank of the nearest auto which had been standing on the pier. The destroyer was to leave Ibiza at two-thirty, call at San Antonio an hour later, and leave San Antonio about four-thirty. Because the English warships had refused to transport dogs, I assumed the Germans would not take Moritz along, and sadly I handed the leash to Eulalia Noguera, hoping Moritz would protect her, as she promised to care for him.

"He shall eat exactly as if you were here," Eulalia said, which is worth more than a library filled with treaties with Italy and Germany.

A small group of women were standing fearfully on the edge of the plaza as we passed, suitcases in hand. We stopped to say good-bye to them. I remember particularly Antonia and her three small daughters who had been born in America. In front of Cosmi's was a disconsolate group of men, those who were too tired and discouraged to take shelter from air raids. Pedro of the Royalty had tears in his eyes. Ferrer for once spoke in a low tone of voice, but cordially. Rigoberto, haggard, approached us. I have never seen such complete despair.

"One cowardly act after another," he said. "The only reason I am not leaving is because I cannot. Good-bye."

I told them we would go to some town near the border, where we could get money from America, and return as soon as it was possible. The suitcases were piled in, we seated ourselves as best we could, and the auto started moving through the empty town and on across a landscape from which the light had died. It was certain that the fascists were coming, and as we rode along I could not forget Ferrer, Pep Salvador, Captain Juan, Carlos, old Miguel Tur, our communist potter at Cala Llonga, Guarapiñada, all the men who were marked for slaughter. I had asked Pep Torres to try to get away with us, but sadly he had refused.

When we reached the tangent from which the port and the walled city could be seen, the destroyer was lying at anchor in the harbor. Stink of decaying fish. We skirted the cove and the wrecks of fishing vessels, zigzagged through smashed remnants of walls and approached a small group of Ibicenco men and some German officers and sailors. The young German in command, soft-voiced and with the gentlest manners, came forward to receive us and spoke in English. Ramon was standing near by, but no sight of Cosmi. I did not dare to inquire. I gave Ramon all the *pesetas* I had left and asked him to pass them on to Pep Torres. We stepped into the waiting launch as our suitcases were loaded into a tender, nodded to our fellow-passengers and the propeller began churning.

Two poodles yapped and a Sealyham growled. It seemed that the Germans were tolerant of dogs. Too late. Extinction of propeller. And as we drifted neatly to the gangplank I saw Cosmi reclining in an easy-chair.

"Ah, *la famille*," he said, for the benefit of all and sundry. Trust Cosmi to be exactly there and calmer than any of us.

They made us all comfortable on the quarter deck, and the English-speaking officer smiled and asked us please to be careful as we were going to make thirty miles an hour. There was some delay, tense for me because of Cosmi. I remained at his side, and then a miracle took place for the benefit of Cosmi and me, a sign in the sea and the sky. For there was, yes, unmistakably sailing and passing not fifty yards astern, the *Isabel Matutes*, and silently, almost impossibly thankful, we saw who it was at the wheel—Mateo, and waving to us, clowning, Cosmi's brother Pep Salvador, and bashfully smiling, Captain Juan and young Carlos. Also Fernando, the honeymooning schoolmaster quite brideless. A dozen others. And safely, before our eyes and the noncomprehending kind eyes of our German officers and crew, those good men sailed away to open stretches of the sea, to choose their own destination and not to be shot against the wall. At the rail, Cosmi in his dirty shirt and torn trousers. Did they see us? I think so. And of the dead empty city (white flag) and stench of fishes and our orange peel of town life and promise, we counted seventeen good men sailing to safety and the future, and if only our German craft would start and get clear, perhaps there would be a future, after all.

Cosmi, smiling and inscrutable, and at last propeller, and swinging, now moving, elastic of distance, and we turned, not to pass Santa Eulalia and Arabie and Cosmi's wife, small son and life's savings and shores and coves of dreams, but the other way.

Uncertain click of stereopticon—and the rushing sea.

Postscript

THE day after we left Ibiza, Italian troops landed there and set up another fascist administration. This information was published in the newspapers of Southern France and barely mentioned in Paris. All mail and passenger service and supplies of food were cut off, except through Italian sources. The island was used as a rebel base, and after the usual warnings to the small surviving remainder of the civilian population, government planes bombarded the port towns early in April and, according to the London newspapers, destroyed most of the houses.

I have been unable to learn of the fate of my republican friends who escaped on the schooner Isabel Matutes, *but Cosmi, who went away with us, representing himself to be an Algerian cook, was appointed government purchasing agent on board a steamer which carries food supplies from Odessa to Valencia. The vessel, which I shall not name, is still active in this work.*

Near the end of May, the German battleship Deutschland, *at anchor in the shadow of Ibiza's ancient fortress, was bombed by government aviators after having fired at the government planes. The dispatches mentioned merely that the island was a "rebel base."*

According to Associated Press *reports issued the next day, the Italian and rebel troops, who arrived within a few hours after I was taken off on* Die Falke, *herded four hundred Republicans, among whom must have been most of the male characters in this book, and killed them with machine-guns through the small Moorish windows.*

My continuous and repeated efforts to obtain direct news of my republican comrades and friends in Santa Eulalia, the ones who could not get away, have been thus far without result. Those who have died, I am sure have died bravely. The others are fighting, or dissembling in order to risk their lives for liberty when the opportunity presents itself.

It was a privilege to be associated with such courageous, high-minded men and women, and their enemies will do well to be afraid of them as long as they are above ground.

E. P.

June 14, 1937.